WHITEHEAD and GOD

Prolegomena to Theological Reconstruction

Laurence F. Wilmot

Wilfrid Laurier University Press

Canadian Cataloguing in Publication Data

Wilmot, Laurence F., 1907-
   Whitehead and God

Bibliography: p.
Includes index.
ISBN 0-88920-070-X

1. Whitehead, Alfred N., 1861-1947 – Theology.
2. God – History of doctrines – 20th century.
I. Title.

B1674.W354W55   192   C79-094144-9

Wilfrid Laurier University Press
Waterloo, Ontario, Canada   N2L 3C5

To my wife, Hope,
who ventured with me, at home and
abroad, to complete the study
underlying this book

Preface

This book is intended as a contribution towards the renewal of theological discourse in the final quarter of the twentieth century. It presents the findings from personal research into the development of the concept of God in the philosophy of Alfred North Whitehead, and the application of his conceptual tools in a re-examination of the writings of some fourth-century Christian theologians in their efforts to provide answers to the problems posed for the Church by Arianism. The research was prompted by Whitehead's recommendations addressed to theologians in *Adventures of Ideas*.

The book consists of twelve chapters and is divided into two parts. An introductory chapter seeks to set Whitehead's philosophy within the context of contemporary movements in both philosophy and theology, to disclose the extent to which he raises fundamental questions which are puzzling theologians today, and indicate the relevance of his thought for Christian theology. Chapters II-IV investigate the variety of Whitehead's approaches to reality—through science, religious experience, and philosophy, and his selection of a model for his own cosmological scheme—tracing the early development of his thought from mathematics to science, to the philosophy of science, to a realization of the necessity for metaphysics to provide an overall picture of the universe to replace the seventeenth-century cosmology which has dominated thought for two hundred years but has now been shown to be unsatisfactory as a fundamental interpretation. Whitehead is convinced that the universe as disclosed in modern scientific observation calls for an alternative doctrine of organism, and in his Lowell Lectures, in 1925, he is commencing to prepare the ground for the metaphysical task. In this work we also gain an indication of the importance which Whitehead attaches to religion and, in the published lectures, a chapter is introduced in which God is declared to be metaphysically necessary as the principle of concretion.

Whitehead is aware of the extreme limitations of metaphysics; what further can be known about God must be gathered from empirical evidence which is provided in the documents of the religions of the world. Chapter III examines Whitehead's report on his own investigations of religious records and which formed the subject matter of his second series of Lowell Lectures. We discover here a number of clues as to the direction of his subsequent thought, among them the declaration that the central religious dogma in question today is: What do you mean by "God"? All other problems, he insists, are subsidiary to this, and it proves to be an extremely difficult question to answer with any degree of certainty. The very variety of reports on the nature of God constitutes one of the central problems for Whitehead. He recognizes that each of the extreme views cannot be true to the complete exclusion of the others, and suggests it will be necessary to find a mediating position. He is impressed with the important qualifications which were brought into religion by the early preaching of Christianity but, in this series of lectures, treats Jesus rather as a prophet and founder of one of a number of religions. His examination of oriental religions convinces him of the necessity for an impersonal substructure of the universe, if he would be guided by the consensus of opinion of the great world religions simply taken as historical phenomena.

In Chapter IV we examine Whitehead's treatment of cosmological systems which have been influential on the western world, particularly those of Plato and of Newton and the seventeenth-century philosophers, and his reasons for selecting the Platonic as most suitable to the needs of the twentieth century. We also examine the influence of F. H. Bradley on Whitehead's thought, particularly the problem of God as treated in the final chapters of the *Essays on Truth and Reality,* in which Bradley insists on the necessity for the immanence of God in the world as well as being its Maker and Sustainer. Part of Whitehead's response to Bradley at this point is his call for a secularization of the concept of God's functions in the world. He insists that discourse about God must not be limited to the human self-consciousness, but must be applied to his relations to the world of nature, without in any way detracting from or invalidating the significance of religious experience.

In Chapter V we analyze the metaphysical system, paying particular attention to those categories which will bear directly upon the concept of God and of his agency in the world. Our investigation discloses that Whitehead is engaged on a fundamental metaphysical search for ultimate meaning in the universe which is here viewed as a creative advance into novelty. He postulates an impersonal ultimate "creativity," and God is declared to be the "primordial creature" of creativity. Other important categories which are investigated are those of "actual entity," "eternal object," "prehension," "subjective aim," and note is taken of the need which Whitehead found throughout this discussion for a secularization of the concept of God's functions in the world, leading to his declaration of there being three natures in God. In the developing system these are termed the "primordial," "consequent," and "superjective" natures respectively, but in later chapters of *Process and Reality* the superjective function is incorporated into the other two natures.

Analysis of the concept of God, undertaken in Chapter VI, discloses that it is a revised Platonic version. God is declared to be the "creature of creativity" with respect to his relation to the ultimate, and to be "primordial" with respect to everything which comes to be in the universe; the actualities of which the universe is composed all presuppose his primordial ordering of "creativity" and of the "eternal objects," whereas he merely presupposes the general metaphysical character of creative advance. We examine the unusual language by means of which Whitehead seeks to describe the activities of God in bringing about a universe which is a self-creative process; how God initiates each actuality and sustains its process as it passes into the immediacy of his own life. God is said to be transcendent and immanent, but also to be a creature transcended by the creativity on the one hand, and on the other hand is declared to be *causa sui*. A serious attempt is made to sort out the meanings to be attached to the terminology within the context in which it occurs, while pointing out tendencies which become apparent as the work proceeds.

Our analysis of the final chapter of *Process and Reality* discloses that a twofold development is taking place in Whitehead's thought about God. On the one hand, he would appear to be incorporating into his conception of God elements of Neo-Platonism, although he at no time mentions Plotinus; and on the other hand, ideas drawn from the New Testament are exercising an increasingly important influence upon his thought. It becomes evident that, at the conclusion of *Process and Reality*, two conflicting cosmologies are confronting the one mind and will call for clarification of the issues and for decision if the system is to present a consistent picture of the universe.

In Chapter VII we present a brief selection of appraisals of Whitehead's cosmology which help to bring into focus the conflicting problems which Christian theologians experience as they seek to utilize the process philosophy as a basis for a Christian interpretation of the universe. Archbishop William Temple, in his Gifford Lectures, delivered in 1932-33, acknowledges his indebtedness to Whitehead in his analysis of the world as apprehended, but insists that the category of the ultimate calls for further explanation and that God as limited by Whitehead's definitions is not capable of performing all that is ascribed to him. John B. Cobb, Jr., 1965, utilizing Whitehead's cosmology, seeks to construct a Christian Natural Theology, and is criticized by Langdon Gilkey for his failure to note that the system as set down in *Process and Reality* cannot express the Christian vision of reality. Our chapter concludes with an examination of some recent discussions which have focused on God and creativity, and the viability of Whitehead's God for Christian Theology, including a dialogue between Lewis Ford and Robert C. Neville.

Part II of the book, entitled "Research and Discovery," traces the subsequent development of Whitehead's thought through his Princeton Lectures, and his next major philosophical work, *Adventures of Ideas*. In the former, entitled *The Function of Reason*, Whitehead identifies the objective of the next phase of his search as being the location of a "counter agency" which, he declares, is necessary to account for the emergence of mental activity and the evolution of mankind in a universe which, physically, appears to be wasting away. *Adventures of Ideas* traces the history of the activation of two or three ideas in promoting the arrival of mankind at civilization. In a section entitled "Cosmologies," Whitehead reports his discovery of three culminating phases within a period of approximately twelve hundred years which, taken together, constitute the threefold revelation of Christianity. These are identified as: (i) Plato's conviction, expressed in his later Dialogues, of God as a persuasive, and not a coercive, agency; (ii) Jesus Christ, regarded now as an exemplification of the nature of God and of his agency in the world; and (iii) the fourth-century formulation of the Christian faith in response to the challenge of Arianism. Both the negative judgments which Whitehead now pronounces against Platonism and his positive affirmations of the superiority of the Christian formulations are of such importance as to warrant an investigation of the sources from which he drew these various insights. The remaining chapters of this section are, accordingly, taken up with an investigation into and an evaluation of the sources.

Our examination of the sources, in Chapter IX, discloses that Plato in his later thought does enunciate this novel conception of God as a persuasive agency and that this has an important bearing on his understanding of man and of his responsibility for the formation of his own character by the decisions which he makes in the face of circumstances. We find, moreover, that this conviction of man as responsible agent before God was not confined to the Greeks, but had received partial exemplification in the lives of the founders of the faith of Israel. Whitehead's conviction that this idea, which was an intellectual discovery in Plato, had received exemplification in the life of a man who lived in a particular historical context is born out by our research. Jesus Christ is declared by his followers to be in himself a disclosure of the nature of God and of his agency in the world as persuasive love.

It was the metaphysical implications of the fourth-century theological writings which finally convinced Whitehead of the superiority of the Christian over the Platonic answer to the problem of "God," and, in order to clarify the questions with which the Christian theologians were faced at that time, in Chapter X we investigate the climate of opinion, disclosing important developments in Platonism which was the prevailing philosophy of the fourth century. A twofold development brought to its full extent by Plotinus, resulted in a conception of the extreme transcendence of God and of a graded hierarchy of three divine hypostases; analysis of the Arian creed discloses a conception of God remarkably similar to the Plotinian One, and a graded hierarchy declared to be by creation and by the will of God. A comparison of Plotinus, Arius and Whitehead discloses that there are a number of similarities and differences, and some striking parallels between Whitehead and Plotinus, on the one hand, and between Whitehead and Arius, on the other. It becomes evident that the problems which beset Whitehead's metaphysical scheme are those which Arius posed for the Christian Church in the fourth century.

In Chapter XI we undertake an analysis of aspects of the theology of Athanasius; the fundamental problems facing him in the fourth century and Whitehead in the twentieth are discovered to be similar, and Athanasius' empirical and teleological approach would be very attractive to Whitehead. Examination of *contra Gentes* and the treatise *On the Incarnation* discloses the importance which Athanasius attaches to the Christian doctrine of creation as a prerequisite to understanding the Incarnation, which is interpreted as both a sacrifice for sin and a demonstration in a human life of the nature of God and of his agency in the world. The Christian doctrine of the mutual immanence of the three divine Persons in the one God, all unqualifiedly divine, is located in Athanasius' polemical *Discourses against the Arians,* and his development of the doctrine of the Holy Spirit as the mode of God's operations in the world in both creation and sanctification is located in the *Letters to Serapion.* Each of these affirmations is compared with Whitehead's interpretation in *Adventures of Ideas* and it becomes evident that these are the sources of the insights which lie behind Whitehead's judgment of the superiority of the Christian over the Platonic concept of God and his relation to the world.

In our concluding chapter we briefly recapitulate to show the development which was taking place in Whitehead's thought about God throughout his life; that he acknowledged having received from the Christian theologians insights which enabled him to reject the Platonic cosmology which had dominated his own philosophical system, and declared that the discovery made by the fourth century theologians should be incorporated into general metaphysics. We seek to apply the Christian insights to the philosophy of organism and by so doing to re-structure that philosophy in order that it may serve as the raw material for a Christian philosophical theology.

Further implications of our findings are to the effects that the present scientific world view is one which is particularly susceptible of a Christian interpretation, that the approach and arguments of Athanasius in the fourth century are illuminating for the twentieth, and that his clear differentiation between the Christian and the Platonic cosmology will be of assistance in the present theological debate, enabling theologians to identify elements of Neo-Platonic thought which are a source of much confusion in contemporary discourse about God.

Laurence F. Wilmot

Winnipeg, Manitoba
March 31, 1978

Acknowledgements

I wish to express appreciation to Professor D. C. Williams, of the Department of Philosophy, Harvard University, who in the summer of 1960 encouraged me to pursue my research into the sources of Whitehead's various ideas of God; to the late Dr. A. M. Farrer and Keble College, for fellowship extended to Hope and me during the two years 1961-63; to the Professors in the faculties of Philosophy and of the Honour School of Theology, whose lectures were always interesting and informative—particularly those of Drs. Henry Chadwick, H. N. D. Kelly and Canon David Jenkins in Patristics; to Dr. Paul Henry, S.J., Sarum Lecturer for the year 1962-63, for the insight that the Neo-Platonic climate of opinion was an important factor in the dilemmas facing the Church at Nicaea; to Dr. G. B. Caird, for his lectures on New Testament Theology; and to the succession of priest-students at St. Augustine's College, Canterbury, during the four years 1963-67, who attended my lecture-seminars and helped me think through a number of the problems in theology facing the Church during those years.

I wish also to express appreciation to Professors Lewis S. Ford, of Pennsylvania State University, and John B. Cobb, Jr., of Claremont School of Theology, both of whom read the original manuscript and made helpful suggestions for revision, and to Professor Brenton Stearns of the Department of Philosophy of the University of Winnipeg for his encouragement that I should seek publication.

This book has been published with the help of a grant from the Canadian Federation for the Humanities, using funds provided by the Social Sciences and Humanities Research Council of Canada.

Contents

Abbreviations

Following are the abbreviations and editions of Whitehead's works used in the footnotes:

AI   *Adventures of Ideas.* New York: The Macmillan Company, 1932; Cambridge: Cambridge University Press, 1933.

CN   *The Concept of Nature.* Cambridge: Cambridge University Press, 1920.

ESP   *Essays in Science and Philosophy.* New York: Philosophical Library, 1947.

FR   *The Function of Reason.* Princeton: Princeton University Press, 1929; Beacon Paperback ed., 1958.

MT   *Modes of Thought.* New York: Cambridge University Press, 1938; third impression, 1956.

PR   *Process and Reality: An Essay in Cosmology.* New York: The Macmillan Company, 1929; Harper Torchbook ed., 1960. (Page numbers in parentheses refer to the edition published at Cambridge by the Cambridge University Press.)

PNK   *An Enquiry Concerning the Principles of Natural Knowledge.* Cambridge: Cambridge University Press, 1919; second edition, 1925; reprinted, 1955.

RM   *Religion in the Making.* New York: The Macmillan Company, 1926; reprinted, 1933.

SMW   *Science and the Modern World.* Cambridge: Cambridge University Press, 1926; reprinted, 1933.

N.E.B. *The New English Bible: New Testament.* Oxford: Oxford University Press, 1961.

Part 1

The Search for Categories of Interpretation

Chapter I

The Legacy of the Sixties

Throughout the past two decades Christian theology has been passing through a state of ferment which shows few signs of abating. No sooner does the debate settle down in one part of the English speaking world than it breaks out in another. A whole succession of writers, each professing membership of the Christian Church and expressing his desire to remain a member and to be considered in good standing, has called in question first our "image" of God, then the person and work of Jesus Christ, and finally the very being and existence of God himself, even to the point of suggesting that we should do well to give up using the word "God" for a generation.[1] From yet another quarter comes the suggestion that far from it being merely the case that "God is dead," as Nietzsche had declared, the problem now is that the *word* "God" is dead. The real problem of understanding the Gospel today, it is maintained, consists in the difficulty of finding any meaningful way to speak of God.[2] From being a question of communication, of finding a suitable language with which to speak of God, the debate has come to centre on the question as to whether or not there be God in any real sense of that word.

After two decades of this kind of theologizing in the negative mode, we are prompted to enquire why the "new" theology is unable to say anything constructive. Why are its results mainly negative? The answer to this question must be sought in the presuppositions of thought from which the theologians have been working. Investigation will disclose that, in the main, this type of theologizing has resulted from the attempt to apply the principles and methods of reductive analysis to Christian theology; consequently, their efforts had in them the seeds of failure from the beginning. Professor A. J. Ayer, in discussing the work of the reductive analysts in philosophy, explains that whereas from the time of the early Greeks philosophers have been concerned basically with the search for what reality there is, the efforts of the analysts "mainly take the form of trying to show that something, which there appears to be, is not."[3] The application of the method to

[1] J. A. T. Robinson, *Honest to God* (London: SCM, 1963), pp. 7, 8.
[2] Paul van Buren, *The Secular Meaning of the Gospel* (London: SCM, 1963), pp. 102-103.
[3] A. J. Ayer, *The Concept of a Person* (London: Macmillan, 1963), p. 12.

theology has brought the request that theology be translated into anthropology and that Christological statements should accordingly be translated into statements about man.[4] From calling for the "non-objective" use of the word God, the debate has proceeded to the conclusion that "God is dead," by which they mean that all meaning has finally been drained out of the term "God" as it has been used in theological dialogue. It becomes evident in the pages of these writers that it is not a helpful procedure to apply the verification principle as the criterion of meaningfulness to theological statements.

Had the new theologians been more thoroughly acquainted with Ayer's works they would have realized the futility of attempting to theologize in these terms. It was one of the avowed aims of Professor Ayer when he wrote *Language, Truth and Logic*, to eliminate both metaphysics and theology by declaring them to be meaningless.[5] He sought to achieve this by setting up the "verification principle" of the Logical Positivists as the sole criterion of the meaningfulness of propositions. The effect of this move was to limit meaningful discourse to propositions of common sense and of the sciences, i.e., propositions which can be subjected to an empirical test. If we accept the major premise advanced by Ayer, his arguments are unanswerable.

It would seem self-evident, in the face of this avowed aim of the positivists that a theologian, if he would achieve any worthwhile statement of the faith, must reject at the outset this reduction of meaningful discourse to that of the empirical sciences, for his task brings him directly into the area of evaluation and of aesthetic appreciation both of which transcend the limits of scientific investigation. Yet, Paul van Buren, in his book *The Secular Meaning of the Gospel*,[6] evidently accepts the verification principle as though it were a scientifically established principle of meaningfulness from which he is required to work if he is to be understood. Setting out from such presuppositions, he very quickly finds it necessary to deny the reality of "God" and recommends that the term should be abandoned. The balance of his book has to do with a serious effort to translate the Gospels into anthropological terms and yet to retain some reality in the way of confrontation for the experience of self-awareness which comes to those who read the Gospels; his book stands as a reminder that acceptance of the positivist position is not a satisfactory basis for theological enquiry. Having accepted the verification principle as the criterion of meaningful discourse, van Buren comes to the conclusion that theology is "out," and urges concentration upon anthropological studies.

What of the group of writers who accept the other major denigration of positivism, namely, that metaphysics is "out"? In this group we find Harvey Cox, William Hamilton and Thomas Altizer, each of whom commences from the presupposition that because we are living in the "post-metaphysical" era we must search for a new basis for

[4] van Buren, *The Secular Meaning of the Gospel*, p. 103.
[5] A. J. Ayer, *Language, Truth and Logic* (2nd ed.; Dover, 1946), p. 115.
[6] van Buren, *The Secular Meaning of the Gospel*, pp. 103-105.

theologizing if we would speak to the 20th century. Cox in his *Secular City*,[7] Hamilton in his *New Essence of Christianity*,[8] and Altizer and Hamilton in their *Radical Theology and the Death of God*[9] each set out from the presupposition that metaphysics is utterly dead and that, therefore, all the language in which Christian theology has been stated is out-moded. Ergo, all that the Church has said throughout the centuries, and particularly the formal statements of the Creeds, is meaningless to our age.

According to Harvey Cox we are left with the "secular city" and the problems of politics and social values and, strange as it may seem in the light of his rejection of metaphysics, with a confrontation by the God of the Bible, who ever or what ever he may prove ultimately to be. Cox appears to desire to throw history out also and yet to retain the confrontation of God and man in the existential moment—the moment of decision in economic and political life in the reordering of the life of urban man. Clearly, there is a metaphysical structure presupposed in the universe implied in this thinking, even though it is denied any reality by its author. This becomes more evident in both Hamilton and Altizer who have accepted the Hegelian dialectic as the structure of the universe and then find themselves in the role of the antithesis to the Hegelian Absolute. Their viewpoint is patterned very closely upon that of the renegade Hegelian, Ludwig Feuerbach, who, in his *Essence of Christianity*,[10] gives the classic interpretation of the antithesis to Hegel's thesis on the Absolute Spirit. Feuerbach declares that, rather than it being the case, as maintained by Hegel, that the Universe is the clothing of the Absolute Spirit who therein becomes incarnate, the very idea of God and Absolute are mere projections of the human spirit; that it is man's nature to idealize and that this aspect of his nature has been objectified and split off from its true basis in the human spirit and declared to be God. Having posited all his goodness in God, man, says Feuerbach, is left with only negative aspects and so prostrates himself before his self-made deity and accuses himself of having no good in him. Religion, says Feuerbach, is a psychological trick which man unwittingly performs upon himself, and recommends that men should now recognize religion for what it is and assume their rightful heritage in the earth by claiming that which is their own. Feuerbach became steadily more atheistic and materialistic in his outlook and ended in pure humanism. Altizer and Hamilton are more truly Hegelian in their stance of waiting. Having accepted the Hegelian dialectic as the way in which the universe works, they are caught in the web of their own unexamined metaphysical presuppositions; it is their fate to have ar-

[7] Harvey Cox, *The Secular City* (London: SCM, 1965).

[8] William Hamilton, *The New Essence of Christianity* (London: Darton, Longman and Todd, 1961).

[9] Thomas Altizer and William Hamilton, *Radical Theology and the Death of God* (New York: The Bobbs-Merrill Company, 1966).

[10] Ludwig Feuerbach, *The Essence of Christianity*, trans. by George Eliot (New York: Harper Torchbooks, 1957), pp. 14, 97-99, 230, 270-71.

rived on the scene at the time in history when the antithesis of the Hegelian dialectic is uppermost and so they can do nothing but wait. God is "dead" and there is nothing we can do about it today, but, if we wait, perhaps someone will come along with a synthesis one day before too long. And so they are waiting, but for whom? or for what? They do not know and there does not seem much hope for modern man along this road.

It becomes evident that if we accept the thesis of logical positivism both theology and metaphysics are "out" and the modern disciples of the variety of new theologies are each in their own way demonstrating the strength of Ayer's arguments provided that we accept his major premise. But, why should we? Why should we accept the verification principle as the sole criterion of meaningful discourse? John Wisdom[11] was quick to point out that the verification principle is itself one of a class of metaphysical propositions, namely, positivistic propositions, and that, according to the limitation which it places upon meaningful discourse, is itself a meaningless utterance, for it is not possible to verify it in these terms. It may be a useful test to apply to propositions to discover whether they come under the class of scientific statements— i.e., refer to matters which can be investigated by one or other of the physical sciences. But to limit meaningful discourse to the propositions of the sciences would constitute an arbitrary decision as unacceptable to the scientist as to others. Alfred North Whitehead's reply to the challenge of positivism was to point out that were scientists to accept the strictures placed upon language by this school there would be no progress in science, for advancement in any scientific field is achieved only by the employment of creative imagination.[12]

Had the new theologians been more observant of trends in philosophical thinking they would have realized that logical positivism was no longer philosophically acceptable, as Ayer had himself declared in 1960. In his inaugural lecture, in taking the chair as Wykeham professor of Logic in the University of Oxford in 1960, Professor Ayer acknowledges that the verification principle "suffers from a vagueness which it has not yet been found possible to eradicate" and expresses a doubt of its adequacy "as a means of distinguishing questions of analysis and interpretation from questions of fact."[13] The mistake of those who promoted the theory, he now acknowledges, lay in the assumption that it is possible to supply a neutral record of the facts which is free from interpretation. Philosophy is after all concerned to a certain extent with questions of empirical fact, since it must provide the criteria as to what is to count as a fact. Ayer recognizes that the adoption

[11] John Wisdom, "Metaphysics and Verification," *Mind,* XLVII, and *Philosophy and Psycho-analysis* (Oxford: Blackwell, 1957), p. 51.

[12] Alfred North Whitehead, *Process and Reality: An Essay in Cosmology* (New York: Harper Torchbooks, 1960; first published, New York: Macmillan, 1929), p. 20 (18ff., Eng. ed.), and *Adventures of Ideas* (Cambridge: Cambridge University Press, 1933), pp. 160-65.

[13] A J. Ayer, "Philosophy and Language," being the first chapter in *The Concept of a Person* (London: Macmillan, 1963), pp. 20-21.

of criteria implies the acceptance of a given conceptual system, and that the appraisal of conceptual systems falls within the province of philosophy. In coming to this conclusion, Professor Ayer has left positivism behind and is recommending that philosophers should undertake basically metaphysical tasks as part of their responsibility. He is here recognizing that it will be necessary for philosophy to bring under review from time to time the conceptual systems and categoreal features which form the presuppositions of statements put forward by a wide variety of specialists in a great many fields of investigation and in ordinary conversation.

In the closing section of the lecture, Ayer returns again to this question of the necessity of challenging the presuppositions of the sceptic's arguments. The current philosophical emphasis on fact, as opposed to theory, has been overdone, he concludes.[14] The claim to dispense with theory has all too often been simply a way of masking assumptions which had better be openly recognized, and he now recommends to philosophers that they give themselves to this wider task. He has not lost his distrust for speculative metaphysics, but this is not sufficient ground for limiting the scale of philosophy:

> ... there is no reason to suppose that the only concepts which are worth investigating are those that have a comparatively narrow range, or that all that we can usefully do is to describe how concepts of this kind are actually employed. It is equally possible, and perhaps of more importance, to examine the architectonic features of our conceptual systems; to apply analytical techniques to the investigation of categories.[15]

There is a remarkable similarity between Ayer's language at this point and the language of Whitehead in the introductory chapter of *Process and Reality*. Whitehead is insistent that there are no brute matters of fact,[16] but that each can be understood only by its metaphysical interpretation as an item in a world with some systematic relation to it. Philosophy, he insists, does not initiate interpretations. "Its search for a rationalistic scheme is the search for more adequate criticism and for more adequate justification, of the interpretations which we perforce employ."[17] Actually, Whitehead's whole philosophical venture constitutes his endeavour to carry out just such an appraisal, which Ayer is now, thirty years later, insisting is a vital part of the philosophical task.

Both Ayer and Whitehead are reaffirming an aspect of experience whose recognition lies at the root of any meaningful theological interpretation. Whitehead pays more attention to the part played by the imagination in the metaphysical undertaking than does Ayer, though it is implicit in his request quoted above that we should look for concepts having a wider range, that we examine the architectonic features of our

[14] Ibid., p. 33.
[15] Ibid.
[16] Whitehead, *Process and Reality*, p. 21 (19). (Pages numbered in parentheses in this footnote and in subsequent footnotes are from the English version published by the Cambridge University Press.)
[17] Ibid., p. 22 (19-20).

conceptual system, and that we should investigate the categories employed in discourse; each of these calls for the exercise of creative imagination in an effort to discern meanings which, while present, have been neglected or simply not seen by a too facile acceptance of limited definitions of terms. There is, Whitehead points out, a constant interplay between science and metaphysics in which imagination plays a fundamentally important part; he illustrates this from the part played by speculative imagination in the discovery of the planet Pluto, and concludes; that "speculative extension beyond direct observation spells some trust in metaphysics, however vaguely these metaphysical notions may be entertained in explicit thought."[18]

Whitehead is under no misapprehension as to the extreme difficulties of the metaphysical undertaking: "Our metaphysical knowledge is slight, superficial, incomplete. Thus errors creep in. But, such as it is, metaphysical understanding guides imagination and justifies purpose. Apart from metaphysical presuppositions there can be no civilization."[19] In a later chapter on "Science and Philosophy"[20] he traces the process whereby slowly and quietly the truths of science are evolved and in turn replaced by larger truths in the light of further coordination until the Newtonian cosmology, which had held the spotlight for more than two centuries, has broken down[21] and is being replaced by another more in accordance with the facts. He concludes that it is now the task of the philosopher "to discover a doctrine of nature which expresses the concrete relatedness of physical functionings and mental functionings, of the past with the present, and also expresses the concrete composition of physical realities which are individually diverse."[22] Professor Ayer, in his recognition of the necessity for some conceptual system by which man seeks to bring order into his experience, is of one mind with Whitehead at this point. There are at the present time a number of cosmological interpretations held by groups of physicists by means of which they seek to interpret their findings. The very variety of such metaphysical schemes constitutes a call to philosophers to examine, as Ayer recommends, "the architectonic features"[23] of the categories employed. In the concluding paragraphs of his essay on "Philosophy and Language,"[24] he puts forward a number of concrete proposals for further investigation, among which is the suggestion that the time has come when our static concepts, such as that of a physical object, might well be replaced with some more dynamic concept, and asks the question: "Might not substantially the same facts be expressed in a language reflecting a universe of discourse in which the basic particulars were momentary events?"[25] Without

[18] Whitehead, *Adventures of Ideas*, pp. 163-64.
[19] Ibid., p. 164.
[20] Ibid., p. 179.
[21] Ibid., p. 200.
[22] Ibid., p. 201.
[23] Ayer, *The Concept of a Person*, p. 33.
[24] Ibid., p. 34.
[25] Ibid.

singling out any specific philosopher, Ayer is here recommending that philosophers should now reinvestigate Whitehead's whole approach to reality as a potentially fruitful undertaking.

Ayer is at one with Whitehead also in his recognition of the extreme difficulty of the task of the revision of the presuppositions of our thought, and points out that "very often when these alleged entailments are of philosophical interest, their validity is in dispute. The meaning of the crucial terms is just what needs to be settled."[26] Whitehead deals with this problem in considerable detail in the first chapter of *Process and Reality*; this is in fact the subject of the chapter and underlies his whole philosophical venture. He defines speculative philosophy as "the endeavour to frame a coherent, logical, necessary system of general ideas in terms of which every element of our experience can be interpreted."[27] Weakness of insight and deficiencies of language are, he maintains, the factors which prevent philosophers from ever finally formulating their metaphysical first principles.[28] It is part of the task of the philosopher, he suggests, to redesign language just as the scientist redesigns pre-existing appliances.[29] But it is just at this point that the appeal to facts is difficult, because the adequacy of the sentences in which we seek to give expression to the facts is what is mainly at issue. The problem, he suggests, lies in the fact that "every proposition refers to a universe exhibiting some general systematic metaphysical character,"[30] and in "proposing a fact must, in its complete analysis, propose the general character of the universe required for that fact."[31]

Whitehead insists that the proper objective of philosophy is the elucidation of immediate experience and the gradual elaboration of categoreal schemes; but the categories of such a system, rather than being dogmatic and final, are "tentative formulations of the ultimate generalities."[32] It aims at being so universal in its applicability that it finds illustration in every aspect of human experience, aesthetic, religious, social and scientific; and one of the central objectives of Whitehead's system is the fusing of religion and science into one rational scheme of thought. "Philosophy," he explains, "finds religion, and modifies it; and conversely, religion is among the data of experience which philosophy must weave into its own scheme."[33] Both religion and science require metaphysical interpretation of their categories of thought for the elucidation of their meaning, and in turn, each provides important data which must be given full consideration by the metaphysician in his task of generalization. Furthermore, religion and science each have an important influence upon the other. "Science finds religious experiences among its percepta; and religion finds

[26] Ibid., p. 31.
[27] Whitehead, *Process and Reality*, p. 4 (3).
[28] Ibid., p. 6 (4).
[29] Ibid., p. 16 (14).
[30] Ibid.
[31] Ibid., p. 17 (15).
[32] Ibid., p. 12 (11).
[33] Ibid., p. 23 (21).

scientific concepts among the conceptual experiences to be fused with particular sensitive reactions."[34]

Whitehead's major philosophical works were written while he was in America on the faculty of philosophy of Harvard University, and were published at a time when logical positivism was reaching the zenith of its influence in England and on the continent of Europe. He consistently repudiates positivism and presses on with the metaphysical task which he considers to be essential as providing the framework within which more specialized investigations may be carried on. His writings were largely neglected in England and have not since received the attention there that they merit. His secularization of the concepts of God's function in the world shocked the susceptibilities of some of his early reviewers, and his final statement in *Process and Reality* suffers from elements of incoherence which renders its full comprehension that much more difficult. Many of his early readers failed to take seriously his reminder that the most that the metaphysician can say about the ultimate are of the nature of "tentative formulations,"[35] pointing beyond themselves and awaiting confirmation or otherwise from experience. Examination of his writings subsequent to the publication of *Process and Reality* discloses that Whitehead's thought about God continued to evolve, or shall we say that he continued to ponder the ultimate generalities at the base of all experiences, and there are important further clarifications in later writings, particularly *Adventures of Ideas*.

When he wrote *Process and Reality*, Whitehead was convinced that the ultimate essence or sub-structure of the universe must be impersonal, and that process is ultimate. He expressly acknowledges that his view as expressed therein has many affinities with some strains of Indian or Chinese thought.[36] But, in a series of lectures delivered in the winter of 1937-38, he suggests that the discussion of process has run into exaggeration at this point, and states in correction, that "the essence of the universe is more than process."[37] There are factors in the universe, he acknowledges, to which the notion of process does not apply. Some of those he had already indicated in an earlier work, in which he came to the conclusion that "apart from some notion of imposed Law, the doctrine of immanence provides absolutely no reason why the Universe should not be steadily lapsing into lawless chaos."[38] It will be one aim of the present essay to trace the variety of Whitehead's approaches to, and his attempts at a clarification of his thought about God and the world, with a view to disclosing the sources of the insights which led him to this conviction of the necessity for the "more than process," and to evaluate its importance for contemporary dialogue about God.

[34] Ibid., p. 24 (22).
[35] Ibid., p. 12 (11).
[36] Ibid., p. 11 (9).
[37] A. N. Whitehead, *Modes of Thought* (3rd imp.; Cambridge: Cambridge University Press, 1938), p. 137.
[38] Whitehead, *Adventures of Ideas*, pp. 146-47.

A contemporary reader, however, may well ask how Whitehead, whose major philosophical writings were published in the decade following 1925, can possibly have any relevance to the present theological debate. Perhaps it may suffice, as a preliminary reply, to call attention to the extent to which Whitehead, throughout his philosophical investigations, was asking and searching for satisfactory answers to just those questions which are giving deep concern to the Church in the secularized society in which it is set today. To cite a few of the more obvious examples:

1. It is a major complaint of Whitehead against the theologians of the Christian Church, from the fifth century to the present day, that they have failed to develop the logical implications of their faith because a false image of God has clouded their minds, preventing them from discerning the real significance—for their understanding of man and the universe—of the discoveries made and recorded in the formulations of the faith at which they finally arrived and expressed in the Church's creeds. He suggests that "the notion of the absolute despot has stood in the way";[39] and he accuses the Church of idolatry, in that it has fashioned God in the image of an imperial ruler and has largely neglected its Galilean origin.[40] In Wittgensteinian terminology, the Christian theologians have been suffering from "aspect blindness"[41] in the matter of their image of God. When Bishop Robinson urged, at the time of the publication of his book, *Honest to God*, that "our image of God must go,"[42] he was therefore simply reiterating something which Whitehead had urged thirty -five years earlier as a prime requisite for progress.

2. A second illustration is contained in Bonhoeffer's agonized question as, from the ordeal of a Nazi concentration camp, he contemplated the task of the Church and asked: "How do we speak . . . in a secular fashion of God?"[43] His cry echoes and reiterates Whitehead's plea, in 1927, that "the secularization of the concept of God's functions in the world is at least as urgent a requisite of thought as is the secularization of other elements in experience."[44] Examination of the context in which Whitehead makes his plea discloses that he is concerned with the problem with which Bonhoeffer was wrestling in his cell.

3. In *Religion in the Making*, published in 1926, Whitehead analyzes religious experience to disclose the dominant ideas which are common to the great world religions, and declares that today there is but one religious dogma in debate, to which all other religious dogmas

[39] Ibid., p. 218.
[40] Whitehead, *Process and Reality*, pp. 519-21 (484-85).
[41] Ludwig Wittgenstein, *Philosophical Investigations*, trans. by G. E. M. Anscombe (Oxford: Basil Blackwell, 1963), Pt. II, xi, p. 213e.
[42] Robinson, *Honest to God*. (The phrase was the title to an interview which he had with the *Sunday Observer* on the Sunday before publication [March 19].)
[43] Dietrich Bonhoeffer, *Letters and Papers from Prison* (2nd ed., 1956; London: SCM Press, 1953), p. 123.
[44] Whitehead, *Process and Reality*, p. 315 (294.

are subsidiary, namely: "What do you mean by 'God?'"[45] The question is repeated by Bonhoeffer, in his *Letters*,[46] which for the most part consist of a cross-questioning of himself on this vast theme in search for answers which will be relevant to the needs of twentieth century man in a secular world. This is a fundamental question, because it is concerned with the ultimate meaning of the universe and of man's life on the earth. What do we mean by "God"? The different religions each give a different answer and along with it a whole reinterpretation of the meaning of human life and society. Bishop Robinson reiterates the question,[47] and the response to his book discloses that it is the question which is uppermost in the minds of multitudes today. Upon the answers which it receives in the lives of religious people in this generation may well depend the future of civilization as we know it.

4. Bishop Robinson's second book, in which he suggests that perhaps a new reformation of Christianity is under way, takes its title from a chapter in Whitehead's *Adventures of Ideas*. In a chapter entitled "The New Reformation,"[48] Whitehead puts forward the thesis that a new reformation is under way, which he believes is of the nature of a re-formation; he urges that there is evidence of a new response to the "divine persuasion"[49] in many parts of the world and that this constitutes a fresh opportunity for the Christian Church provided that its leaders are willing to equip themselves by a re-examination of the historical origins of their faith. He is convinced that if they will carry out this exercise with an open mind, they will discover aspects of the Christian message which have gone largely unheeded and undeveloped throughout the centuries. He is critical of the older metaphysical undertaking, but insists that it is impossible to reason about ultimate meaning and values without engaging in metaphysical thinking and expression. He recommends that theologians undertake this task today with a view to a revision of the theological vocabulary, and concludes: "I suggest that the development of systematic theology should be accompanied by a critical understanding of the relation of linguistic expression to our deepest and most persistent intuitions."[50]

It becomes evident that Whitehead, forty years ago, was raising questions identical to those which have been at the base of the theological ferment of the past two decades. It is not merely the case that he asks the same type of question, but that they are asked in the terminology in which they are being raised today—so much so that the questions raised by the "new theologians" might well have been lifted right out of Whitehead's major works, essays and lectures in which he sought to provide clarification on the nature of God and of his relation to the

[45] A. N. Whitehead, *Religion in the Making* (New York: Macmillan, 1926), pp. 67-68.
[46] Bonhoeffer, *Letters and Papers from Prison*, p. 179.
[47] Robinson, *Honest to God*, p. 24.
[48] John A. T. Robinson, *The New Reformation* (London: SCM Press, 1965), and Whitehead, *Adventures of Ideas*, Ch. X.
[49] Whitehead, *Adventures of Ideas*, pp. 205, 206.
[50] Ibid., p. 209.

world, and urged upon theologians the need to re-think and re-state the implications of their faith.

It is reasonable to assume that one who is so accurate in diagnosing the nature of the problems which lie before the Church may well have discovered some clues as to the direction in which solutions may be found. He is convinced that the future course of history depends upon the decision of his generation as to the relation between science and religion,[51] and one of the major aims of his whole philosophical venture is to bring about a rapprochement between science, religion and philosophy. He is not surprised that there should be conflict between science and religion for both have always been in a state of continual development and the clash, he insists, "is a sign that there are wider truths and finer perspectives within which a reconciliation of a deeper religion and a more subtle science will be found."[52] The fact of the conflict does not worry him, but what is a cause of concern is the fact that for over two centuries religion has been on the defensive, and that a weak defensive, throughout a period of unprecendented intellectual progress. He is convinced that religion will not regain its old power until it can face change in the same spirit as science does; its principles may indeed be eternal, but its thought-forms and modes of expression must change with the advance of knowledge.

[51] A. N. Whitehead, *Science and the Modern World* (Cambridge: Cambridge University Press, 1926), pp. 224-25.
[52] Ibid., p. 229.

Chapter II

The Variety of Whitehead's Approaches to Reality: The Approach through Science

Alfred North Whitehead was born in 1861 at Ramsgate, in the Isle of Thanet, Kent, England. He attended Sherbourne School in Dorsetshire; he distinguished himself in mathematics and in 1880 proceeded to Trinity College, Cambridge, where he was successively scholar and then Fellow. He was bracketed fourth wrangler in the mathematical tripos of 1883 and in the following year was elected a Fellow and put on staff as an assistant lecturer. His first book, *A Treatise on Universal Algebra with Applications,* was published in 1898; this was an attempt to integrate new developments in algebra and geometry which had been put forward by Hermann Grassman, W. R. Hamilton, and Boole. It was a highly original piece of work, and the reputation based on it led to the election of Whitehead as F.R.S. in 1903. At this point Whitehead seemed set on a career as a pure mathematician.

Through Mathematics to the Physical World

Bertrand Russell came up to Cambridge in 1890 and became an attached disciple of Whitehead. They went together to Paris to attend congresses on mathematics and philosophy where they heard an account of the work of Giuseppe Peano of Turin, who had invented a new ideography for use in symbolic logic. They recognized this to be vastly superior to anything previously known and devoted themselves to its development. They believed it might lead to the solution of the problem of the foundation of mathematics. After ten years' work together they arrived at the conclusion that mathematics is part of logic and published their findings in the three volumes of *Principia Mathematica,*[1] which appeared in the years 1910-13.

Throughout these years Whitehead continued to follow up his interest in the application of mathematics to physics and in 1905 presented to the Royal Society (in the same year in which Einstein's first paper on Relativity appeared) a paper "On Mathematical Concepts of

[1] Bertrand Russell and A. N. Whitehead, *Principia Mathematica* (Cambridge: Cambridge University Press, Vol. I, 1910; Vol. II, 1912; Vol. III, 1913).

the Material World" in which he discussed alternative theories of relativity and presented several proposals for their unification into a single theory of the material world. He stated his object as being to initiate the mathematical investigation of various possible ways of conceiving the material world. His biographer suggests that this memoir is important in the history of Whitehead's philosophical development, because it presents his first criticism of "scientific materialism."[2]

In the ten years following the publication of *Principia Mathematica* Whitehead was engaged in the application of the principles developed in it to the study of science. It had been the intention of the joint authors that there should be a fourth volume, written chiefly by Whitehead, and treating of geometry. Russell, in the Preface to his book, *Our Knowledge of the External World*, mentions that in this volume he has stated in a popular form some insights which he owes to Whitehead and which shortly would find a more exact expression from Whitehead's pen in a fourth volume of the *Principia*.[3] This fourth volume, however, was never published and no explanation was given, other than the fact that about this time the association of the two ceased.

By this time Whitehead is voicing his criticism of the classical concept of the material world and commencing the elaboration of a new concept from a different empirical base. Three papers, "Space, Time and Relativity" (1915); "The Organization of Thought" (1916); and "The Anatomy of Some Scientific Ideas"[4] (1917, are the first of his writings which would ordinarily be called philosophical. These were shortly followed by two books, *An Enquiry Concerning the Principles of Natural Knowledge*[5] (1919), and *The Concept of Nature*[6] (1920), in which Whitehead presents a new philosophy of natural science, with special application to physics.

In *The Principles,* Whitehead informs the reader that his aim is to bring three main streams of thought, the scientific, the mathematical and the philosophical to bear upon the problem of discovering a more adequate language for the interpretation of the universe as disclosed in scientific investigation. He explains that in this study he is "concerned only with Nature, that is, with the object of perceptual knowledge, and not with the synthesis of the knower with the known."[7] He is searching for a terminology which will enable him to unravel the perplexity as to what it is that is known in human knowledge, and concludes that, under

[2] Victor Lowe, "Whitehead's Philosophical Development," in *The Philosophy of Alfred North Whitehead,* ed. by Paul A. Schilpp (New York: Tudor), p. 35.

[3] Bertrand Russell, *Our Knowledge of the External World* (London: Unwin Brothers, 1914), Preface, p. 8.

[4] All three are now available in *The Aims of Education,* by A. N. Whitehead, in a Mentor Book published by the New American Library, copyright 1929, by the Macmillan Company.

[5] A. N. Whitehead, *An Enquiry Concerning the Principles of Natural Knowledge* (Cambridge: Cambridge University Press, 1919).

[6] A. N. Whitehead, *The Concept of Nature* (Cambridge: Cambridge University Press, 1920).

[7] Whitehead, *The Principles of Natural Knowledge,* Preface, p. vii.

the circumstances, there will be an incompleteness in the investigation: "it raises more difficulties than those which it professes to settle."[8]

In both *The Principles* and *The Concept of Nature,* Whitehead is concerned with the method of Extensive Abstraction and deals with problems of congruence, space, time and motion; and with the distinction between objects and events. He seeks here to limit the study of nature to an examination of what is observed, a position which he found himself compelled to abandon later. For example, in *The Concept of Nature,* he states that "the modern account of nature is not as it should be, merely an account of what the mind knows about nature; but it is also confused with an account of what nature does to the mind."[9] This, he suggests, has had disastrous results for both science and philosophy, and particularly for philosophy. But, five years later, in his Lowell Lectures in 1925, he expresses a point of view which is in sharp contrast to this, stating with approval that "the effect of physiology was to put mind back into nature."[10]

Here we find Whitehead moving out of the realm of mathematics, by way of a philosophy of mathematics and the physical sciences, into the realm of philosophy. He is building up at this time what has been called the "furniture of the universe," in his theory of "events," "objects," and "extensive abstraction," by means of which he seeks to clarify thought about the physical world. It is a fundamental premise of his thinking that a scientific system must seek to render nature intelligible and therefore predictable; but in a period of rapid scientific change this is exceedingly difficult, and, in the second edition of *The Principles of Natural Knowledge* (published in 1924), he acknowledges that the paradoxical nature of many statements in the first edition is due to the fact that, at the time of writing, his own thought was unclear: "The true doctrine, that 'process' is the fundamental idea, was not in my mind with sufficient emphasis."[11] He is feeling his way to a greater clarity of thought; as he applies his new conceptual tools in the interpretation of experience fresh problems demand that he push his thought yet further, and, in the preface to the second edition of *The Principles,* he indicates his hope to "embody the standpoint of these volumes in a more complete metaphysical study."[12]

In his Lowell Lectures, delivered in 1925, Whitehead undertakes a major revision of the prevalent scientific cosmology, which has been rendered obsolete by recent scientific discoveries. His method here is to survey the origins and development of modern science with a view to disclosing the notions about ultimate reality which dominated the period. There persists throughout the whole period of three hundred years "the fixed scientific cosmology which presupposes the ultimate

[8] Ibid., p. viii.
[9] Whitehead, *The Concept of Nature,* p. 27.
[10] A. N. Whitehead, *Science and the Modern World* (Cambridge: Cambridge University Press, 1926), p. 184.
[11] Whitehead, *The Principles of Natural Knowledge* (2nd ed., 1924), p. 202.
[12] Ibid., Preface, p. ix.

fact of an irreducible brute matter, or material, spread throughout space in a flux of configurations,"[13] and upon this edifice was built the philosophy of scientific materialism. Modern science has outgrown this static conception of nature, and developments in physics, in biology, in physiology, and psychology all call for a revision of cosmology. Whitehead is convinced that we are entering upon an age of reconstruction in religion, in science, and in political thought. The time has come, he suggests, when we must revise all our notions of the ultimate character of material existence; he recommends that we abandon traditional materialism in favour of an alternative doctrine of organism.[14] The doctrine of inert substance is now metaphysically unintelligible, in the light of recent scientific disclosures as to the nature of the components of the physical world. The changed outlook calls for a metaphysical interpretation, and Whitehead is beginning, in *Science and the Modern World,* to construct the elements of such a scheme.

The universe presents itself to our attention as a process of becoming which is the becoming of actual entities, and Whitehead finds that there is needed a ground of becoming, as explanation of the fact of there being a universe, and of its being this particular universe. The particularity of events, he suggests, requires a principle of "limitation of antecedent selection"[15] among an infinite variety of possibilities. This is his discovery of the need for "God as the Principle of Concretion"[16] and of ultimate limitation. God is here described as an "attribute of the substantial activity"[17] (which in the fully developed system is designated as the Ultimate, creativity). His existence is declared to be "the ultimate irrationality,"[18] inasmuch as no metaphysical reason can be given as to why the universe should be as it is. "God is not concrete," says Whitehead, "but he is the ground for concrete actuality. No reason can be given for the nature of God, because that nature is the ground of rationality."

The point which Whitehead wishes to emphasize here is that while metaphysics is unable to state anything about God, it is a metaphysical necessity that we postulate his presence as the "principle of determination" if we would give any account of the order and structure which is disclosed in the actualization of events. At this point we have reached the limit of rationality. Whitehead reflects that Aristotle, at a similar point in his metaphysics, found it necessary to introduce a Prime Mover, who was not of much value for religious purposes, and he expresses a doubt as to "whether any properly general metaphysics can ever, without the illicit introduction of other considerations, get much farther than Aristotle."[19] But the conclusion at which Aristotle arrived does nonetheless, he maintains,

[13] Whitehead, *Science and the Modern World,* p. 22.
[14] Ibid., p. 47.
[15] Ibid., p. 221.
[16] Ibid., p. 216.
[17] Ibid., pp. 220-21.
[18] Ibid., p. 222.
[19] Ibid., p. 215.

represent a first step without which no evidence on a narrower experiential basis can be of much avail in shaping the conception. For nothing, within any limited type of experience, can give intelligence to shape our ideas of any entity at the base of all actual things, unless the general character of things requires that there be such an entity.[20]

Whitehead here declares himself to be convinced both of the necessity and the limitations of natural theology; it is necessary, to provide a framework within which to interpret religious intuitions and experience; and it is limited, in that it depends upon the insights of religious experience to provide content in the form of illustrations and examples, and indicate the nature of the being so designated. "What further can be known about God must be sought in the region of particular experiences, and therefore rests on an empirical basis."[21]

Before leaving the discussion of God in *Science and the Modern World,* Whitehead makes an important comment in the final paragraph of this chapter which provides insight into the presuppositions of his own thought about God at this time, and also gives a clue as to the direction in which we may expect him to move. He suggests that both medieval and modern philosophers have paid God "metaphysical compliments" in their desire to safeguard his religious significance. "He has been conceived as the foundation of the metaphysical situation with its ultimate activity."[22] Whitehead's objection, at this time, against letting God be God in this manner is that we thereby make him responsible for all the evil in the world as well as the good. There is a very real element of truth in this assessment; in fact, the reality of the evil in the world constitutes for the Christian theologian one of the most acute problems which he must face. The alternative which Whitehead here proposes, of conceiving God as merely the "supreme ground for limitation" is the Platonic conception in which God is said to be responsible only for the good in the world. As so conceived, Whitehead explains, "It stands in his very nature to divide the Good from the Evil, and to establish Reason 'within her dominions supreme.'"[23]

The objection to this attempt at the solution of a most difficult problem is that, while we exonerate God from blame we do so at the price of reducing him to the status of a finite agent, and are left with the problem of evil, and the totality of the universe of which it is a feature, without any explanation. The problem persists, how can we conceive of God as author of creation and simultaneously the supreme ground for limitation in the becoming of actual entities in a process of self-creation? Only a deeper apprehension of the nature of God and of his process of creation and of his purpose for mankind can provide the clues to an understanding of this problem which continues to be the most acute question posed for those who would argue for the Christian

[20] Ibid., pp. 215-16.
[21] Ibid., p. 222.
[22] Ibid.
[23] Ibid., p. 223.

revelation of God. Such clues as we do have emerge from a clearer grasp of the full implications of Christ's revelation of God as Eternal Love, and can lead, if not to the solution of this problem, at least to its reduction to manageable proportions.

It cannot be solved by exonerating God from responsibility for the universe; this leaves us without any explanation for the fact of there being a universe, and we are virtually back with Bradley and his conception of a finite God.[24] The problem posed here will receive further consideration in our study of the metaphysics; for the present, it is sufficient to note that Whitehead's judgment is itself a metaphysical decision whose source will be found in the Platonic presuppositions of his thought at this time. What is abundantly clear, is that, once God has been admitted as necessary to an understanding of the scheme, questions concerning his nautre and his relation to the world press for an answer.

Summing up: In this chapter we have traced the development of Whitehead's thought through his mastery of mathematics, to an interest in the application of mathematical studies to the investigation of the physical universe; we have noted that from this point his mind moved to the philosophy of science, and to a recognition of the necessity of metaphysical construction to provide a framework within which the particularity of things might be comprehended in their inherent interrelatedness; there is a growing recognition of the importance of religious and aesthetic experience as a source of intuitions as to the nature of things. His investigations of modern science have led to a recognition of the necessity for God as the principle of concretion and of limitation to account for the fact of there being a universe. While this conclusion is a metaphysical judgment, metaphysics is itself incapable of discovering the nature of God. If anything further is to be known about God, it must be sought in the region of particular experiences; and we are not surprised to discover that Whitehead's next move is an examination of the empirical evidence in the records of the great World Religions.

[24] F. H. Bradley, *Essays on Truth and Reality* (Oxford: Clarendon Press, 1914), pp. 428ff.

Chapter III

The Variety of Whitehead's Approaches to Reality: His Investigation of Religious Experience and Expression

In his analysis of the universe as disclosed by the sciences, White-head has become convinced of the need for God as the principle of limitation and of concretion in the organic process of the world. He recognizes that in this affirmation he has gone beyond the realm of the sciences into stating a metaphysical assumption. This is not the only possible reply to the situation disclosed by science; Bertrand Russell, with whom he had worked for ten years on the production of *Principia Mathematica,* arrived at the same point in his analysis of the fundamental elements of physical nature and agreed with Whitehead that "events, not particles must be the stuff of physics."[1] There is, he acknowledges, a vast field, traditionally included in philosophy, which scientific methods are not adequate to explore, and states, "I do not myself believe that philosophy can either prove or disprove the truths of religious dogmas."[2] Whitehead would be in accord with Russell on both counts, but he insists that there are empirical evidences in the records of religious experience which provide data to be taken into account by both science and philosophy. Russell rejects this evidence and apparently remained fixed in his early conviction that all is due to chance happenings;[3] their difference on this matter of fundamental faith constitutes the parting of the ways in their philosophical endeavour. Whitehead finds Russell's position unsatisfactory as an explanation because it fails to explain anything, and constitutes a denial of the very order disclosed throughout the universe, an orderliness which is the opposite of chaotic movement. Some principle of limitation and of order is necessary to account for the universe, and, in this sense, God is a metaphysical necessity, but metaphysics is unable to say anything about him beyond that which may be gathered from observation from human experience. Whitehead is here recognizing both the necessity and the limitations of metaphysics in arriving at an understanding of

[1] Bertrand Russell, *A History of Western Philosophy* (New York: Simon and Schuster, 1945), p. 832.
[2] Ibid., p. 835.
[3] Bertrand Russell, "A Free Man's Worship," *Mysticism and Logic* (Middlesex: Penguin Books, 1918) (A270), Ch. III, pp. 51ff.

the meaning of human existence in the world. God is necessary to the metaphysical situation disclosed by the sciences, but his nature and relationship to the world can be known only as they are discerned in particular experiences at great moments in the history of mankind.

Whitehead devotes the Second Series of Lowell Lectures[4] to an analysis of religious dogmas with the purpose of discovering what type of justification can be found for belief in religious doctrines. He analyzes the four elements or factors which are found in all religions, namely, ritual, emotion, belief and rationalization, and concentrates his attention on the fourth, namely, the process of rationalization by which religions free themselves from outmoded forms of expression. His analysis proceeds on the assumption that character and conduct depend, in the long run, upon intimate convictions held by the individual. While the conduct of human life is conditioned externally by the environment, it receives its final quality, on which its real worth depends, from the internal life which is the self-realization of existence. "Religion," says Whitehead, "is the art and the theory of the internal life of man, so far as it depends upon the man himself and on what is permanent in the nature of things."[5] He concedes that social relationships are of great importance for religion, because no one lives an absolutely independent existence, but they are only a part. Behind all collective emotions, he asserts, there is "the awful ultimate fact, which is the human being, consciously alone with itself, for its own sake."[6] The heart and core of religion, he maintains throughout this study, "is what the individual does with his own solitariness." His readings have disclosed that religion runs through three stages, if it evolves to its final satisfaction. "It is the transition from God the void to God the enemy, and from God the enemy to God the companion."[7]

Great moments of crisis in the lives of the founders and reformers of the world religions have been productive of insights into the nature of reality and these have later been incorporated into the dogmas of particular faiths. It becomes clear from his readings that religion bases itself primarily upon a small selection from the common experiences of men, and in this sense must be regarded "as one among other specialized interests of mankind whose truths are of limited validity."[8] On the other hand, the great religions claim that while they trace their origin and their major conceptions to unique occasions in the lives of exceptional individuals, these are of universal validity, and are to be applied by faith to the ordering of all experience and at all times. Whitehead concludes from this that religion holds an important middle position between the abstractions of metaphysics and the particular principles which apply to only some among the experiences of mankind; particular in its time and place for origination, it nonetheless claims universal validity and application for its principles.

[4] A. N. Whitehead, *Religion in the Making* (New York: Macmillan, 1927).
[5] Ibid., p. 16.
[6] Ibid.
[7] Ibid., pp. 16-17.
[8] Ibid., p. 32.

Whitehead's major concern in this study is to investigate religious doctrines or dogmas which have emerged as religious geniuses sought to formulate truths disclosed in moments of religious intuition. He sums up his conclusions in the declaration, which has been repeated in the contemporary theological dialogue, that "Today there is but one religious dogma in debate; What do you mean by 'God'?"[9] All other questions are subsidiary to this, because the answers here will determine what may be said upon the others. Among a bewildering variety of beliefs and practices, the records of the great world religions disclose that there are three main simple renderings of the concept of God or of the Ultimate before the world, each of which, throughout the history of thought has been so interpreted as to be mutually exclusive of the other view. Whitehead gives these as (i) the extreme doctrine of immanence, found mainly among the Eastern Asiatic religions; (ii) the extreme doctrine of transcendence, as portrayed in the Semitic religions; and (iii) the extreme doctrine of monism as in various forms of philosophic monism.[10] Each of these points of view, Whitehead insists, is bearing witness to some genuine intuition into the nature of things and cannot simply be brushed aside as meaningless; we must seek a reconciliation by a more searching analysis of the terms employed to give expression to their faith. He believes it to have been part of the genius of Christianity that it has not adopted any one of these clear alternatives, but has, at least in decisive issues, subordinated its metaphysics to the religious facts to which it appeals; whereas Buddhism has from the beginning been a metaphysical system generating a religion, Christianity has been a religion seeking a metaphysic.[11] It has consequently been much more able to adjust to the changing climates of opinion throughout its long history. At its inception it inherited the simple Semitic concept, but with important qualifications, many of which were introduced by its founder.

Whitehead is impressed with the extent to which the beginnings of Christianity constitute an illustration of the rationalization of a religion, a process which was being carried out by Jesus Christ throughout his active ministry and was completed after his death and resurrection by his disciples—a process whereby the simple Semitic concept of God received important qualifications and the religion was transformed. Whitehead indicates five such qualifications which were of the utmost importance for the foundation and development of Christianity:

(1) The association of God with the Kingdom of Heaven, coupled with the explanation that "The Kingdom of Heaven is within you";

(2) The concept of God under the metaphor of a Father;

(3) The expansion of the implications of this notion in the two Epistles of John and in the Fourth Gospel, culminating in the doctrine that "God is Love";

[9] Ibid., p. 67.
[10] Ibid., pp. 68-69.
[11] Ibid., p. 50.

(4) In the Gospel according to John, by the introduction of the doctrine of the Logos, a clear move is made towards the modification of the notion of the unequivocal personal unity of the Semitic God.

(5) By the insistence on the immanence of God. The notion of immance, Whitehead suggests, must be discriminated from that of omniscience. The Semitic God is omniscient; but, in addition to that, the Christian God is a factor in the universe.[12]

Each of these five important developments which he located in the New Testament played a part in the formation of Whitehead's expression of his thought about God in the final chapter of *Process and Reality*.

Christianity, however, is but one of a number of religious expressions which must be taken into consideration by the metaphysician. Whitehead in his study of world religions is seeking empirical evidence which will enable him to formulate some satisfactory categories of explanation. Rational religion, he insists, must have recourse to metaphysics for the scrutiny of its terms; but he is equally insistent that religion contributes its own independent evidence which must be taken into account by the metaphysician.[13] If the enquiry into religious experience is to be helpful, however, it must take into account the wide variety of expressions of religion and be based, so far as is possible, upon some consensus of opinion among world religions as to the nature of ultimate reality. Religious experience, Whitehead declares, "consists of a certain widespread, direct apprehension of a character exemplified in the actual universe."[14] The religious person views the universe from a more comprehensive perspective than the non-religious. His faith may be expressed in graphic accounts of the experiences which brought the insight to him, but will include certain metaphysical presuppositions which are an important part of his faith. These, Whitehead suggests, will be held to be well founded "in so far as we trust the objectivity of the religious intuitions."[15]

Whitehead is here expressing essentially the principle of interpretation enunciated by Anselm in the Fides Quaerens Intellectum of the *Proslogion*,[16] and by Augustine before him in his oft-quoted saying "Crede ut intelligas,"[17] a principle which will play an important part in the later formulation of Whitehead's thought. It is this objectivity which is being denied by many of the writers in the New Theology; van Buren, for example, considers he is simply reporting a fact in stating that "the solution proposed by existential theologians consists of eliminating all 'objectification' of God in thought and word,"[18] and proceeds to criticize them for not going far enough; his

---

[12] Ibid., pp. 72, 73.
[13] Ibid., p. 79.
[14] Ibid., p. 86.
[15] Ibid.
[16] Anselm, *The Proslogion*.
[17] S. Augustine, in Sermon 118:1; also in Joan, Evang. 29,6.
[18] Paul van Buren, *The Secular Meaning of the Gospel* (London: SCM, 1963), p. 83.

own recommendation, under the circumstances, is that the word "God" be dropped from the vocabulary of theological discourse. Whitehead correctly at this point puts his finger on the essence of the problem facing the theologian and calls attention to the inherent relation between trust in the objectivity of religious intuitions and recognition of the validity of the metaphysical foundations. He is searching for metaphysical categories disclosed in the doctrines of the great world religions, hopeful that these may provide some clues as to the nature of ultimate reality.

Analysis and comparison of the concepts of God in the various religions convinces Whitehead that "religious experience cannot be taken as contributing to metaphysics any direct evidence for a personal God in any sense transcendent or creative."[19] Readings in Confucian, Buddhist, and Hindu philosophy disclose that all are at one in disclaiming the intuition of any ultimate personality substantial to the universe. There may very well be in these religions personal embodiments, but the substratum is impersonal. Whitehead finds, moreover, that Christian theology has also, in the main, adopted the position that there is no direct intuition of such an ultimate personal substratum, but that our belief in God as personal is based upon inference. He suggests that in this the theologians were following Greek thought. The Greek thinkers based their procedure on the Pythagorean notion "of a righteousness in the nature of things, functioning as a condition, a critic, and an ideal."[20]

These considerations will have an important bearing upon Whitehead's formulation of the first principles of his metaphysical system. A rational appeal to religious experience must seek the widest possible agreement among intuitions as to the ultimate nature of things, and Whitehead concludes that if there is to be any concurrence on this question, it is against the conception of a personal substratum to the universe. Lest this decision be taken as final, however, Whitehead introduces a warning note to the effect that on "a question of rational interpretation, numbers rapidly sink in importance."[21] There may well be intuitions which first emerge into consciousness under exceptional conditions and which are later found to be of universal significance. The emergence of the great religions has, as a matter of fact, resulted from just such supreme moments in the lives of founders, and the question which must ultimately be faced is whether it is possible that some one of these has provided intuitions which more adequately portray reality than others. At this point in his development Whitehead is imbued with the need for seeking a consensus of opinion on the question of the nature of ultimate reality, and he settles for an impersonal ultimate.

Another metaphysical principle which becomes evident in the analysis of the universe as disclosed in the physical sciences and in

[19] Whitehead, *RM,* pp. 86-87.
[20] Ibid., p. 63.
[21] Ibid., p. 66.

biology, and which Whitehead now finds confirmed by the religious experience of mankind, is the interrelationship of the individual and society, each formative of the other. The topic of religion, he says, is individuality in community. There are physical occasions and there are mental occasions and the mental occasion is derivative from its physical counterpart; it is of the nature "of a perceptivity issuing into value-feeling, but it is a reflective perceptivity."[22] Whitehead is insistent upon the interrelationship between the physical and the spiritual. "A mental occasion is an ultimate fact in the spiritual world, just as a physical occasion of blind perceptivity is an ultimate fact in the physical world. There is an essential reference from one world to the other."[23] The philosophy of organism will seek to refute the validity of the Cartesian dichotomy between mind and matter by a demonstration of the essential interrelatedness of all things in the organic process of the universe.

In the third and fourth lectures in this series Whitehead is bringing together the findings of his analyses of the universe as described in the sciences and in religious experience and is engaged in the task of formulating the categories by means of which he will undertake the construction of his metaphysical system. He seeks to isolate the formative elements which jointly constitute the actual temporal world; it is an empirical task because "we know nothing beyond this temporal world and the formative elements which jointly constitute its character."[24] His investigations have disclosed at least three such formative elements which are now listed as

(i) the creativity whereby the actual world has its character of temporal passage into novelty;

(ii) the realm of ideal entities, or forms, which are in themselves not actual, but are such that they are exemplified in everything that is actual, according to some proportion of relevance;

(iii) the actual but non-temporal entity whereby the indetermination of mere creativity is transmuted into a determinate freedom. This non-temporal actual entity is what men call God—the supreme God of rationalized religion.[25]

God is here identified as the ordering principle without which there would be no order, and without order, there would be no world.[26] In this Whitehead is extending the argument of Kant, who saw the necessity for God in the moral order, but denied the validity of the argument from the cosmos; Whitehead is here challenging this position and extending the argument from design to the whole universe. This he does by finding the foundations of the world in the aesthetic experience which he believes to be prior to both the cognitive and the conceptive experience. "The actual world is the outcome of the aes-

[22] Ibid., p. 102.
[23] Ibid., p. 103.
[24] Ibid., p. 90.
[25] Ibid.
[26] Ibid., p. 104.

thetic order, and the aesthetic order is derived from the immanence of God."[27]

In the concluding lecture Whitehead is commencing to work out the interrelationships of the three formative elements which he has discerned as together constituting the character of the universe, and is moving in the direction of a differentiation of the various operations of God in the actualization of the world—a process which is carried to its completion in his metaphysical system, as disclosing different aspects of the nature of God. We recall that in *Science and the Modern World* God was required by the metaphysical situation as the Principle of Concretion to account for the fact of there being a universe. He had also pointed out at that time that rightness of limitation is essential for growth of reality.[28] This aspect of the situation is now carried further. "Unlimited possibility and abstract creativity can procure nothing";[29] before creativity can achieve anything real it must acquire a character and this it acquires in the primordial creative act which is the primordial nature of God. God is declared to be the principle of limitation by which the universe is given a particular direction in its process of becoming, and creativity is everywhere informed by the eternal objects which are the primordial nature of God. It is now pointed out that every actual entity which comes into being, from the primordial nature of God to the most minute proton or neutron provides an element of limitation and a condition for the possibilities of creativity in any specific situation. That which is already actual provides the basis for further groupings of the elements into new concrescences under the limitation provided by God in his provision of the initial subjective aim of each. In this way God provides the direction for each new concrescence and ensures that it will be a particular entity with specific potentiality for becoming, conditioned, on the one hand, by the eternal objects which comprise its subjective aim, and on the other by the data provided by the specific universe of the space-time continuum. "The limitation, and the basis arising from what is already actual, are both of them necessary and interconnected,"[30] Whitehead declares, and sums up the situation in the significant statement that "The whole process itself, viewed at any stage as a definite limited fact which has issued from the creativity, requires a definite entity, already actual among the formative elements, as an antecedent ground for the entry of the ideal forms into the definite process of the temporal world."[31]

Here we see Whitehead arriving at a realization of the necessity of there being some principle of origination. He is concerned about the actual "temporal" world, which is experienced by us and is investigated by science, and he is raising the ultimate question of origination.

---

[27] Ibid., p. 105. It is interesting to note that Aquinas says something very similar. See *Philosophical Texts*, ed. by T. Gilby (New York: Oxford University Press), p. 111, "The poetic reasons for all things made are in the Word" (*Summa Theologica* 1a. xxxiv. 3).

[28] A. N. Whitehead, *Science and the Modern World*, pp. 220-21.

[29] Whitehead, *RM*, p. 152.

[30] Ibid.

[31] Ibid.

Everywhere in the universe, in the physical, mental, emotional, and moral realms there is creativity; things come to be, creative forces are at work in the world; they are not working blindly, but in harmony are producing this particular universe which has evolved a finite variety of entities, some of which have developed the ability to conceptualize their experience and so to reflect and to think and communicate their thoughts one to another. The question which finally presses for an answer is that of origination. What is the principle of origination of the world of things and people? Whitehead suggests that at whatever stage it is viewed, the process "requires a definite entity, already actual among the formative elements, as an antecedent ground for the entry of ideal forms into the definite process of the temporal world."[32]

Whitehead's investigations have brought him to the conviction of the necessity for an aboriginal actuality which, as antecedent ground, must not itself be a part of the process, but must "differ from actuality in process of realization in respect of the blind occasions of perceptivity which issue from process and require process."[33] The actual entities or "occasions" in process of becoming "build up the physical world which is essentially in transition."[34] God is the ground antecedent to the transition which is the actual world, and Whitehead sees that in order to be the "ground" of the universe in process of becoming he "must include all possibilities of physical value conceptually, thereby holding the ideal forms apart in equal conceptual realization of knowledge."[35] Thus, the ideal forms, as pure potentials, are not just somewhere in a realm of forms as for Plato, but, "as concepts, they are grasped together in the synthesis of omniscience."[36] The language employed here is similar to that of Plotinus in describing his Intellectual-Principle, the Second Hypostasis in his divine hierarchy. This statement, however, might equally be regarded as a commentary upon the question of the Psalmist: "Is there knowledge in the most high?,"[37] to which Whitehead replies, yes, indeed, there must be, otherwise it would not be possible for us men. There is both knowledge and evaluation by which there is established an order in the relevance of ideal forms for concrescence in the actual world. This realization, in turn, compels Whitehead to recognize that God's goodness constitutes a limitation, and he concludes that God cannot be "in all respects infinite,"[38] for the essence of valuation is selection of one as against another. God is good, he is not evil—"unlimited fusion of evil with good would mean mere nothingness"[39]—chaos. It was Plato's recognition of the necessity of order and harmony which led him to reject the Homeric gods and to

[32] Ibid.
[33] Ibid., pp. 152-53.
[34] Ibid., p. 153.
[35] Ibid.
[36] Ibid.
[37] Psalm 73:11.
[38] Whitehead, *RM,* p. 153.
[39] Ibid.

assert that God is good and the author only of good; and Whitehead likewise concludes that "the limitation of God is his goodness."[40]

Whitehead now presses forward to the conclusion of his argument; God "is complete in the sense that his vision determines every possibility of value."[41] It is this vision (further defined in *Process and Reality* as "God's envisagement"[42]) that makes possible a world and determines what kind of a world it will be; his complete vision "co-ordinates and adjusts every detail."[43] The phraseology calls to mind Plotinus'[44] itemization of the various objects of the universe and the world which have come into being by means of Soul, and Athanasius' description of the same as being due to the operation of the Word and Good God, and his later and more explicit description of the Creation of the world by God the Father, through His Word, and in the Holy Spirit—the Word being the agency of God in Creation and the Holy Spirit being His mode of operation in bringing the world into being and sustaining the creative process which is the universe. Whitehead suggests that God's complete vision co-ordinates and adjusts every detail, and consequently it cannot be said that God is growing in knowledge as the actual world takes shape, because what comes to pass is simply the concretion of his purposes for the development of the world. He now goes on to suggest that "this ideal world of conceptual harmonization is merely a description of God himself."[45] In this sense, God is his purpose, and Whitehead equates the Kingdom of Heaven and God. "Thus the nature of God is the complete conceptual realization of the realm of ideal forms."[46] At this point in Whitehead's thought, the realm of Plato's Forms is being gathered into the nature of God, who is being identified with the Second Hypostasis of Plotinus' System, the Intellectual-Principle.

Whitehead is here attempting a synthesis of the findings of his research into the great religions of the world, and is bringing together the conception of God as portrayed in the Christian Gospel and the fully developed Platonic system in an effort to equate them. On the one hand, he wants to say that "the Kingdom of heaven is God,"[47] and on the other to speak of the primordial nature of God as "the complete conceptual realization of the realm of ideal forms."[48] And yet there is another sense in which he wishes to keep the forms apart as in the Platonic Dialogues; "The forms," he declares, "belong no more to God than to any one occasion."[49] It becomes evident that a number of

[40] Ibid.
[41] Ibid.
[42] Whitehead, *PR*, p. 70 (60).
[43] Whitehead, *RM*, pp. 153-54.
[44] Plotinus, *Enneads*, V. 1, 2. Eng. ed. by Paul Henry, S.J., trans. by Stephen McKenna (London: Faber & Faber, 1956), p. 370.
[45] Whitehead, *RM*, p. 154.
[46] Ibid.
[47] Ibid.
[48] Ibid.
[49] Ibid., p. 157.

conflicting ideas are struggling for inclusion within Whitehead's concept of God.

Moreover, Whitehead, in addition to thinking of God in his work of antecedent envisagement and of concretion, is working out a formula for another side to God's nature, according to which he is seen to be also at work within the actual world, taking to himself the values of those entities which are in process of becoming; both the good and the evil inherent in each situation enter into God's nature and there become transmuted, so that he brings good out of a situation which appears to be mere wreckage. This aspect of his nature will be developed fully in *Process and Reality* to become the Consequent Nature of God, but the fundamentals of that development are clearly stated here. The Kingdom of Heaven, Whitehead declares, "is the overcoming of evil by good."[50] Each actual occasion contributes to the total situation a ground partly good and partly bad and in this way limits the possibilities of the immediate future; but, on the other hand, because this occasion, with all its shortcomings, enters into and is transmuted in the nature of God, this ideal or possible consequent as it stands in God's vision is also added to the total situation and so there is a possibility of the realization of a deeper and fuller satisfaction in the consequent.

Here we find the gradual development of a further aspect of Whitehead's concept of God, namely his consequent nature, whereby God meets each occasion afresh each day and seeks to bring from the situation the maximum good which is possible for it, having in mind the freedom of choice which is inherent in the process of self-creation of all actual occasions. In this way God brings good out of evil, and utilizes what would normally be termed wreckage for the building up of some part of his Kingdom. "His purpose is always embodied in the particular ideals relevant to the actual state of the world."[51] Every act, Whitehead suggests, leaves the world with a deeper or a fainter impress of God, and the passage of time is now defined as the journey of the world towards the gathering of new ideas into actual fact, and it may lead upward or downward, depending upon individual response to the challenge of the present situation. It is in this sense that God is, as Whitehead has put it, the lure for adventure, meeting us where we are today and leading us on to the next stage of our pilgrimage which is made possible or necessary by our past reactions and attainments or lack of them. "Whatever ceases to ascend, fails to preserve itself and enters upon its inevitable path of decay."[52] The aspect of decay is particularly observable in the physical realm, and both here and in *The Function of Reason* (1929), Whitehead calls attention to the two aspects which the universe displays: "On one side it is physically wasting, on the other side it is spiritually ascending."[53] Some scientists envisage the

[50] Ibid., p. 155.
[51] Ibid., p. 159.
[52] Ibid., pp. 159-60.
[53] Ibid., p. 160, and also *The Function of Reason* (Beacon Paperback ed., 1958; Princeton: Princeton University Press, 1929).

entire wasting away of the physical world; but there is another aspect, in which our universe is seen to be passing to new creative conditions, so that the question, "What will the future hold?" becomes a further question, "What are we today making possible for tomorrow?" The study concludes with a summing up of the total situation:

> The present type of order in the world has arisen from an unimaginable past, and it will find its grave in an unimaginable future. There remain the inexhaustible realm of abstract forms, and creativity, with its shifting character ever determined afresh by its own creatures and God, upon whose wisdom all forms of order depend.[54]

The twin themes of order and of limitation are fundamental to any understanding of the universe, as necessary today in the age of science as in Plato's day. But when Whitehead sums up the things that remain, what he re-affirms is basically the Platonic view of the ultimate realities as the forms, creativity and God. If we compare with the above the concluding phrase in the final sentence of the third lecture it will become abundantly evident that this is exactly what Whitehead meant to say at this time, and that his presuppositions at the conclusion of *Religion in the Making* are those of the later Dialogues of Plato. The universe, he declares, "exhibits a creativity with infinite freedom, and a realm of forms with infinite possibilities; but that this creativity and these forms are together impotent to achieve actuality apart from the completed ideal harmony, which is God."[55] Here in these two important summary passages, we have a clear enunciation of the Platonic triad of the Forms, the Receptacle (creativity) and God, whose place in the scheme is that of the Demiurgos of the *Timaeus,* bringing such order as is possible into the situation, but limited by the other aspects of reality. It is true, as we have pointed out, that in the final chapter he is moving in the direction of inclusion of the Forms within the being of God, but this has not yet taken place; the Forms, we are told here, "belong no more to God than to any one occasion."[56]

[54] Whitehead, *RM,* p. 160.
[55] Ibid., pp. 119-20.
[56] Ibid., p. 157.

Chapter IV

The Variety of Whitehead's Approaches to Reality: Philosophical Investigations and the Selection of a Cosmological Framework

In the Preface to *Process and Reality* Whitehead gives some indication of the extensive research into philosophy which preceded the writing of his metaphysical system. He declares that he is going behind Kant to the "phase of philosophic thought which began with Descartes and ended with Hume"[1] but warns the reader that he is going to emphasize those elements in the writings of these philosophers which subsequent philosophers have put aside. He considers that John Locke anticipated the philosophy of organism but that this aspect of his thought has largely been neglected. He here reiterates his intention to "bring the aesthetic, moral, and religious interests" of mankind "into relation with those concepts of the world which have their origin in natural science."[2]

Whitehead acknowledges his indebtedness to Bergson, William James, John Dewey and Bradley; particularly the latter, with whom he states he has in the main body of his own work been in sharp disagreement, but that the final outcome of his system is not so greatly different, and concedes that in the final chapter on "God and the World" the approximation to Bradley is evident. He is quite explicit on this point and declares that "if this cosmology be deemed successful, it becomes natural at this point to ask whether the type of thought involved be not a transformation of some main doctrines of Absolute Idealism onto a realistic basis."[3] In the light of this claim it becomes important to examine Bradley's thought, particularly in its final expression in the *Essays on Truth and Reality* in which Bradley gives expression to his puzzlement and dissatisfaction with some of his conclusions about the nature of ultimate reality.

[1] A. N. Whitehead, *Process and Reality: An Essay in Cosmology* (New York: Harper Torchbooks, 1960; first published, New York: Macmillan, 1929), Preface, p. v.
[2] Ibid., p. vi.
[3] Ibid., p. viii (vii).

Another point of emphasis in the Preface calls for attention if we would understand the direction in which Whitehead's thought is moving. He is writing a cosmology which he hopes will provide a basis for the interpretation and comprehension of the wide variety of human experience in the sciences, in aesthetics, in morality and religion. He calls attention to two cosmologies which at different periods have dominated European thought, namely, "Plato's *Timaeus* and the cosmology of the seventeenth century, whose chief authors were Galileo, Descartes, Newton, Locke."[4] He suggests that he will seek a fusion of the best elements of these two previous schemes with such modifications as are called for by the advance of knowledge in our own day.

In the final chapter of the cosmology the weight which Whitehead has given to the respective systems which have preceded him becomes at once a basis for interpretation of the whole and provides a limitation upon the meaning to be ascribed to the ultimate categories in the system. As Whitehead states in the concluding sentences of the first chapter of Part V, "God and the World introduce the note of interpretation. They embody the interpretation of the cosmological problem in terms of a fundamental metaphysical doctrine as to the quality of creative origination, namely, conceptual appetition and physical realization."[5] This being the case, it becomes important to examine and compare at least briefly the Platonic and the Newtonian scheme for clues as to the presuppositions of Whitehead's thought as he approaches an interpretation of the ultimate meaning of things.

(i) *The cosmological framework: Newton, Plato and Whitehead*

Whitehead describes the cosmology of the seventeenth century as being based partly on a mixture of theology and philosophy and partly due to the Newtonian physics. But Newtonian physics is no longer acceptable as a fundamental statement, and Whitehead declares that the system which he is formulating is basically Platonic, in the sense that: "If we had to render Plato's general point of view with the least changes made necessary by the intervention of two thousand years of human experience in social organization, in aesthetic attainments, in science, and in religion, we should have to set about the construction of a philosophy of organism."[6] Our examination of the second series of the Lowell Lectures disclosed that the presuppositions of Whitehead's thoughts about God and the World at that time were Platonic,[7] and this fact becomes particularly evident in his discussion of the order of nature in *Process and Reality*.[8] Here he compares and contrasts the *Timaeus* of Plato and the *Scholium* of Newton. The *Scholium* is a statement of details abstracted from the process of nature in which "space, and time, and material masses, and forces, are alike ready-made for the

---

[4] Ibid., p. ix (ix).
[5] Ibid., p. 518 (483).
[6] Ibid., p. 63 (54).
[7] See above, p. 29.
[8] Whitehead, *PR*, pp. 127ff. (115ff.).

initial motions which the Deity impresses throughout the universe."[9] The concept of God implied here and throughout Newton's writings, is that of Deism, of a God transcendent to the world, and of a world complete—a finished product—brought into being by divine fiat. Whitehead complains that he finds no hint in the *Scholium* of "that aspect of self-production, of generation, of φύσις, of natura naturans, which is so prominent in nature."[10] The *Scholium*, consequently, provides no basis upon which to extract "either a theism, or an atheism, or an epistemology, which can survive a comparison with the facts . . . and finally, physics has now reached a stage of experimental knowledge inexplicable in terms of the categories of the *Scholium*."[11]

Whitehead concedes that if we compare Plato's *Timaeus* with Newton's *Scholium* as a scientific statement, the *Timaeus* will appear, in comparison, simply foolish. But there is another aspect of the *Timaeus* which is lacking in the *Scholium* and which gives to Plato's myth a timeless quality; it is a cosmology, an "endeavour to connect the behaviour of things with the formal nature of things."[12] It presents the universe as a process of becoming and as the work of subordinate deities, rather than *causa sui*. Whitehead holds that, in its evolutionary doctrine, the organic philosophy is reiterating something emphasized in the *Timaeus*, in which the origin of the present cosmic epoch is traced back to an aboriginal disorder. Plato's doctrine, he maintains, has puzzled critics obsessed with the Semitic theory, and because Newton, who held this theory, made no provision for the evolution of matter, its non-evolution has been a tacit presupposition of modern thought. Until very recently the only alternatives open were "either the material universe, with its present type of order, is eternal; or else it came into being, and will pass out of being, according to the fiat of Jehovah."[13] Today, however, developments in scientific knowledge are demanding that the whole subject be re-investigated and re-formulated, and Whitehead insists that in appealing to Plato he is appealing to the facts against modes of expression which have been prevalent during the past few centuries, but which can no longer be accepted as a fundamental statement.[14] He recommends that a more acceptable mode of expression will be found in the writings of Plato and Aristotle for whom "the process of the actual world has been conceived as a real incoming of forms into real potentiality, issuing in that real togetherness which is an actual thing."[15] This would appear to be an accurate statement of the thought of Aristotle, who taught that the universe was the result of the informing of matter, but to be a misstatement of the teaching of Plato, for whom the Forms were eternal models, in a realm of Forms in the heavens, which are only mirrored or imaged in the material world. It is

[9] Ibid., pp. 143-44 (130).
[10] Ibid., p. 143 (129-30).
[11] Ibid., p. 144 (130-31).
[12] Ibid.
[13] Ibid., p. 146 (133).
[14] Ibid., p. 147 (133-34).
[15] Ibid., p. 147 (134).

interesting to note that A. E. Taylor, for whom Whitehead had a great admiration, taught as Platonic doctrine[16] virtually the position which Whitehead here takes, and it is possible that he is at least partly responsible for the novel turn which the Forms take in Whitehead's hands.

It is important to an understanding of Whitehead's organic philosophy to realize that he did pattern the system upon the Platonic cosmology, because he found in Plato's myth a forthright account of the origination of the universe which, he was convinced, contained genuine intuitions into the nature of reality, and he was particularly impressed with the insight that "the creation of the world is the incoming of a type or order establishing a cosmic epoch. It is not the beginning of matter of fact, but the incoming of a certain type of social order."[17]

Whitehead, however, in taking over and utilizing the Platonic cosmology, subtly changes the meanings of terms and concepts in a manner designed to transpose the whole onto a more realistic basis.

Plato was the first to introduce into Greek Philosophy the conception of creation by a divine artificer. His Demiurge, however, is not an omnipotent creator, but is more like a human craftsman, who must have materials to work upon; so the task of the Demiurge is not to create the materials out of which the universe is composed, but rather to introduce some intelligible order into a condition of disorder which he "takes over." Neither does he create the patterns or models in the likeness of which he constructs the visible. There are, for Plato, two orders of existence, the intelligible and unchanging model, the Forms, and the changing and visible copy, which is not self-subsistent, but requires the support of a medium in which it appears, much as a reflection requires a mirror to hold it. Plato, therefore, found it necessary to introduce a third factor, the Receptacle, "as it were the nurse— of all becoming,"[18] as that "in which" qualities appear, as fleeting images seen in a mirror. The Receptacle has a nature of its own from which it never departs. But it has no qualities of its own "before" the qualities enter it, unlike the gold, which has its own sensible qualities. Timaeus suggests that "we shall not be deceived if we call it a nature invisible and characterless, all-receiving, partaking in some very puzzling way of the intelligible and very hard to apprehend."[19]

Plato's notion of a Receptacle as a necessary and permanent matrix of all becoming finds its counterpart in Whitehead's system in "creativity"; but whereas in the Platonic myth the Receptacle is the "third factor" in the situation, Whitehead finds it necessary to declare "creativity" to be the ultimate in the philosophy of organism.

[16] A. E. Taylor, *Commentary of the Timaeus*, Preface, pp. ix, x; also his discussion of 35b, 1-3, the account of the becoming of the physical world on p. 131. See also his *Plato: The Man and His Work* (London: Methuen, 1929), p. 440.

[17] Whitehead, *PR*, p. 147 (134).

[18] Plato, *Timaeus*, 49A; cf. F. M. Cornford, *Plato's Cosmology: The "Timaeus" of Plato translated with a running commentary* (4th imp., 1956; London: Routledge and Kegan Paul, 1937), p. 177.

[19] Plato, *Timaeus*, 51A-B; Cornford, *Plato's Cosmology*, p. 186.

Moreover, it is important to notice that, whereas in Plato's myth the Receptacle is simply the medium in which the visible comes to be—the matrix of all becoming—and is finally identified as Space, in Whitehead's system, "creativity" is that substantial activity which is the ground of all becoming and is a dynamic category. In this respect, Whitehead's category of the ultimate is in strong contrast to both Plato's Receptacle and Aristotle's prime matter, both of which are passive recipients, in the one case of the "images" of the Forms and in the other of the Forms or Universals themselves. There is an element of similarity, even here, however, inasmuch as creativity is characterized by the eternal objects which are prehended by actual entities in process of concretion. By designating "creativity" to be the ultimate in his system, Whitehead seeks to incorporate into it all the values inherent in the conceptions of both Plato and Aristotle, and to carry forward his plan of transposing the whole onto a realistic basis.

Comparison of the three philosophers (Plato, Aristotle, and Whitehead) in their selection of that aspect of experience which will be regarded as ultimate provides an illustration of the importance of first principles in determining the direction of the system as a whole. The language which Whitehead employs in explaining the nature of his "ultimate" is practically identical with that of Timaeus in interpreting the Receptacle, which has, he declares, "a nature invisible and characterless, all-receiving,"[20] and takes on the appearances of those images which it receives. Whitehead declares that "creativity is without a character of its own . . . it cannot be characterized, because all characters are more special than itself,"[21] but is always found under conditions, and is described as conditioned. By selecting this dynamic aspect of experience as the ultimate in his philosophy, Whitehead seeks to solve one of the most persistent problems which has puzzled philosophers from the earliest times until the present day, namely, how to reconcile change and changelessness.

The universe as described by Whitehead in *Process and Reality* is a self-creative process, in contrast to the conception of a static universe of the older physical theory, and as suggested in much Christian literature about the creation of the world by divine fiat, as though it were "a self-sufficient completion of the creative act, explicable by its derivation from an ultimate principle which is at once eminently real and the Unmoved Mover."[22] It was one of the fundamental aims of Whitehead's philosophical venture to replace this static conception with a dynamic interpretation portraying the universe as a continuous process of self-creative activity in which each actual entity exercises a measure of choice and in turn makes its own contribution to the totality which is the universe. In "creativity" Whitehead has isolated an element which is more ultimate than either Plato's Receptacle or Aristotle's "matter"; but "creativity" is going to require further elucidation before

[20] Plato, *Timaeus,* 51A; cf. Cornford, *Plato's Cosmology.*
[21] Whitehead, *PR,* p. 47 (42-43).
[22] Ibid., p. 519 (484).

it will be adequate to account for the fact of the creative universe of which it is one expression. By making "creativity" itself the ultimate in his metaphysical system, Whitehead seeks to develop a complete cosmological scheme in which the process is the reality. He adopted the Platonic framework because it fitted best the needs of the situation disclosed by the empirical sciences and in ordinary experience; the universe as presented to us is a creative process. The adoption of the Platonic cosmology will, however, have important consequences for Whitehead's development, because the adoption of a framework involves acceptance of limitations upon the meanings to be attached to major categoreal notions; in particular, it will have a most important bearing upon the concepts of the ultimate nature of reality, upon the nature of God and his relation to the world. Whitehead is aware of this difficulty and remodels the categories accordingly, but nonetheless, the Platonic framework will exercise an important influence upon the development of the system and will affect the final interpretation.

(ii) God, religious experience, and the Absolute: The influence of Bradley

If Whitehead drew the framework and the structure of his system from Plato, his reading of F. H. Bradley, particularly his later *Essays on Truth and Reality*,[23] posed some of the most acute problems which troubled the philosophers of his day, and called for an attempt at a solution by anyone who sought to bring together into a unified system the insights of science, religion and philosophy. Bradley is a typical philosopher of the Hegelian tradition for whom the idea is the real and all else is at most an appearance of the Absolute idea. In the end all differences, all goodness and evil, God and religion, all alike are dissolved into the Absolute. Bradley is himself disturbed about some of the consequences of his philosophy, especially for the practice of religion.

Whitehead, in the Preface to *Process and Reality*, acknowledges his indebtedness to Bradley; he indicates that while in the main body of his work he is in sharp disagreement with him, yet in the final interpretation in which he is seeking to answer the question "What does it all come to?"[24] he is approximating to Bradley's position. He expresses the hope that he has succeeded in transforming some of the main doctrines of Absolute Idealism onto a realistic basis. This he accomplishes, in part, by rejecting Bradley's Absolute as a meaningless term and substituting in its place as the ultimate in his system a feature of the universe (the substantial activity) as actualized and characterized only in the process of becoming of actual entities which are the reality of the universe as described by Whitehead.

Whitehead is here specifically affirming what Bradley denies. The process, Bradley declares, while it moves within Reality, "is not Reality itself";[25] and explains that "to take God as the ceaseless oscillation and

---

[23] F. H. Bradley, *Essays on Truth and Reality* (Oxford: Clarendon Press, 1914).
[24] Whitehead, *PR*, Preface, p. viii (vii).
[25] F. H. Bradley, *Appearance and Reality* (London: George Allen and Unwin, 1925), p. 448.

changing movement of the process, is out of the question"[26] for him. He reverts to this problem again in the concluding section of the *Essays*. Whereas his theory of the Absolute carries the implication that change is only appearance and is therefore unreal, he is compelled to recognize that for him, as for everyone else, the world is full of change. This question of "how change stands to that which changes or shows change,"[27] he expostulates, is one which you cannot get rid of "unless you will set up the abstraction of change as real by itself, or as even perhaps the main or only reality of things."[28] It is this element of experience which Bradley branded as an abstraction which Whitehead declares to be the reality in his system, and by so doing seeks to reconcile the factor of change with the changeless. Facts as actual finite events are for Bradley the "lowest and most untrue forms of appearance,"[29] while Whitehead constitutes the event as "the unit of things real."[30] For Bradley, "God is but an aspect, and that must mean but an appearance, of the Absolute,"[31] whereas for Whitehead he is the one non-temporal actual entity.

For Bradley God is a finite being, and while he will allow that God may be personal for the religious consciousness, yet finds himself compelled, in consistency to his philosophical principles, to differentiate between this and the Absolute. "If you identify the Absolute with God," he declares, "that is not the God of religion."[32] If, on the other hand, you separate them, then "God becomes a finite factor in the whole."[33] He is reduced to the status of an appearance and this, Bradley realizes, would not be a satisfactory conclusion for the religious person. He recognizes that it is necessary for religion to have some doctrine, however little, and is equally certain that such doctrine will not be ultimate truth. He recommends that if the problem of religion is to be discussed rationally at all, there is needed first an enquiry into the essence and end of religion, which will call for two indispensable steps. "We must get some consistent view as to the general nature of reality, goodness, and truth, and we must not shut our eyes to the historical facts of religion."[34] Having settled our terms of reference in regard to religious truth, we must, in the second place, he suggests, acquaint ourselves with the nature of scientific truth, for otherwise we will be unable to deal rationally with any alleged conclusion between religion and science. Whitehead's metaphysical endeavour appears to be an attempt to follow Bradley's recommendations, with the important exception that Whitehead takes his start from an investigation into the

[26] Ibid., p. 446.

[27] Bradley, *Essays on Truth and Reality*, p. 471.

[28] Ibid.

[29] Bradley, *Appearance and Reality*, p. 449.

[30] Whitehead, *Science and the Modern World* (Cambridge: Cambridge University Press, 1926; cheap ed., 1933), p. 189.

[31] Bradley, *Appearance and Reality*, p. 448.

[32] Ibid., p. 447.

[33] Ibid.

[34] Ibid., p. 452.

nature of the universe as disclosed in experience and investigated by science, and he finds reality in those very features which Bradley had declared to be appearance. In presenting his ideas to the public, however, Whitehead appears to be following the steps suggested by Bradley and the title of his presentation suggests both the similarity and the difference between his own and Bradley's presentation.

In the *Essays on Truth and Reality* Bradley discusses a number of problems which within the terms of his philosophy he is unable to solve. He insists upon the necessity for a clear distinction between God and the Absolute. God is not the Absolute, but, along with everything else, is an appearance of Reality; in fact, for Bradley, God has no meaning outside of the religious consciousness. As such, "God" is a limited concept, useful for practical purposes and having such reality as an appearance may have, but must not be confused with the Absolute or the universe. Bradley recognizes, however, that such a conception of God as finite is not satisfactory as an object of worship, and at this point he faces a dilemma which he is unable to resolve. He recommends that we settle for inevitable inconsistency in religion and proceed upon the assumption that a personal God is not the ultimate truth about the universe. He rejects the conception of God as utterly transcendent and pleads that some way must be found by which to speak of the immanence of God as the indwelling Life and Mind and the inspiring Love, as well as being its Maker and Sustainer.[35] As he contemplates the universe in all its variety and complexity, he feels that nothing short of a "necessary pantheism" could account for it, but he can see no way of stating this consistently with views of an individual "Creator."[36]

Unable to find a way of reconciling this dilemma in which his philosophy has placed religion, Bradley now urges the need for a new religion which will recognize and justify all human interests and supply an intellectually defensible formulation of faith; he is not at all optimistic that this is possible:

> Whether we shall get this new religion, and, if so, whether by modification of what exists or in some other way, I am unable to surmise. But it is not, so far as I see, in the power of philosophy to supply this religious demand. And I much doubt the possibility of a religious doctrine able in the end to meet our metaphysical requirements of ultimate consistency.[37]

Bradley's difficulties here are accentuated by his Hegelian interpretation of persons as understood in the legal relationship of standing over against, or as parties to an agreement; it is understandable that it should be thought wholly inappropriate that the Absolute should stand in such relation (an external relation) to anything else. His limited notions of personality in relation both to God and to man preclude the possibility of Bradley's discovery of the solution of the problem which he poses. In the final chapter of *Process and Reality*, Whitehead appears

---

[35] Bradley, *Essays on Truth and Reality*, p. 436.
[36] Ibid.
[37] Ibid., p. 446.

to be seeking to meet these problems left by Bradley and at the same time retain a consistency with his own metaphysical system. The problem, as posed by Bradley, is threefold:

   (a) the demand for an ultimate principle other than God;
   (b) how to account for the creative origination of the universe, without denying;
   (c) the reality of the indwelling presence of God within nature, and as the constituting factor of the religious consciousness.

(iii) How shall we speak about God? Whitehead's call for a secularization of the concepts of God's functions in the world

The problem faced by Whitehead throughout *Process and Reality,* and which becomes particularly acute in the final chapter, is that of interpretation. "What does it all come to?"[38] He is endeavouring to bring together into one consistent system the findings of his study of religious doctrines, and insights provided by the sciences, and the long tradition in the history of philosophy. His major problem is that of finding a suitable terminology with which to speak of the ultimate realities. We have become aware in our study of Bradley that, in part at least, his problem is constituted in the fact that the language which is being employed in theology is limited to attempts to interpret religious subjective experience and Bradley finds difficulty in applying this directly to the universe. Whitehead is convinced that theology must extricate itself from this delimitation of its field of concern and find a terminology suitable to speak of God in relationship to the universe.

This approach is fundamental to Whitehead's whole outlook, and in *Process and Reality* he states explicitly that "the secularization of the concept of God's functions in the world is at least as urgent a requisite of thought as is the secularization of other elements in experience."[39] His concern here is the need to find a language adequate to speak of the fundamental motivation and direction of the activity, not only of conscious human experience, but of the lower orders of organic and inorganic nature. The request comes in a discussion of non-statistical judgments which, he points out, "lie at a far lower level of experience than do the religious emotions."[40]

Whitehead is at this point facing the most acute language problem in the whole undertaking; how can he formulate a set of concepts adequate to the origination and ongoing process of the universe? God's role in the universe is formative and constitutive through his characterization of creativity for novel occasions of actualization, through his constitution of the relevance of groups of eternal objects for concrescence in specific occasions, and in specific instances, from the fact that he gives to each concrescent actuality its initial subjective aim at definiteness. The need to formulate language by means of which

[38] Whitehead, *PR*, pp. viii (vii) and 518 (483).
[39] Ibid., pp. 315-16 (294).
[40] Ibid., p. 315 (294).

to speak of God in terms of these various functions among others leads Whitehead to a realization of the urgency for the secularization of the concept of God's functions in the world. This, he declares, is just as urgent a need as the secularization which has taken place in terminology applied to other elements of experience, such as those which the sciences investigate. There is no possibility of misunderstanding Whitehead's meaning here; he is quite explicit in differentiating the various aspects of the problem: "the concept of God is certainly one essential element in religious feeling." There is no intention here to minimize the importance of the concept of God in religious experience. His concern is to emphasize that it must not be limited to this one sphere of experience of the most highly advanced group of organisms, but applies with equal force to all of nature. God is necessary, indeed, to religious feeling, "but the converse is not true; the concept of religious feeling is not an essential element in the concept of God's function in the Universe."[41]

Whitehead, at no time in *Process and Reality*, makes any direct reference to Schleiermacher, but he leaves the reader in no doubt that he is concerned to supersede that whole trend of theological thinking which originated with Schleiermacher and which has resulted in a tendency to delimit the scope of theological investigation to the comparatively narrow field of the religious consciousness. "In this respect," Whitehead complains, "religious literature has been sadly misleading to philosophic theory."[42] Whitehead, throughout *Process and Reality*, is concerned to find a way of speaking about the universe which will lead to a deeper understanding of the meaning of things; he is convinced of the immanence of God at work in the world and in the lives of men; he also believes in some sense in transcendence, but that God is not to be equated with the Ultimate. In the final chapter of *Process and Reality* he believes he has devised a more adequate language than has heretofore been available with which to speak of God in those relations as they are disclosed in the workings of nature and in the religious experience of mankind.

Summary

Our examination of Whitehead's approaches to reality has disclosed that the *Timaeus* of Plato provided the structural pattern and the major categoreal notions of his cosmology, including the notion of a creator God who is more of a craftsman than a creator, whose major role is that of bringing order into a situation relatively chaotic, and who is limited in what he may accomplish by other elements which do not owe their origin to his activity. From the philosophy of Bradley he received the notion of an Ultimate principle which is impersonal, and of a God who is finite, somewhat after the manner of the Platonic God. Bradley also posed for Whitehead the problem of differentiating in

---

[41] Ibid.
[42] Ibid., p. 316 (294).

some manner between the various functions of God and speaking of him accordingly, with a strong emphasis upon the necessity of accounting for the immanence of God in the world. From the world religions he believed himself to have received confirmation of the conviction of the impersonality of the substructure of the Universe, and in his assessment of the extreme views of transcendence, of immanence, and of monistic pantheism, he became aware of the necessity for some mediating position in order to account for the full wealth of experience. Each of these several studies pointed to the great complexity of the subject and impressed upon Whitehead the importance of devising a terminology which would be expressive of the variety of functions exemplified in the total situation under review.

Whitehead believes that in "creativity" he has found a metaphysical category of the Ultimate which will account for the becoming and perishing of the actual entities which constitute the universe without the necessity for a personal creator. Rejecting the conception of an Absolute which could be related to nothing and replacing it with an ultimate which is exemplified (characterized) in each actual entity in its process of becoming, he seeks to remove the contradictions which had appeared to be irreconcilable in Bradley's system, to interpret the universe as a self-creative process each of whose actualities receives its initial subjective aim from God conceived as the primordial exemplification of the Ultimate.

We are now prepared to analyze and evaluate the various categoreal notions by which Whitehead seeks to describe God and his relation to the world.

Chapter V

Whitehead's Metaphysical System

Whitehead's metaphysical system is an attempt to provide a philosophical framework within which to understand the universe of which we are a part—the world and ourselves, our aspirations, achievements, and hopes for the future. An existential concern presses upon the philosopher to find a modus vivendi adequate for himself and others of his generation. It is his declared aim to bring the findings of all his earlier studies into focus in "a system of ideas which bring the aesthetic, moral and religious interests into relation with those concepts of the world which have their origin in natural science."[1] He explains that one of the main reasons why he is embarking on such an ambitious venture is the realization that all scientific theory is dominated by some such scheme which, while it may not be acknowledged by those who engage in scientific research, is no less influential in guiding imagination and, if inadequate, as the older scientific cosmology has been proven to be, may be a hindrance to progress in understanding.

In his metaphysical system Whitehead seeks to promote growth in understanding by providing an alternative scheme which will be capable of criticism and improvement in the light of larger knowledge; he warns the reader that the categories which will be gradually elaborated in the scheme, while they are essential to the progress of discussion, must on no account be regarded as more than "tentative formulations of the ultimate generalities,"[2] which may well have to be altered as the investigation proceeds, or alternatively, may acquire, and require to be given recognition as having, depth and importance which was not evident at the commencement of the undertaking. As he has already disclosed in earlier writings, Whitehead is convinced that "the event is the unit of things real,"[3] and feels compelled to ask the metaphysical question as to "what the fact of the reality of an event is in itself."[4]

In *Process and Reality* Whitehead undertakes to provide a metaphysical description of the universe as a self-creative process of which God is the principle of origination and of order. His earlier

---

[1] A. N. Whitehead, *Process and Reality: An Essay in Cosmology* (New York: Harper Torchbooks, 1960; first published, New York: Macmillan, 1929), Preface, p. vi.

[2] Ibid., p. 12 (11).

[3] A. N. Whitehead, *Science and the Modern World* (Cambridge: Cambridge University Press, 1926; cheap ed., 1933), p. 189.

[4] Ibid., p. 116.

investigations have disclosed that God is necessary as the principle of concretion, of order and of limitation, as the only way in which to account for the fact of there being a universe and for its being the kind of universe that it is. According to the philosophy of organism the final real things of which the world is made up are "actual entities" or "actual occasions," and we must enquire first what the fact of the reality of an "actual entity," or "actual occasion," or "event" is in terms of White-head's philosophy. Ivor Leclerc[5] points out that this category in White-head's system signifies the general metaphysical category of "that which is," and that cognate terms in other philosophical systems are " οὐσία ," "substance," and "monad." He suggests that the phrase may also bear the secondary connotation of "what that is which is," i.e., of a certain conception of the *nature* of an "actual entity."[6] But the metaphysical category of "actual" entity does not logically entail any particular conception of the nature of an actual entity; the discovery of that nature is the object of the metaphysical undertaking.

Whitehead rejects monism because it is unable to account for the experienced plurality of entities and is unable to explain the fact of change and of disorder in the world. On the other hand, he also rejects theories of two or more different kinds of actual entity, such as Descartes' doctrine of two kinds of substance. According to Whitehead's theory, all actual entities are generically of one kind: "God is an actual entity, and so is the most trivial puff of existence in far-off empty space."[7] He agrees that there are gradations of importance and diversities of function, but insists that "in the principles which actuality exemplifies all are on the same level."[8] This is reiterated over and over again throughout the discussion of the system; "God's existence is not generically different from that of other actual entities, except that he is 'primordial' in a sense to be gradually explained."[9]

The problem for metaphysics, as Aristotle had stated it, is "what is οὐσία ?"—the problem of determining those features which are completely generic to that which is without which it could not *be*; reality must, in some fundamental sense, be unitary, and must be changeless; yet, experience yields a universe which is composed of many entities in a constant process of change. The problem posed for the philosopher is that of adjusting the changeless to the factor of change. The traditional solution to this problem has been to regard an actual entity as essentially "changeless." While conceding that for many purposes of life the notion of an enduring substance sustaining qualities expresses a useful abstract, Whitehead insists that it is not satisfactory as a fundamental statement of the nature of things and that as a metaphysical statement it is sheer error. The existence of such "entities" is derivative from that of

[5] Ivor Leclerc, *Whitehead's Metaphysics, An Introductory Exposition* (London: George Allen & Unwin, 1958), p. 53.
[6] Ibid.
[7] Whitehead, *PR*, p. 28 (24).
[8] Ibid., p. 28 (24-25).
[9] Ibid., p. 116 (103).

actual entities.[10] Whitehead, therefore, rejects the conception of an actual entity as enduring self-identically the same amidst change. The world of our experience is in constant change, and it is this process which must be accounted for in the metaphysical system. He points out that it was one of the weaknesses of Descartes' system that he failed to account for change and endurance; for him the existence of an actuality is instantaneous and endurance is the mere succession of instantaneous facts. In treating "enduring entities" as actual substance, Descartes commits what Whitehead has termed "the fallacy of misplaced concreteness."[11] Furthermore, Descartes' instantaneous substances, since they are devoid of process, and accordingly of activity, cannot themselves be the reason for, or the cause of, the process consisting in the transition to successive substances. He requires some other activity or entity to be the "power and act" of creation,[12] and is consequently driven back to the acknowledgment of God as the only true substance, all other entities being dependent upon him for their existence, and ends with three kinds of substance, namely, enduring entities, mental entities, and God.

Whitehead maintains that the existence of an actual entity cannot be either "instantaneous" or a "changeless endurance." On the contrary, it is of the very essence of his system that an actual entity's "being" is constituted in its "becoming."[13] This is Whitehead's principle of process; the process is the reality, and all other meanings of "process" are derivative from this root meaning. He rejects the idea of a continuous process of becoming, and describes his system as a theory of atomism, of "epochal" units of becoming, in each of which the process of becoming is completed, or reaches its "satisfaction" and becomes "objectively immortal" and, as such, possible data for successive concretions. By this means he seeks to solve the problem of "change" and "changelessness." Each actual entity becomes itself by a process of prehension whereby it grasps into the unity of its own subjective form other actual entities of its immediate environment which thereby become components of its concrescence.

A prehension, Whitehead reminds the reader, always has a reference to an external world and involves emotion, purpose and valuation. It has what he describes as a "vector character."[14] The "ontological principle" of the philosophy of organism lays it down as a guide to understanding that the reasons for things are always to be found in the composite nature of definite actual entities—"in the nature of God for reasons of the highest absoluteness, and in the nature of definite temporal actual entities for reasons which refer to a particular environment. The ontological principle can be summarized as: no actual

[10] Ibid., p. 122 (109-10).
[11] Ibid., p. 11 (9); also cf. *Science and the Modern World*, p. 64.
[12] Leclerc, *Whitehead's Metaphysics*, pp. 65-66, and Descartes' *Principles of Philosophy*, Part I, 51. I am indebted to Ivor Leclerc for calling this to my attention and sorting out this aspect of Whitehead's argument.
[13] Whitehead, *PR*, pp. 34-35 (31).
[14] Ibid., p. 28 (25).

entity, then no reason."[15] There is a togetherness of actual entities which results from their prehensions of each other; this Whitehead calls a nexus, and the ultimate facts of immediate experience are actual entities, prehensions, and nexūs (plural for nexus). These are a few of the primary notions, but in order to understand the revolutionary nature of the philosophy of organism it will be necessary to look briefly at a few of the more important categories and categoreal conditions, of which there are in all a total of forty-five, each of which he requires because it receives exemplification in some aspect of experience. The most important of these is the category of the Ultimate.

Every philosophical system finds the necessity for an ultimate principle of interpretation which is only capable of characterization through its accidental embodiments; in the philosophy of organism this ultimate is termed "creativity," and "God" is its primordial, non-temporal accident.[16] In earlier works God is described as an attribute of the substantial activity,[17] and later as "the completed ideal harmony" without which creativity and the forms are powerless to achieve actuality;[18] but in the metaphysical system, God is specifically stated to be an "accident," and Whitehead is careful to explain his purpose in designating "creativity" as the ultimate. He is differentiating his system from monistic philosophies, such as that of Spinoza or of absolute idealism, in which this ultimate is God, who is also equivalently termed the Absolute.

By adopting as the ultimate in his system the impersonal substantial activity which is everywhere exemplified in actual entities, and designating it "creativity," Whitehead is making a decision which will have important consequences for the development of the metaphysical system. He justifies this action on the grounds that both philosophers and theologians, by ascribing to God "eminent" reality, have separated him from the universe, depicting him as a totally transcendent deity imposing his will upon the universe and man, much as an oriental potentate imposes order upon his subjects. This conception of God, he maintains, is responsible for the tragic persecutions and inhumanity which have been so prominent in some phases of Christian and Mohammedan history, and it so dominated the minds of seventeenth-century scientists, such as Isaac Newton, and others of his day, as to prevent them from asking fundamental questions which would otherwise have occurred to them naturally. Newton, Whitehead explains, held the Semitic theory of a "wholly transcendent God creating out of nothing an accidental universe,"[19] and consequently made no provision for the evolution of matter. In terms of metaphysical insight, he finds the *Timaeus* of Plato is much superior to Newton's *Scholium*.

There are other reasons why Whitehead chose an impersonal aspect of the universe to serve as the ultimate in his system rather than

[15] Ibid.
[16] Ibid., p. 11 (9).
[17] Whitehead, *SMW,* p. 221.
[18] Whitehead, *RM,* pp. 119-20.
[19] Whitehead, *PR,* p. 146 (133).

God. His researches into the religious experience of mankind had disclosed that the religions of India and China were in agreement in postulating an impersonal substratum to the universe.[20] There may be personal manifestations in some expressions of these religions, but the underlying substratum is an impersonal process. Another important influence upon his thought at this time was that of F. H. Bradley, and particularly his final thoughts about the nature of ultimate reality as expressed in his *Essays on Truth and Reality,* in which Bradley insists that the Absolute is not God; this, he considers, is quite unthinkable, because God is related to the religious consciousness and it was fundamental to Bradley's thought about the Absolute that it is not related to anything. He consequently insists that "a personal God is not the ultimate truth about the Universe, and in that ultimate truth would be included and superseded by something higher than personality."[21] Whitehead rejects Bradley's conception of the Absolute as the ultimate; such a conception is too abstract to be of any service in the philosophy of organism in which the interrelationship of all actualities whatsoever is a fundamental principle.

In some respects, however, the language which Whitehead employs to speak of his ultimate is similar to that of Bradley, who declares that the Absolute must not be equated with its appearances, and yet that it "appears in its phenomena and is real nowhere outside them";[22] Whitehead likewise declares of his ultimate that it "is the universal of universals characterizing ultimate matter of fact,"[23] and which apart from its "accidents is devoid of actuality."[24] But Whitehead makes a careful distinction between the two systems. In monistic systems the ultimate is allowed a final, "eminent" reality, beyond that ascribed to any of its attributes,[25] and Whitehead feels this to be illegitimate. By selecting for his ultimate an observable feature of the universe he seeks to transpose the whole discussion onto a realistic basis and so to provide a scheme which will be adequate for the interpretation of the universe as a self-creative process. The universe, he declares, is a process of creative advance into novelty, and its ultimate principle of interpretation is "creativity."

The metaphysical situation is further clarified by Whitehead's explanation that in the philosophy of organism, "creativity" will replace Aristotle's category of primary matter."[26] Creativity is not itself an actual entity, but is rather the basic activity of self-creation which is generic to all individual actual entities. It is, Whitehead says, "without a character of its own in exactly the same sense in which the Aristotelian

---

[20] See above, p. 23.
[21] F. H. Bradley, *Essays on Truth and Reality* (Oxford: Clarendon Press, 1914), p. 432.
[22] F. H. Bradley, *Appearance and Reality* (London: George Allen and Unwin, 1925), p. 411.
[23] Whitehead, *PR,* p. 31 (28).
[24] Ibid., pp. 10-11 (9).
[25] Ibid.
[26] Ibid., pp. 46-47 (42).

'matter' is without a character of its own. It is that ultimate notion of the highest generality at the base of actuality."[27] It is, moreover, impossible to characterize creativity, because all characters are more special than itself, but it is always found under conditions and is described as conditioned.

While Whitehead identifies his ultimate, "creativity," with the part played by Aristotle's "matter," there are important distinctions in the understanding of the two notions which constitute the reason why Whitehead selected "creativity" as the ultimate in his system. Leclerc points out that while they are similar, inasmuch as both are "that which takes different forms, that which exists only in its individualizations,"[28] yet Whitehead conceives the ultimate in his system "as *activity*, creative activity, and in doing so is specifically maintaining that *to the 'ultimate,'* and to no other element in an actuality, is to be ascribed the efficacy whereby the ultimate takes different forms."[29] In this aspect of its function, the ultimate of Whitehead's system is a dynamic category in contrast to the static "matter" of the Aristotelian system. According to Aristotle, the "efficacy" whereby "matter" takes different forms is not to be ascribed to the "ultimate" itself, but to "form." Whitehead rejects this Aristotelian doctrine, while agreeing with Aristotle that "act," "acting," is a generic feature of actuality. Leclerc suggests that Aristotle at this point was tacitly regarding "form" as the "ultimate," but that as he well realized, "form" cannot fulfil the requirements as an "ultimate." He was later led to identify "form" and "being" and, as a "ground" for the universe, arrived at the notion of an Unmoved Mover. Whitehead, as we have seen, "rejects all theories of a wholly transcendent 'ground' as involving incoherence."[30] He identifies, instead, "being" and "acting" and draws the logical conclusion that the "act" whereby actuality is what it is, is itself the "ultimate." By this move Whitehead was able to constitute the ultimate, "creativity," as the "ground" of the universe, whose ultimate character is that of self-creating activity, and the individual actual entities of which the universe is composed are the "creatures" of this universal "creativity" in the sense that each is an instance of the ultimate.[31]

Whitehead isolates three basic notions, creativity, many, and one, which are ultimate in securing the rhythmic process of the universe, and which together "complete the Category of the Ultimate and are presupposed in all the more special categories."[32] He is careful to explain that the term "one" here does not stand for the integral number *one*, but for the singularity of an entity. The term "many" conveys the notion of "disjunctive diversity" and is an essential element

[27] Ibid., p. 47 (42-43).
[28] Leclerc, *Whitehead's Metaphysics*, pp. 84-85. If the ultimate could be further defined as the Creative activity of God, then this statement of Leclerc would seem adequate; God is his own reason. But this is not what Whitehead is saying here.
[29] Ibid.
[30] Ibid., p. 86.
[31] Ibid., p. 87.
[32] Whitehead, *PR*, p. 31 (28).

in the concept of "being." These two terms, "many" and "one" presuppose each other in all discussion of process. "Creativity" is "that ultimate principle by which the many, which are the universe disjunctively, become the one actual occasion, which is the universe conjunctively."[33] It lies in the nature of things, he declares, that the many enter into complex unity.

The unity which emerges is something novel and diverse from any entity of the "many" which it unifies, and creativity is now declared to be also the principle of novelty. "The ultimate metaphysical principle is the advance from disjunction to conjunction, creating a novel entity other than the entities given in disjunction. . . . The many become one, and are increased by one."[34] Whitehead calls this production of a novel togetherness "concrescence," which is his term for the process of the becoming of an actual entity as an epochal whole.[35] He designates this "microscopic process,"[36] to emphasize that it is but one aspect of the larger rhythmic movement of the creative advance. The second species, which he terms "macroscopic process," denotes the *transition* from particular existent to particular existent; it is, he declares, ". . . the fluency whereby the perishing of the process, on completion of the particular existent, constitutes that existent as an original element in the constitutions of other particular existents elicited by repetitions of process."[37] In this species of process the creativity transcends the individual actual entity, providing the data for subsequent concrescences.

Donald Sherburne calls attention to the importance of keeping these two species of process together as one process with two distinguishable species. Both the production of togetherness and the production of novelty "happen simultaneously: to produce togetherness is to produce novelty, and vice versa."[38] Sherburne concludes that "it is because creativity links in the same set of relationships the production of togetherness and the production of novelty that ongoingness is built into the philosophy of organism."[39] He explains that "ontologically speaking, transition and growth are faces of the same coin" and that, in fact, for Whitehead "microscopic and macroscopic process are equally fundamental as features of that which is really real, since at bottom they are inseparable, though distinguishable."[40] Microscopic process ensures that the becoming of actual entities is a self-creative process completed in each epochal actuality, while macroscopic process ensures the transition from the fading of process in one actuality to its provision of data for "the renewal of the process in the concrescence of actualities beyond that satisfied superject."[41] Leclerc, in his account,

[33] Ibid., p. 31 (28).
[34] Ibid., p. 32 (28-29).
[35] Ibid., pp. 32 (29) and 321 (299).
[36] Ibid., pp. 326-27 (304).
[37] Ibid., p. 320 (298).
[38] Donald Sherburne, *A Whiteheadian Aesthetic* (New Haven: Yale University Press, 1961), p. 22.
[39] Ibid.
[40] Ibid., p. 23.
[41] Whitehead, *PR*, p. 134 (121).

concludes that "this conception secures too the *existence* of the universe without the need of a transcendent creator to account for its existence."[42] That this was Whitehead's intention there can be no doubt, but it leaves many questions unanswered, and it will be necessary to enquire whether "creativity" as defined by Whitehead at this point is able to bear the full extent of origination which he ascribes to it.

Another important category in Whitehead's system is that of "eternal object." The individuality of each actuality in the universe is constituted by the ultimate, "creativity," taking a particular "form of definiteness." These "forms" are Platonic ideas, but with a difference; they resemble more the Aristotelian universals. They are entities, because they exist, not as themselves actual, but as components of actual entities. Because Whitehead's conception of them differs somewhat from earlier thought, he terms them "eternal objects." Their nature does not consist in their process of becoming, therefore they cannot be included among "actual" entities; but they are the determinants of the definiteness of the process of acting of actual entities. Whitehead employs the term "ingression" to express this "informing" or determining of the definiteness of actualities by eternal objects. They are in some sense antecedent to the actualities in which they are becoming ingredient, but Whitehead does not conceive of them as existing in some kind of Platonic world of Forms; this, however, may require some qualification, for the eternal objects can exist only as "ingredients" in actual entities.[43] They are, in their very nature, timeless or eternal and given as potentials for becoming; by their nature, they must have ingression in some actuality, but there is nothing in their nature to determine which actuality they shall have ingression into.

Whitehead insists that the conception of a universe in which there is growth, development, and process presupposes the notion of potentiality;[44] actual entities and eternal objects are seen in his system as contrasting entities constituting respectively the two types of "actuality" and of "pure potentiality," which "require each other in the reciprocal roles of example and character."[45] The eternal objects are "given" as data for particular actualities, but we must not ascribe to them any activity whereby they have ingression into any particular actuality. Decision as to which eternal objects shall have ingression into an actuality lies with the actual entity in process of concrescence; it must select or "decide" from among potentialities, which will be received and which discarded. Whitehead explains that "just as 'potentiality for process' is the meaning of the more general term 'entity' or 'thing,' so 'decision' is the additional meaning imported by the word 'actual' into the phrase 'actual entity.'"[46] Potentiality, however, is not restricted to the eternal

[42] Leclerc, *Whitehead's Metaphysics*, p. 87. See also William J. Garland, "The Ultimacy of Creativity," *The Southern Journal of Philosophy*, 7/4 (Winter, 1969-70), 361-76.

[43] Whitehead, *PR*, pp. 73 (63), 38 (34-35), and 70 (60).

[44] Ibid., p. 72 (62); cf. also Whitehead, *Modes of Thought* (Cambridge: Cambridge University Press, 1956), p. 136.

[45] Whitehead, *MT*, p. 97.

[46] Whitehead, *PR*, p. 68 (58-59).

"entities"; all entities are potentials and an actual entity, having achieved its "satisfaction," or completed its process, becomes objectively immortal and a potential for ingression into successive actual entities. An actual entity is, therefore, seen in a twofold aspect, and Whitehead suggests the hyphenated word "subject-superject" as its exact description. It may be seen as a "subject" with respect to its own process of becoming and as "superject" with respect to its objective immortality for ingression into another actual entity in process of becoming.[47] The subject-superject is the end which the activity aims to achieve, whereby it receives incorporation into the ongoing process by transition.

We have been describing the process of becoming of an actual entity, but must now push our enquiry farther back and ask why does one actuality emerge rather than another in a particular environment, and how does it arise? We have already touched on this briefly in our earlier description of an actual entity,[48] but must now look at it rather more carefully. Whitehead designates this element the category of "prehension," and considers it so important that he devotes five *categories of explanation* to its definition.[49] According to the philosophy of organism, the initial stage of an actuality is an act of unconscious perception of data, an act of perceptually "grasping" and "including" them as its "objects," and this action is what Whitehead terms "prehension"; in fact, he states that "the essence of an actual entity consists solely in the fact that it is a prehending thing (i.e., a substance whose whole essence or nature is to prehend)."[50] Analysis of an actual entity discloses it to be a concrescence of prehensions which have originated in its process of becoming.

Whitehead isolates three factors which are in every prehension: (a) the "subject" which is prehending, namely, the actual entity in which that prehension is a concrete element; (b) the "datum" which is prehended, which is that part of the environment which is relevant to that concrescence; and (c) the "subjective form" which is *how* that subject prehends that datum. A distinction is made according to the data prehended; there are "physical prehensions" whose data are other actual entities, and "conceptual prehensions" whose data are eternal objects. Moreover, as already indicated above, consciousness is not necessarily involved in the subjective forms of either type of prehension. It is simply the description of the vector quality of the relationship (feeling) at the base of each actuality by which it selects from the environment those elements which will receive incorporation into concrescence. There are accordingly two species of prehensions: (a) "positive prehensions" which are termed "feelings," and (b) "negative prehensions" which are said to "eliminate from feeling."[51]

[47] Ibid., pp. 43 (39) and 339 (313).
[48] See above, pp. 43-44.
[49] Whitehead, *PR*, p. 35 (31-32), sections x-xiv incl.
[50] Ibid., p. 65 (56).
[51] Ibid., p. 35 (31-32).

Examination of the process of concrescence discloses that prehension is the experience by which that which was objective data enters into the subjectivity of the actual entity in question. It involves the evaluation of the data for acceptance or discard in accordance with the subjective aim dominating the activity of self-creation. The being or existence of the actual entity is constituted by the process of growing together, concrescence, of the data into a novel unity, towards the achievement of its subjective aim, as final cause. It is inherent in Whitehead's system that an actual entity must be conceived as one epochal whole of becoming, and the question which now presses for an answer is that of origination; how does an actual entity—an epochal whole of becoming—commence? Or, in Whiteheadian terminology, where does it receive its initial subjective aim? Whitehead recognizes that he has come to a focal point in the investigation:

> This doctrine of the inherence of the subject in the process of its production requires that in the primary phase of the subjective process there be a conceptual feeling of subjective aim; the physical and other feelings originate as steps towards realizing this conceptual aim through their treatment of initial data.[52]

In other words, the subjective aim is required from the beginning of the process as providing the direction and focus of the concrescing activity. There can be no activity without aim; the aim must be involved at the outset, and cannot therefore be generated by the activity. From whence, then, can the initial aim derive?

By the ontological principle, the subjective aim must itself come from somewhere, which means, according to the philosophy of organism, from some actual entity.[53] Moreover, since it is a conceptual feeling, and since it arises in the primary phase of the actuality in question, it must be a primary conceptual feeling, or what Whitehead describes as a conceptual reproduction.[54] The question arises: what, then, is the physical prehension from which it arises? The problem is complicated by the fact that the vast multiplicity of data available for concrescence do not carry any regulative principle for their synthesis;[55] yet, according to the ontological principle, that "regulative principle"—i.e., the subjective aim—must derive from some actual entity. This situation, Whitehead explains, requires the admission of a non-temporal actual entity as the primordial source of the subjective aim at definiteness, and so he arrives at the conviction of the necessity for God as the origination of the process: "In this sense God is the principle of concretion; namely, he is that actual entity from which each temporal concrescence receives that initial aim from which its self-causation starts."[56] The initial phase of the concrescence is also

---

[52] Ibid., p. 342 (316).
[53] Ibid., p. 373 (345).
[54] Ibid., pp. 39-40 (36). Categoreal Obligation IV; and pp. 379-82 (350-53), Category of Conceptual Valuation explained; cf. also pp. 364-65 (337).
[55] A. N. Whitehead, *Adventures of Ideas* (Cambridge: Cambridge University Press, 1933), p. 328.
[56] Whitehead, *Process and Reality*, pp. 374 (345) and 342 (316-17).

conditioned by the world in which the actuality arises, and God and the world together constitute jointly the character of the creativity for the initial phase of each novel concrescence.[57] Once so constituted, the subject is a process of self-creative activity whose decisions are directed by its subjective aim at definiteness; by a process of positive and negative prehensions it will achieve its concrescence into subject-superject.

Whitehead concedes that, inasmuch as each actual entity derives from God its initial subjective aim, there is a sense in which God can be termed the creator of each temporal actual entity. A phrase such as this, however, is apt to mislead by its suggestion that the ultimate creativity of the universe is to be ascribed to God's volition, whereas, according to the philosophy of organism, "the true metaphysical position is that God is the aboriginal instance of this creativity, and is therefore the aboriginal condition which qualifies its action."[58]

What are we to make of this suggestion of Whitehead's that "it is the function of actuality to characterize creativity, and God is the eternal primordial character"?[59] Leclerc warns against assuming that it implies that God is in the past of all other actualities, in the sense that "God was once the solely existing actual entity";[60] such a conception of God, he suggests, would violate all the categories of Whitehead's system. A consistent metaphysical pluralism, he insists, "cannot hold that creativity originally had only a single instantiation."[61] Leclerc presses Whitehead's definition of "actual entity" to its logical conclusion: "By the ontological principle and the category of relativity, all actual entities require 'data'; thus God as an actual entity can no more be without other actual entities than they can be without God."[62] But this only points up the difficulties in which the system is involved at the point of final interpretation. How can God be described as a "unique actual entity,"[63] as Leclerc has correctly interpreted Whitehead's meaning, and provide the direction for the concrescence of all other actual entities, if he is himself in process of concrescence and requiring these others for his existence? There appears to be a fundamental contradiction here which will require to be overcome if the system is to provide an interpretation of the universe. The implications of Leclerc's suggestion are that God and the actual entities are simply two sides of one movement.

It would seem necessary to assume that there must be a sense in which God stands outside the process, or at least, is in some sense distinguished from the process, if he is to be the principle of concretion, of order, and of limitation, and to provide some direction to the creative activity, thereby constituting it this specific universe. In this sense, God is, and must remain, unique, in order that he may provide

[57] Ibid., p. 374 (346).
[58] Ibid., p. 344 (317-18).
[59] Ibid.
[60] Leclerc, *Whitehead's Metaphysics*, p. 194.
[61] Ibid., p. 195.
[62] Ibid.
[63] Ibid., p. 193.

the criterion of judgment and the principle of interpretation of the process as a whole. To meet the paradoxical nature of this situation, Whitehead suggests a differentiation in the nature of God in so far as he must be said to be primordial, to account for the fact of there being a universe; and yet he also wants to say that God is in process of becoming with every other created fact, and, in this sense, must be said to be "with all creation"[64] and involved in temporality, and in some sense be said to be consequent.

We have now arrived at the central problem in the interpretation of the universe according to Whitehead's cosmological scheme, and we turn to an analysis and evaluation of the various categoreal notions by which he seeks to describe God and his relation to the World.

[64] Whitehead, *Process and Reality,* p. 521 (486).

Chapter VI

Analysis of the Concept of God in *Process and Reality*

It is important to notice, at the commencement of our analysis of Whitehead's concept of God, the sequential order in the operation of two fundamental presuppositions of his system: the actual entities in their process of concrescence presuppose a primordial ordering of creativity by God, whereas God in his "unity of conceptual operations," "merely presupposes the general metaphysical character of creative advance."[1] He is, in fact, the "primordial exemplification"[2] of the creativity, providing the element of order in the general metaphysical situation without which there would be chaos. The particularities come to be within an ordered world and could not become were the order not everywhere operative within the universe, as the general background, and inherent in every aspect of the process; even those aspects which seem to be chaotic require the general background of order, for "disorder" is, Whitehead suggests, a relative term, expressing the lack of importance possessed by the defining characteristics of the societies in question beyond their own bounds.[3] In order for creative advance to be possible, there must be general stability and order, and Whitehead is emphatic that "the primordial nature of God is the acquirement by creativity of a primordial character."[4]

Inasmuch as God is an "actual entity" of a unique kind it will be well to review, however briefly, the structure of an actual entity. In his analysis of this category, Whitehead identifies three phases of the epochal process of becoming.[5] In the first place, each actual entity arises out of the "objectifications" in the actual world relative to it as its "efficient" cause or causes, and, in this sense, "has the character 'given' for it by the past."[6] But each specific process of concrescence arises by virtue of the "subjective aim" at "satisfaction" which it receives from God as the principle of concretion, and has the subjective character which constitutes its "final cause" or "lure." And thirdly, it has what Whitehead describes as its "superjective" character, by which in achiev-

---

[1] A. N. Whitehead, *Process and Reality: An Essay in Cosmology* (New York: Harper Torchbooks, 1960; first published, New York: Macmillan, 1929), p. 522 (487).
[2] Ibid.
[3] Ibid., pp. 141f. (128).
[4] Ibid., p. 522 (487).
[5] Ibid., p. 134 (121).
[6] Ibid.

ing its "satisfaction" (i.e., completing its own process of becoming) it becomes new data, qualifying the transcendent creativity in successive concretions, and remains as an element in the content of creative purpose. This means that actualities beyond that satisfied superject will be enriched or impoverished accordingly.

In the *Timaeus* of Plato, Whitehead found an attempt at an interpretation of the universe in terms which were other than religious. Plato's Demiurge is not a religious figure; at no time is it suggested that he be worshipped. The aim of the myth is to extend knowledge and understanding and to provide insight into the nature and workings of the universe as a process of becoming. Whitehead takes over the general scheme and builds upon it. To meet the complexity of the situation presented by the facts of experience and further disclosed in the sciences, and in an attempt to provide a metaphysical description of the complex interrelatedness of God and the World, he introduces an element of complexity into his concept of the nature of God.[7] Having already analyzed the nature of an actual entity as threefold, Whitehead now announces that the nature of God is threefold in exactly the same manner, except for one important difference, constituted in the fact that God is primordial, and therefore has no past, whereas all other actual entities are temporal. The attempt at a differentiation of various aspects of the nature of God according to his operations in the universe, a process which was being initiated in the closing sections of *Religion in the Making* (1926), is here carried to its completion in a threefold characterization of the nature of God, commencing with his primordial nature, which is here described as "the concrescence of a unity of conceptual feelings, including among their data all eternal objects."[8] Under this designation an attempt is being made to describe in terms applicable to human subjectivity the activity of God in bringing about the co-ordination of the full multiplicity of the eternal objects "into relevant lures of feeling severally appropriate for all realizable basic conditions."[9] This had earlier been described as God's "envisage-ment"[10] of the full wealth of potentiality for concrescence in the world. In the secularization being carried out here by Whitehead, this is described as God's subjective aim, which, in religious language, in New Testament terms, would be said to be "the eternal purpose of God." Whitehead is insistent that, according to the philosophy of organism, "God's existence is not generically different from that of other actual entities, except that he is 'primordial.'"[11]

If God is primordial, and the process is the outcome in activity of his "envisagement" of the world, then it is understandable that the world which becomes will in some ways manifest God's nature, and if he is creative Love, then it is reasonable that the world should be process

[7] Ibid., p. 134 (121-22).
[8] Ibid., p. 134 (122).
[9] Ibid.
[10] Ibid., p. 50 (46).
[11] Ibid., p. 116 (103).

with direction; inasmuch as he is creative, it is understandable that the process of the universe should be a creative advance into novelty with an element of spontaneity and of choice allowed to each entity in its process of actualization. We might say that it is characteristic of the class of created universes that they should bear some likeness to their creators and that this specific universe is discovered to be generically like its creator in the relationship of creature to creator. At least, this seems to be the direction in which Whitehead's thought is moving in some sections of the final chapter of *Process and Reality*.

God also has, according to Whitehead, a "consequent" nature which is "the physical prehension by God of the actualities of the evolving universe,"[12] and is otherwise described as "the weaving of God's physical feelings upon his primordial concepts,"[13] and in this aspect of his nature he is declared to be involved in temporality. In other words, according to the philosophy of organism, God, in his consequent nature, is in process of "becoming with every other creative act."[14] In this aspect, God is conceived by Whitehead as finite, and his "being" is constituted by a process of becoming. Whitehead is careful to point out that God's conceptual nature, i.e., his primordial nature, is unchanged by reason of its final completeness; "but his derivative nature is consequent upon the creative advance of the world."[15] As consequent and derivative, this aspect of God's nature is temporal along with the temporality of every other actual entity. But because of the all-inclusiveness of God's aboriginal envisagement, his primordial nature is non-temporal or eternal. This involvement of God "in unison of becoming"[16] is an attempt to do justice to the fact of the interrelatedness of all aspects of the universe, and to give expression to the process of valuation which is constantly sifting and sorting the wheat from the straw in the dynamic process of the actual world in such a manner that "each novel actuality in the temporal world contributes such elements as it can to a realization in God free from inhibitions of intensity by reason of discordance."[17] In other words, the universe, in its process of becoming, matters to God; he is with each actuality and as it achieves such satisfaction as is the outcome of the totality of its process, he transmutes and conserves all the good which can possibly be brought out of the complex situation of that actuality, objectively immortal, in that specific epoch, and available for further concrescence.

Here we encounter, says Whitehead, a third nature of God, namely, his "superjective" nature, which is further described as "the character of the pragmatic value of his specific satisfaction qualifying the transcendent creativity in the various temporal instances."[18] Attention is called to this aspect of God's nature in the final section of *Religion*

[12] Ibid., p. 134 (122).
[13] Ibid., p. 524 (488).
[14] Ibid., p. 523 (488).
[15] Ibid., pp. 523-24 (488).
[16] Ibid., p. 523 (488).
[17] Ibid., pp. 134-35 (122).
[18] Ibid., p. 135 (122).

in the Making, in which it is pointed out that, in addition to the ground for future concrescences which is constituted in the objective immortality of each completed actuality, God also adds to the situation the ideal consequent as it stands transmuted in his vision. In this way, Whitehead states, every event becomes "a base in actual fact to which he [God] provides the ideal consequent"[19] and by means of which he is able to become "a factor saving the world from the self-destruction of evil."[20] In the light of this insight, Whitehead draws the conclusion that "the power by which God sustains the world is the power of himself as the ideal. He adds himself to the actual ground from which every creative act takes its rise."[21] It is in this context that God functions as the principle of concretion, giving to each new occasion as it arises its initial subjective aim, which becomes the final cause determining the direction in which it moves in its process of concretion; and so the "world lives by its incarnation of God in itself."[22] By adding his vision of the ideal consequent as the potentiality of the specific situation, God qualifies the transcendent creativity in the various temporal instances.[23]

Each of these three aspects of the nature and the character of God is further developed as attention is focused on the "creative phases in which the universe accomplishes its actuality"[24] but there follows here, in Chapter III of Part II, a paragraph in which Whitehead makes explicit a number of points which are fundamental to an understanding of the conception of God which is being developed throughout *Process and Reality.* "This is the conception of God," he reminds his readers, "according to which he is considered as the outcome of creativity, as the foundation of order, and as the goal towards novelty."[25] Order and novelty are here further described as "but the instruments of his subjective aim which is the intensification of 'formal immediacy.'"[26] A further important point is made in the statement to the effect that "every actual entity, including God, is a creature transcended by the creativity which it qualifies."[27] Finally, there is a most important statement to the effect that God is *causa sui* in respect to his own existence, and that temporal occasions are also *causa sui,* after having received from God the initial subjective aim from which the self-causation of each commences. This is further clarified by the statement to the effect that:

> to be *causa sui* means that the process of concrescence is its own reason for the decision in respect to the qualitative clothing of feelings. It is finally responsible for the decision by which any lure for feeling is admitted to

[19] A. N. Whitehead, *Religion in the Making* (New York: Macmillan, 1926), p. 156.
[20] Ibid.
[21] Ibid.
[22] Ibid.
[23] Whitehead, *PR,* p. 135 (122).
[24] Ibid., p. 532 (496).
[25] Ibid., p. 135 (122).
[26] Ibid.
[27] Ibid.

efficiency. The freedom inherent in the universe is constituted by this element of self-causation.[28]

This conception of God as the "outcome of creativity" and a "creature transcended by the creativity which it qualifies," which is nonetheless "*causa sui*" and is the "foundation of order" and the "goal towards novelty," is patterned after the Platonic model, but with subtle and important differences in emphasis. It is a notion of God as "an actual entity immanent in the actual world, but transcending any finite cosmic epoch—a being at once actual, eternal, immanent, and transcendent."[29] It is this conception of God, re-stated and applied on a cosmic dimension, which Whitehead hopes will provide the interpretation of the whole metaphysical scheme, and we must now turn to Part V for an examination of it.

The various aspects of God's nature are fully developed and summarized in the final chapter. The "primordial nature" of God, which has already been described as comprising "the unconditioned conceptual valuation of the entire multiplicity of eternal objects,"[30] is now further defined as "the unlimited conceptual realization of the absolute wealth of potentiality"[31] and is declared to be "not *before* all creation, but *with* all creation."[32] He is eternally present to each actual entity in its process of becoming and to each actual occasion, giving to each its initial subjective aim towards the realization of something of the wealth of potentiality which is possible for it in that environment: in this way, God is with all creation, making for creative advance into novelty.

Whitehead hastens to point out that his primordial nature is an abstraction from God's full actuality, and insists that in this aspect we must ascribe to him neither fullness of feeling, nor consciousness. But, although only an aspect of God, his primordial nature is regarded as being absolutely fundamental to all actuality whatsoever: "He is the unconditioned actuality of conceptual feeling at the base of things; so that, by reason of this primordial actuality, there is an order in the relevance of eternal objects to the process of creation."[33] The general metaphysical character of the universe is that of a creative advance, the advance into novelty being the primordial characterization given to creativity by the primordial nature of God, and we are now provided with a description of the agency of God prior to the temporal world, operative within the metaphysical framework which appears to be simply matter of fact, much as in the Platonic cosmology.

> His unity of conceptual operations, is a free creative act, untrammelled by reference to any particular course of things. It is deflected neither by love, nor by hatred, for what in fact comes to pass. The *particularities* of the actual world presuppose *it*; while *it* merely presupposes the *general*

28 Ibid.
29 Ibid., p. 143 (130).
30 Ibid., p. 46 (42).
31 Ibid., p. 521 (486).
32 Ibid.
33 Ibid., p. 522 (486-87).

metaphysical character of creative advance, of which it is the primordial exemplification.[34]

This is as much transcendence as Whitehead will permit to God in the system; he is the sole non-temporal actual entity and in that sense is unique, and is primordial; earlier in the work this operation of God had been described as "envisagement";[35] now it is the one "free creative act"[36] which presupposes the metaphysical structure of creativity. "The transcendence of God is not peculiar to him. Every actual entity, in virtue of its novelty, transcends its universe, God included."[37] He will allow that God transcends "any finite cosmic epoch—a being at once actual, eternal, immanent, and transcendent,"[38] but this may be said also of every actual entity. Inasmuch as its very nature is such as to constitute it a novelty, it transcends the universe out of which it has emerged. This limitation on the transcendence allowable to God is repeated in many other passages throughout *Process and Reality*. He speaks also of the "transcendent creativity"[39] which is qualified by the superjective nature of God. Whitehead is much more clear in his own mind about the immanence of God, which he considers to be fundamental to an understanding of the process of the universe, and which he designates the "consequent nature" of God.

In spite, however, of the limitations which Whitehead has imposed on the transcendence of God in the system, it becomes increasingly an actual factor in the creative process as the system is developed. This will become evident from the following brief summary of Whitehead's account of the primordial nature of God:

1. Creativity acquires a primordial character—the primordial nature of God constitutes, according to Whitehead's scheme, the origination of the process of creation.[40]

2. In his primordial nature, God is unconditioned; in fact, this aspect of his nature is constituted of the complete envisagement of all eternal objects whatsoever, and of their order of relevance to the process of creation; it ensures order and limitation in the universe by this primordial ordering.[41]

3. God's envisagement of the universe is a free creative act, unhindered by any actual world, because his action at this stage is non-temporal.[42] He does not determine the actual course of events, but rather provides, by his unity of conceptual operations, for a universe in which there will be the maximum opportunity for freedom of choice within the framework of the world of eternal forms, and of the limita-

[34] Ibid., p. 522 (487).
[35] Ibid., p. 70 (60).
[36] Ibid., p. 522 (487).
[37] Ibid., p. 143 (130).
[38] Ibid.
[39] Ibid., p. 135 (122).
[40] Ibid., p. 522 (487).
[41] Ibid.
[42] Ibid.

tions which are imposed upon the present by previous concrescences throughout the temporal process. In spite of the restrictions imposed by Whitehead upon his primordial nature, God is here being conceived as fulfilling functions which in the ordinary usage of language constitute the meaning of personality (or, to put it at the lowest level, can only be conceived as issuing from personal action).

4. The suggestion that God is not deflected either by love or by hatred for what in fact comes to pass[43] must not be construed as signifying that God in his primordial nature is unmoved, as was Aristotle's Prime Mover, for God's envisagement of the order of creation is described as an urge towards the actualization of his conceptual prehensions. There is thus purpose in the creative advance which it receives from God's envisagement of the future. The particularities of the actual world presuppose this ordering by which it is a universe with dependable laws and conditions making for creative advance.

5. God's "conceptual actuality at once exemplifies and establishes the categoreal conditions."[44] In the first chapter, Whitehead had declared that philosophy would not regain its proper status "until the gradual elaboration of categoreal schemes, definitely stated at each stage of progress, is recognized as its proper objective,"[45] rather than its starting point. These, he warns the reader, will not be regarded in the present work as dogmatic statements, but rather as tentative formulations of the ultimate generalities. But here, at the stage of interpretation, these find reinforcement by their exemplification in the primordial nature of God and their establishment thereby as part of the conceptual totality of the description of creative process.

6. The conceptual feelings, which comprise God's primordial nature, "exemplify in their subjective forms their mutual sensitivity and their subjective unity of subjective aim";[46] they are valuations, Whitehead explains, determining the relevance of eternal objects for each occasion of actuality, implying thereby in God an activity of selection and of fore-ordination.

7. In his effect upon the created order, God's primordial nature elicits a similar response to that which Aristotle ascribed to his Prime Mover. Whitehead states that God "is the lure for feeling, the eternal urge of desire. His particular relevance to each creative act as it arises from its own conditioned standpoint in the world, constitutes him the initial 'object of desire,' establishing the initial phase of each subjective aim."[47] Leclerc points out that what the actual entity prehends is not God as such, in his full concrescence, "but only God as objectified by one of his 'concepts,' namely, the relevant subjective aim."[48]

[43] Ibid.
[44] Ibid.
[45] Ibid., p. 12 (10).
[46] Ibid., p. 522 (487).
[47] Ibid.
[48] Ivor Leclerc, *Whitehead's Metaphysics, An Introductory Exposition* (London: George Allen & Unwin, 1958), p. 196.

Whitehead makes it very evident that creative advance in the universe is made possible, on the one hand, by the "basic adjustment of the togetherness of eternal objects"[49] in the primordial nature of God, as a result of which there is a systematic complex of relatedness among eternal objects which ensures the relatedness of actual entities in the creative advance; and, on the other hand, by the "conceptual adjustment of all appetites in the form of aversions and adversions."[50] These two together constitute the reason why the subjective aim of a concrescing entity will be attracted to one eternal object and repelled by another as not relevant to the fulfilment of its goal or aim. In this sense, God's pure conceptual prehensions involve "appetition" or the "urge toward their realization," without which the eternal objects would be, in Whitehead's words, "a mere isolation indistinguishable from nonentity."[51] Through his divine ordering all things will become actualized, and until this has been accomplished there are, Whitehead maintains, certain deficiencies in God's nature. We are informed that his feelings are only conceptualized and so lack fullness of actuality, and that in this stage God is devoid of consciousness; yet, in his activity of conceptual valuation of the eternal objects, he would appear to perform functions which are usually associated with mind in its highest form. At this stage there is a similarity between Whitehead's primordial nature of God and the Second Hypostasis, the Intellectual-principle, as enunciated by Plotinus in the *Enneads*.[52]

Even in his primordial nature, God is conceived as richer in content than Aristotle's Prime Mover; it is true that in Whitehead's system he is the "lure for feeling,"[53] leading the world by the attraction of love, but he does this in his primordial nature as being the complete envisagement of the world; there is, according to Whitehead, appetition in God, the desire for the fulfilment of that which has been purposed for the world, so that even considered in abstraction there is a suggestion of richness of content awaiting to be disclosed and to receive exemplification.

The Consequent Nature of God

There is, however, another aspect of God's nature, which Whitehead terms his "consequent" nature. In this aspect of his operations God is like the architect turned builder who is now limited by the dimensions of his own plans and specifications, or, as a parent who has brought forth a family and whose life is transformed by the new responsibilities, so that, in the process he becomes a different person. God is at work in the world, in each actual entity, working out his purpose through each society within the world of nature, including mankind. Having envisaged a creative process in which there would be a maximum freedom of choice for each entity in the process of its

[49] Whitehead, *PR*, p. 48 (44).
[50] Ibid.
[51] Ibid., p. 392 (363).
[52] See below, p. 124.
[53] Ibid., p. 522 (187).

becoming, God, in this aspect of his activities, is limited by the world; there is a relativity in the extent to which God is able to achieve his purposes in explicit situations. Whitehead likens him to "the poet of the world,"[54] or to the shepherd watching over his flock; moreover, he "shares with every new creation its actual world"[55]—in human terms, meeting us where we are today, and, in the light of the total environment, transmuted in his presence, he gently leads us so far as we are able to respond.

Whitehead further explains that "God's conceptual nature is unchanged by reason of his final completeness. But his derivative nature is consequent upon the creative advance of the world,"[56] and he is, accordingly, dipolar analogously to all other actual entities. The consequent nature of God is further described as the "realization of the actual world in the unity of his nature, and through the transformation of his wisdom,"[57] and yet again, as the "weaving of God's physical feelings upon his primordial concepts."[58] We are unaccustomed to think of God as having "physical feelings," yet, if we follow consistently in our thinking, is this perhaps implied in the conception of God as creator and sustainer? We employ language implying the activity of purposive thought on the part of God; Whitehead would have us add to this the activity of "feeling." It was his conviction that the Christian religion has been impoverished by an overemphasis upon the intellect, and it was one of his aims in writing *Process and Reality* to recover for our generation a more comprehensive orientation for faith in God as actively at work in the world.[59]

God is here presented as the Master Workman, giving material and living content to his conceptual envisagement of the world. In that initial experience there was no limitation, in contrast to his consequent nature, in which the "world is felt in a unison of immediacy."[60] Here the wisdom of God is presented as an ultimate concern, prehending every actuality for what it can be in such a perfected system—". . . its sufferings, its sorrows, its failures, its triumphs, its immediacies of joy—woven by rightness of feeling into the harmony of the universal feeling, which is always immediate, always many, always one, always with novel advance, moving onward and never perishing."[61] Here the perpetual perishing life of man on earth is lifted up into an eternal relationship, in the immediacy of God's purpose, in which his strivings and his shortcomings are seen in a larger perspective and there takes place a re-evaluation of values, issuing in transformation, with the resultant consequence that "the revolts of destructive evil, purely self-regarding, are dismissed into their triviality of merely individual facts; and yet the good they did achieve in individual joy, in individual sorrow, in the

[54] Ibid., p. 526 (490).
[55] Ibid., p. 523 (488).
[56] Ibid., pp. 523-24 (488).
[57] Ibid., p. 524 (488).
[58] Ibid.
[59] Ibid., pp. 519-20 (484-85).
[60] Ibid., p. 524 (489).
[61] Ibid., p. 525 (489).

introduction of needed contrast, is yet saved by its relation to the completed whole."[62]

Whitehead suggests that the "image under which this operative growth of God's nature is best conceived, is that of a tender care that nothing be lost."[63] Here Whitehead, the visionary, the mystic, contemplating the confused state of the world in the perspective of the purpose of God, conceives of him as continually at work in the universe, working with and within each entity, respecting the element of freedom with which each has been endowed and, in virtue of which it has within it the power to become, to achieve, and to reach some satisfaction; God, he suggests, respects even the wrong choices of men because his purpose is the enrichment of the whole of life by the evolution of spiritual beings through creative decision.

The consequent nature of God is further defined as "his judgment on the world,"[64] but it is a judgment of love; "he saves the world as it passes into the immediacy of his own life";[65] in other words, the operation of God in the world is a process of salvation by incorporation. Here, quite obviously, Whitehead's thoughts are prompted by his meditations upon the accounts of the life of Jesus, as recorded in the New Testament, and particularly in the Fourth Gospel which has profoundly impressed him.[66] It is, he suggests, "the judgment of a tenderness which loses nothing that can be saved,"[67] reminiscent of the great parables of the Lost Coin, the Lost Sheep, the Lost Son,[68] and the story of the feeding of the five thousand, and echoing the words of Jesus at the conclusion: "Gather up the fragments that remain, that nothing be lost,"[69] and the whole placed within the context of the thoughts of the Great Prayer in the seventeenth chapter of John.

At this point a greater wealth of imagery crowds in upon Whitehead's mind; "it is also," he says, "the judgment of a wisdom which uses what in the temporal world is mere wreckage,"[70] recurring to a metaphor which he had introduced in *Religion in the Making*. The source of the imagery for this section is evident; what could be more derelict than the three crosses on the hill of Calvary on that bleak day? It is the symbol of man's brutality to and dehumanization of his fellowmen. Think of the wreckage left behind by the might of Rome, the human wreckage strewn across the centuries in the wake of man's futile, wasteful strife with man! When we recall that Whitehead had lost a son in the First World War,[71] we realize that these are not idle metaphors from his pen.

[62] Ibid.
[63] Ibid., p. 525 (490).
[64] Ibid.
[65] Ibid.
[66] See above, pp. 21-22.
[67] Whitehead, *PR*, p. 525 (490).
[68] Luke 15.
[69] John 6:12.
[70] Whitehead, *PR*, p. 525 (490).
[71] A. N. Whitehead, *Essays in Science and Philosophy* (New York: Philosophical Library, 1947), Part 1, Personal, p. 9.

Implicit in this whole section of Whitehead's treatment of the consequent nature of God is a recognition of the cosmic significance of Jesus Christ as portrayed in the Fourth Gospel—the central theme of the New Testament, that "God so loved the world that he gave"[72] himself, became incarnate and bore the shame of the cross as a physical fact of history. If this message means anything, it surely tells us something about God and the costly nature of his love.

Whitehead insists, moreover, that if we are to understand the consequent nature of God, we require to find a larger perspective in the light of which we may grasp the overall meaning of the creative process. The universe, he suggests, includes a threefold creative act composed of
 (i) the one infinite conceptual realization,
 (ii) the multiple solidarity of free physical realizations in the temporal world, and
(iii) the ultimate unity of the multiplicity of actual fact with the primordial conceptual fact.[73]
It is in the phase of the multiple freedom of physical realizations in the temporal world, he says, that God, in his patience, "is tenderly saving the turmoil of the intermediate world by the completion of his own nature."[74] In other words, Whitehead here gives us his vision of the ongoing purpose of God in the midst of which we find ourselves today. "The sheer force of things," he suggests, "lies in the intermediate physical process: this is the energy of physical production."[75] In the light of the vast expansion of industry, and of man's conquest of nature and of space, what can we say about God and the World? Here, clearly, Whitehead is replying to the conclusions of Philo in Hume's *Dialogues Concerning Natural Religion*. Philo asserts that "The whole [universe] presents nothing but the idea of a blind nature, impregnated by a great vivifying principle, and pouring forth from her lap, without discernment or parental care, her maimed and abortive children!"[76] No, replies Whitehead, this is not a true picture of the universe as disclosed to us; you have not rightly understood the purpose of God—that he works by persuasion and demonstration of his love, to win a free response from those who have it in them to become spiritual beings by the exercise of their freedom of decision.

The two sides of God's nature are now compared and contrasted in terminology which is not always easy to follow; at this point Whitehead would seem to have forgotten his earlier reminder that the reader must keep in mind that the two natures of God are "abstractions"[77] from the reality. John Cobb makes the valid criticism that "too often he deals

[72] John 3:16.
[73] Whitehead, *PR*, p. 525 (490).
[74] Ibid.
[75] Ibid.
[76] David Hume, *Dialogues Concerning Natural Religion, 1779*, Hafner Library of Classics No. 5, edited by Henry D. Aiken (New York: Hafner Publishing Company, 1948), p. 79.
[77] Whitehead, *PR*, p. 50 (46).

with the two natures as though they were genuinely separable."[78] Having noted this tendency, however, it will be well to proceed with our analysis of what Whitehead is endeavouring to express by means of his novel language. In his conceptual experience, God is said to be free, complete, primordial, eternal, actual, deficient, and unconscious; while the other side of his nature, which originated with physical experience, is said to be determined, incomplete, consequent, "everlasting," fully actual, and conscious, and is also stated to be finite.[79]

Whitehead points out that God's nature is now seen to be dipolar, primordial and consequent, analogously to all other actualities. The tendency to impose upon God the limitations of human experience is here carried to its full extent; in human experience, consciousness emerges out of sentience, which in turn is a feature of physical experience; Whitehead here ascribes this same limitation to God in his primordial nature and describes him as in process of coming to consciousness along with other creatures in the creative advance of the world. The implications of this are that God is a part of the process and subordinate to the totality of the creative advance.

The employment of secular concepts by means of which to speak of God enables Whitehead to provide many important insights into the relation in which man stands to the universe, to his fellowmen, and to God. The complexity of the total interrelationship of God, man and the world becomes most evident, and Whitehead does succeed in conveying a sense of the significance of God's activity in the world and of the world's participation in God. But, does it necessarily follow that if each actuality has its reception into God's nature, therefore God is, analogously to all actual entities, in process of becoming along with all creation? The very suggestion of this possibility should be sufficient to warn us that we are making the mistake of treating God as simply one element among others which conspire together to bring the universe into being; it is evident at this point that Whitehead has not pushed back far enough in seeking the ultimate principle upon which all is grounded. Creativity, as such, and as defined by Whitehead, is not able to provide the necessary ground, and we must look behind it to discern that which is more ultimate, and of which it is but one expression.

Consequently, when he comes to the final interpretation, Whitehead faces a dilemma; because God does not, according to his theory in *Process and Reality,* create the world, but is reduced to the status of an ordering principle, the process is in fact declared to be ultimate, and God and the World (now capitalized) are simply two participants in the production of the creative advance. A complex situation is now disclosed, in virtue of which Whitehead declares that it is as true to say one or other of six pairs of contrasted opposites of God or of the World in a process of interrelationships in which it is declared that

[78] John Cobb, Jr., *A Christian Natural Theology* (Philadelphia: Westminster Press, 1965), pp. 178ff.
[79] Whitehead, *PR,* p. 524 (489).

God and the World are the contrasted opposites in terms of which Creativity [now capitalized] achieves its supreme task of transforming disjoined multiplicity [the chaotic state of unordered elements] with its diversities in opposition [declared earlier to be the essence of evil], into concrescent unity, with its diversities in contrast.[80]

By this move Whitehead delivers the system from the charge of pantheism, but he does so only by formally re-asserting the creaturely nature of God as a function and therefore simply an element of the creative process which itself remains without explanation in *Process and Reality*. Here Whitehead indicates clearly that his earlier references to God as the "outcome of creativity" and as the "creature of creativity" are intended to be taken seriously. God is now formally declared to be but one of "two concrescent poles of realization—'enjoyment' and "appetition,' that is the 'physical' and the 'conceptual.'"[81] God's nature, being the conceptual pole, is universal and as such is "unbounded by contradiction."[82]

Applying this interpretation now to the world of experience Whitehead declares that "by reason of his priority of appetition, there can be but one primordial nature of God; and, by reason of their priority of enjoyment, there must be one history of many actualities in the physical world."[83] Each actual entity in the physical world, inasmuch as its process of becoming involves it in temporality, has a history, i.e., its own historic route of occasions in space-time relationships, so that each occasion is simply that occasion and not another. No occasion is repeatable; each is unique, and all actualities whatsoever in the universe are bound together in one interrelated process of advance into novelty. Consequently, while for purposes of analysis we focus attention upon those features only which appear to us to be important, and these alone find a place in our historical records, yet we must not lose sight of the fact that there is but one history of many actualities in the physical world. The whole universe conspires to produce an acorn and "the hairs of your head are all numbered."[84]

The problem with which Whitehead is wrestling is, how can this flux be gathered up into permanence without loss of immediacy, and, on the other hand, how can permanence acquire that which is novel and incorporate it into reality? In *Process and Reality*, Whitehead seeks to resolve the problem by putting God and the World on an equal footing. "God and the World stand over against each other, expressing the final metaphysical truth that appetitive vision and physical enjoyment have equal claim to priority in creation."[85] Both God and the World are here treated as active agents and are mutually enriched by their joint operation. The temporal world, by "embodying" or incar-

[80] Ibid., p. 528 (492-93).
[81] Ibid., p. 528 (493).
[82] Ibid.
[83] Ibid.
[84] Luke 12:7.
[85] Whitehead, *PR*, p. 529 (493).

nating God, brings an enrichment into his nature by the addition of "flux" and the World acquires permanence as it embodies God. The basic Platonic structure of the whole scheme is here being re-affirmed and is further reinforced by the assertion that "the world's nature is a primordial datum for God"[86] even as "God's nature is a primordial datum for the World."[87] A further explanatory paragraph states that "neither God, nor the World, reaches static completion," but that both are "in the grip" of a reality more ultimate than either, namely, "the creative advance into novelty."[88] Creativity, whatever may be its true nature, remains supreme according to the system, but what is Creativity? We are not told, and, until we have the answer to this question, the totality of the process is unexplained. We conclude that the final chapter in *Process and Reality* arrives at the basic question, but fails to provide the answer. What becomes evident throughout this section is that the category of the ultimate, Creativity, is now clearly hypostasized and treated as itself a purposive agency.

We were reminded in the early sections of *Process and Reality* that the categories were merely tentative formulations awaiting confirmation or alteration as the system was developed; it would appear that a re-appraisal is now called for in the case of the category of the ultimate which, in the initial stages of the discussion, was declared to be "without a character of its own,"[89] but is now clearly the controlling principle of the totality of the process. The conclusion of the matter is that, as stated in *Process and Reality*, the system provides no interpretation of the "ultimate metaphysical ground";[90] it gives no reason, for example, why it is a "creative advance into novelty"[91] and not a destructive descent into chaos. Moreover, because creativity is declared to be without a character of its own, God and the World, being both clearly subordinated to Creativity—as the instruments by means of which Creativity achieves its supreme task[92] are unexplained. True, God is declared to be "the primordial created fact,"[93] to be the "outcome of creativity,"[94] and the "creature of creativity,"[95] but where does this leave us when Creativity is declared to be without a character of its own? The same holds true for the "eternal objects"; until we have more clearly defined what we mean by "God," they are without explanation and are simply matter of fact.

There is also at this point in Whitehead's discussion of the final realities a significant change in the language employed to speak about the world. Up to this point in the discussion the world has been

[86] Ibid.
[87] Ibid.
[88] Ibid., 529 (493-94).
[89] Ibid., p. 47 (42).
[90] Ibid., p. 529 (494).
[91] Ibid., pp. 42 and 529 (38 and 494).
[92] Ibid., p. 529 (494).
[93] Ibid., p. 46 (42).
[94] Ibid., p. 135 (122).
[95] Ibid., p. 47 (43).

considered simply as the temporal creative process which is the subject of scientific investigation. The object of the metaphysical exercise is interpretation, and Whitehead is seeking, in this final chapter, to draw together the implications of the cosmological scheme into a final interpretive statement. Throughout *Process and Reality*, with the exception of the final summary in section V of the final chapter, God is spoken of in terms of his functions in the world process as primordial and as consequent. Each temporal entity receives from God its initial subjective aim which constitutes it a process of concrescence.[96] His consequent nature is said to be "the weaving of God's physical feelings upon his primordial concepts,"[97] and is "the realization of the actual world in the unity of his nature, and through the transformation of his wisdom."[98] As we have noted, throughout section IV Whitehead is drawing upon the thought and imagery of the Gospels, but in section V he returns to consider the basic Platonic problem and to the tendency, in both philosophy and theology, to separate the flux from the permanence, leading to inevitable contradiction—a static God on one side and a world reduced to "mere appearance" on the other.

Whitehead is critical of Greek, Hebrew and Christian thinkers who, he suggests, "have embodied notions of a static God condescending to the world, and of a world *either* thoroughly fluent, or accidentally static, but finally fluent—'heaven and earth shall pass away.'"[99] His criticism of these systems is that while they start with a fundamental intuition of a reality which requires to be expressed, they entangle themselves in verbal expressions; the language they employ has the effect of so overstating the two aspects of experience as to end in contradiction, and a failure to recognize that "the problem is double and not single."[100] The real problem, he maintains, is actuality with permanence requiring fluency as its completion; and "actuality with fluency, requiring permanence as its completion."[101]

The discussion which follows makes much more evident the purpose of the unusual language which Whitehead has employed in speaking of God's functions in the world. The problem must be looked at from two different perspectives if its full complexity is to be grasped. From the point of view of God, it "concerns the completion of God's primordial nature by the derivation of his consequent nature from the temporal world."[102] Whitehead has insisted throughout that God as an actual entity is in process of becoming analogously to every other actuality, and we here have the summing up of the whole epochal process which is God achieving "satisfaction." The other side of the

[96] Ibid., p. 343 (317).
[97] Ibid., p. 524 (488).
[98] Ibid.
[99] Ibid., p. 526 (491).
[100] Ibid., p. 527 (491).
[101] Ibid. See the important treatment of this position by Plato in the *Sophist*, 248E-249D, in a very modern sounding discussion in which the Idealists are led to concede that reality must include at least some changing things.
[102] Ibid.

problem concerns the evolving world; in fact, it concerns "the completion of each fluent actual occasion by its function of objective immortality, devoid of 'perpetual perishing,' that is to say 'everlasting.'"[103]

These two perspectives, Whitehead suggests, must be brought
together, if we would understand the significance of the process which
is the universe. The consequent nature of God is now declared to be
"the fluent world become 'everlasting' by its objective immortality in
God."[104] On the other hand, "the objective immortality of actual occasions requires the primordial permanence of God,"[105] because it is
through the activity of God in his primordial nature that "the creative
advance ever re-establishes itself with initial subjective aim derived
from the relevance of God to the evolving world."[106] To grasp the point
here we must envision God as watching over the universe and introducing novelty at those points in the process at which it becomes possible to
achieve progress through fresh creative action. He gives to each concrescent actuality its initial aim at definiteness. Our best efforts fail of
accomplishment, but something has been achieved; this finds objective
immortality in God, and is part of the data for future concrescence. By
reason of God's primordial ordering the creative advance re-
establishes itself and the purpose of God moves forward through the
contributions of the many who have been caught up into the creative
movement; "other men laboured, and ye are entered into their
labours."[107] God's envisagement is relevant to the evolving world.

Here we meet the first suggestion of what Whitehead describes in
the closing section as "the fourth phase" in which the creative action
completes itself, "for the perfected actuality passes back into the temporal world, and qualifies this world so that each temporal actuality
includes it as an immediate fact of relevant experience."[108] This fourth
phase is said to be the present reality of the "kingdom of heaven." It is
"the love of God for the world"[109] and is further described as ". . . the
particular providence for particular occasions. What is done in the
world is transformed into a reality in heaven, and the reality in heaven
passes back again into the world."[110] Both here in the final section and
in the early part of section V Whitehead is stretching language to the
limits in an effort to convey his vision of the ultimacy of the process.
Objective immortality within the temporal world, he explains, does not
satisfy the intuitions of the finer religious minds, who have penetrated
to discern the need for a further factor, namely, "the temporal world
perfected by its reception and its reformation, as a fulfilment of the
primordial appetition which is the basis of all order."[111] In this way,

[103] Ibid.
[104] Ibid.
[105] Ibid.
[106] Ibid., 527 (492).
[107] John 4:38.
[108] Whitehead, *PR*, p. 532 (496-97).
[109] Ibid.
[110] Ibid., 532 (497).
[111] Ibid., p. 527 (492).

Whitehead concludes, "God is completed by the individual, fluent satisfactions of finite fact, and the temporal occasions are completed by their everlasting union with their transformed selves, purged into conformation with the eternal order which is the final absolute 'wisdom.'"[112] This vision of the fulfilment of the purpose of God by the gathering of all things into himself has received a variety of expressions, among which is that of St. Paul who speaks of it as "the fulness of him that filleth all in all."[113]

This brings Whitehead to the point at which a final summary is called for; this, he declares, can only be expressed in terms of a group of antitheses each of which expresses an aspect of the truth, and this, in turn, discloses the need for some unifying principle. Development of the metaphysical scheme has disclosed the complexity of the problem of accounting for the universe. Throughout this whole discussion of the final things the influence of the New Testament upon Whitehead's thought is becoming more evident and is particularly clear in sections IV, VI and VII. But when he comes to summarize the situation in the latter half of section V, it becomes evident that Whitehead is endeavouring to reconcile two conflicting points of view about the nature of ultimate reality which are struggling for expression within his mind. His difficulty is accentuated by the fact that superficially the two viewpoints appear to be saying the same things, but really are not. The main structure of Whitehead's cosmology is Platonic, but into this he is seeking to incorporate Christian insights which he recognizes to be genuine intuitions into the nature of things. In the final summary, however, in the attempt to retain both the unity and the multiplicity as elements of reality, Whitehead finds it necessary to hypostasize not only Creativity, but also the "World," and we are left with a final Platonic triad of Creativity, God and the World, somewhat altered from that given in *Religion in the Making* which concludes with the forms, creativity and God.

In *Process and Reality* the Forms, or "eternal objects" as Whitehead calls them, have been gathered into the primordial nature of God much as, in the Second Hypostasis of his triad, Plotinus incorporates into his Intellectual-Principle all the Platonic Forms. The "World," in Whitehead's summary statement, still conceived as "the multiplicity of finites,"[114] now acquires a metaphysical character and role similar to that of Soul in Plotinus' scheme. In this section, therefore, Whitehead presents the final metaphysical truth as a triad of Creativity, God and the World as together constituting the source of creative origination, a triad in which Creativity is clearly conceived as in some sense prior as providing the general metaphysical ground, and God and the World stand over against each other, representing respectively appetitive vision and physical enjoyment, either of which is the instrument of novelty for the other.[115]

[112] Ibid.
[113] Ephesians 1:23.
[114] Whitehead, *PR*, p. 529 (493).
[115] Ibid.

It will be evident that Whitehead's triad represents a considerable advance on the conception of God as portrayed in Plato's *Timaeus,* and yet there are similarities in that God is declared by Whitehead to be the creature of the ultimate principle conceived as "creativity," and in the fact that the "World" is conceived as a primordial datum for God. It has some definite similarities to the hierarchy of Plotinus, but with important contrasts. One of the major aims of Whitehead's metaphysical endeavour is to provide a rational interpretation of the immanence of God without denying the necessary element of transcendence enabling him to be considered as the principle of concretion and in that sense primordial, whereas the direct consequence of Plotinus' philosophical efforts was to carry the transcendence of God to its utmost extremity in his separation of the spiritual realm from the sensible world, placing him beyond being. Whitehead, on the contrary, seeks to demonstrate the involvement of God in the process which in the philosophy of organism is declared to be the reality. Having said this, however, it will be found that there are a number of similarities between Whitehead's Creativity, God and the World and Plotinus' One, the Intellectual-Principle, and the Soul, in which the latter incorporates elements of Aristotelianism, Stoicism and oriental mysticism into a basically Platonic system. Both the similarities and the contrasts are of sufficient importance to warrant a comparative analysis which will be undertaken at a later point in this essay.[116]

In the two concluding sections of the final chapter an attempt is made to redress the balance by the introduction of basically Christian insights in a further discussion of the primordial and the consequent natures of God in their interrelated activity in the world process. An attempt is made to speak in secular language of the "kingdom of heaven" and God is here being regarded as ultimate and as personal. There is a conflict between Whitehead's remaining Platonism and his emerging Christian convictions. He has not yet discovered the metaphysical solution to the problem as to "the quality of Creative origination," and, until he has solved this problem, it is not possible to enunciate further the relationship of God and the World. Whitehead has gone a long way towards resolution of the puzzles left by Bradley, but the full solution must await clarification of his own thought by further research.

[116] See below, pp. 130ff.

Chapter VII

Some Appraisals of Whitehead's Cosmology

Archbishop William Temple, in his Gifford Lectures delivered in the year 1932-33, draws extensively upon the insights of Whitehead's philosophy of organism and acknowledges his indebtedness to him in his analysis of the world as apprehended; but he subjects Whitehead's final interpretation to a devastating criticism, insisting that the category of the ultimate itself calls for further explanation before it will be adequate to provide the insights into the nature of reality which are required. Temple lays it down as a principle that "the ground of the Universe, by reference to which the universe is explicable or intelligible, must be such that it requires no further explanation of itself."[1] Our analysis has disclosed that it is just at this point that Whitehead's category of the ultimate fails and that this is so actuley evident in the final interpretation that Whitehead finds it necessary to ascribe to Creativity the powers of direction and of purposive activity which by his own previous definition it is precluded from possessing. Creativity as an observed physical law of operation of the universe is incapable of qualifying for the category of the Ultimate in the metaphysical scheme because it is itself one of those features of the universe which requires explanation.

How, then, do we move from a consideration of physical phenomena, such as creativity and the process which is the world, to the explanation of the process itself? Temple finds a clue in Mind itself as apprehended in the world of human experience, and as able to transcend itself and able to initiate action in the physical world; "when Mind, determined by Good, as apprehended, initiates activity, no further explanation is needed."[2]

Whitehead acknowledges this need of the universe for explanation by that which stands outside the flux: "no reason, internal to history, can be assigned why that flux of forms, rather than another flux, should have been illustrated";[3] but the view that the explanation is

[1] William Temple, *Nature, Man and God,* Gifford Lectures, 1932-33 (London: Macmillan, 1934), p. 256.

[2] Ibid., p. 257.

[3] A. N. Whitehead, *Process and Reality: An Essay in Cosmology* (New York: Harper Torchbooks, 1960; first published, New York: Macmillan, 1929), p. 74 (64).

found in the primordial nature of God is not satisfactory because God as defined here is, in Temple's words, "a mere name for a de- sideratum";[4] God must be something other than a ground of possibility if he is to explain the fact of the universe; it does not help to say that God is the principle of concretion if he is no more than this, and as the creature of creativity he is explicitly declared by Whitehead to be less than ultimate.

Temple considers that in his conception of the consequent nature of God, Whitehead is coming very near to the Christian Gospel, but having imposed limitations upon the meaning to be ascribed to the term, he has no valid basis for saying it. Moreover, he gives no reason for the ground of his confidence in "the perfection of God's subjective aim" and the resultant "character of his consequent nature,"[5] other than the suggestion that it would, if true, round off the philosophy of organism. Temple asks the question, how does he know that it is complete in any relevant sense?[6] Whitehead fails to indicate the empiri- cal grounds (data) upon which he bases his judgment.

Temple's final criticism of Whitehead is that in his interpretation of God and the World, "Whitehead surreptitiously introduces thoughts which properly belong to Personality, though ostensibly he stops short at the category of organism."[7] Consequently, the complex totality of God and the World is never explained; we are never given any answers to the basic question of why it is what it is. The answer to such a question could only be found if Whitehead would pass beyond the limitations of organism to Personality—"beyond the notion of inner unification by co-ordination of function to the notion of self- determination by reference to apprehended good."[8]

Whitehead depends upon the notions of God and the World, as interpreted in the final sections of *Process and Reality*, to "embody the interpretation of the cosmological problem in terms of a fundamental metaphysical doctrine as to the quality of creative origination."[9] Our investigation has disclosed that these terms, as defined by Whitehead, fail to provide the interpretation, and to this extent the metaphysical scheme fails. It is one evidence of the humility and greatness of Whitehead that he has been able to recognize deficiencies in his own works and in many cases to initiate a search for their solution before critics had stated their objections. In September, 1932, just prior to the first series of Temple's Gifford Lectures, Whitehead published *Adven- tures of Ideas*, in which he reports the data upon the basis of which he was able to revise his assessment of the relative values of the Platonic and the Christian conceptions of God and the World and in the light of which his metaphysical scheme may be revised and its inadequacies removed.

[4] Temple, *Nature, Man and God*, p. 258.
[5] Ibid., p. 259, quoting Whitehead, *PR*, p. 524 (489).
[6] Ibid., p. 260.
[7] Ibid.
[8] Ibid., pp. 260-61.
[9] Whitehead, *PR*, p. 518 (483).

In the preface to his book, *A Christian Natural Theology*,[10] Professor John B. Cobb, Jr., argues for the need for a Christian natural theology as a basis upon which one may then pass on to consider matters of fundamental Christian belief which are being called in question in our generation, expressing the hope that he might reverse the current trend towards the elimination of the term "God," and instead restore it to meaningful discourse in some real continuity with its historic use. There follows a faithful exposition of Whitehead's general philosophy without in any way calling in question the eligibility of this philosophy to be called Christian. Langdon Gilkey, in a forthright criticism of Cobb's treatment, asks the basic question, "Can the system in question, if its vision remains quite unaltered, express the Christian vision of reality?"[11] His major criticism of Cobb is that this question was not asked at any point in the book. Cobb seems to assume that Whitehead's philosophy is "Christian, in the sense of being deeply affected in its starting point by the Christian vision of reality."[12] In a passage in which he is comparing the task which he has set himself with that which faced both Augustine and Aquinas in their employment of philosophies in the service of theology, Cobb remarks that "Whitehead's work is obviously Christianized in a way Greek philosophy could not have been,"[13] the assumption being that by virtue of the fact that Whitehead lived after the beginning of the Christian era, therefore his philosophy will be "Christianized." Moreover, when we examine Cobb's analysis of Whitehead's concept of God, it becomes evident that this judgment is based upon his findings in the three books *Science and the Modern World*, *Religion in the Making*, and *Process and Reality*; he specifically states that on his findings, "after *Religion in the Making*, nothing really new is added to the doctrine of God. He is an actual entity who envisages and orders the realm of eternal possibilities."[14] The investigation of the development of Whitehead's concept of God concludes with the remark: "Clearly, he retained throughout his life the sense that the ultimate fact is the process itself of which God, the eternal objects, and the temporal occasions are all explanatory."[15]

Here, then, Cobb, while insisting that Whitehead's concept of God does not change significantly after *Religion in the Making*, spells out the elements of the process without apparently realizing that they constitute, not the Christian, but the Platonic vision of reality, and consequently cannot possibly qualify as the metaphysical structure for a Christian theology of nature without first being transformed by confrontation with the Christian doctrine of God. Yet Cobb gives no evidence of having realized this, nor does he apparently realize that Whitehead moved in this direction in *Adventures of Ideas*; he finds in this

[10] John B. Cobb, Jr., *A Christian Natural Theology* (Philadelphia: Westminster Press, 1965).
[11] Langdon Gilkey, *Theology Today*, XXII, No. 4 (January, 1966), 534.
[12] Cobb, *A Christian Natural Theology*, p. 268.
[13] Ibid.
[14] Ibid., p. 149.
[15] Ibid., p. 168.

book relatively little explicit discussion of the doctrine of God and concludes "there was no significant alteration of the major doctrines of *Process and Reality.*"[16]

The remarkable thing is that Cobb makes no reference whatsoever to the discussion which develops throughout Part II of *Adventures of Ideas*, in which Whitehead is dealing with cosmology and in which the whole argument builds up to the important tenth chapter in which he announces his discovery of the uniqueness of Jesus Christ as a revelation of the nature of God and of his agency in the world, and declares that the metaphysical formulation of the faith in the fourth century constitutes a most important advance upon Plato. The absence of any reference to this is all the more remarkable inasmuch as the insights which Whitehead acknowledges having discovered here are those which Cobb requires for the reformulation of the organic philosophy before it can serve as the basis of a Christian theology of nature.

Gilkey raises the very important question of how in Whitehead's thought, God is related to the metaphysical categories descriptive of the other actual entities.[17] This is a problem which Whitehead never did resolve; it was in fact incapable of resolution in the system as outlined in *Process and Reality.* Cobb wrestles with this problem of refraining from attributing to God "any mode of being or relation inexplicable in terms of the principles operative elsewhere in the system,"[18] but without success. Those functions for which God was found to be necessary to the metaphysical system, continually keep appearing throughout the development of the system and setting him apart as being in some special sense unique.

By insisting that God is the "creature of creativity" Whitehead sought to place him among the "actual entities" whose becoming constitutes the ongoing process of the universe; but by suggesting that he is "primordial" and that in this capacity he is "the acquirement by creativity of a primordial character,"[19] he gives to God the unique position of being responsible for the direction of the creative energy and for it being an advance into novelty. Moreover, God's primordial ordering of all the eternal objects determines their relevance to each concrescent occasion, and when we add to this that he also gives to each actuality its initial aim at definiteness, thereby constituting it a process of concrescence, we must confess that God is performing functions which in some sense constitute him unique and different from all other actual entities, and is become, as Gilkey concludes, "not so much an example as one of the presuppositions of the categoreal system."[20]

In the discussion of God and time, this divine uniqueness becomes more evident; Cobb agrees with Whitehead that while actual occasions are temporal, God in his primordial nature is "eternal," and con-

---

[16] Ibid.
[17] Gilkey, *Theology Today*, p. 539.
[18] Cobb, *A Christian Natural Theology*, p. 179.
[19] Whitehead, *PR*, p. 522 (487).
[20] Gilkey, *Theology Today*, p. 539.

sequently unaffected by either time or process; and in his consequent nature he is "everlasting," by which is implied that in him there is no past, but all is in the immediacy of the present. Gilkey's criticism at this point is that neither Whitehead nor Cobb appears to have recognized that the basic ontological difference represented in these attributes of God constitute "fundamental abrogations of the categories descriptive of the other entities which are said to perish literally as soon as they become."[21] These special categories are essential to God in order that he may fulfill his respective functions in the universe and the question which is unsolved is how can God be both transcendent in this necessary sense and yet involved in the actuality of becoming of the actualities.

Cobb suggests as a solution that we regard God as a living person and think of him not as one actual entity, but as a series or route of transient occasions—"an infinite succession of divine occasions of experience."[22] But this will encounter its own peculiar difficulties because the system requires the primordial ordering and structuring of the universe as the very basis of all possibilities of decision and process. Without this prior ordering there could be no universe and therefore the suggestion breaks down. It is only because there is a prior ordering that the emergence of enduring societies such as persons, possessing a measure of freedom of choice becomes possible. Gilkey considers this to be an important methodological move on Whitehead's part, by which he reverses the usual arguments for the existence of God and makes the cosmological argument depend upon the teleological: "there is a world because there is order, and God is essential as the eternal ground of this order among possibility."[23] As the ground for such order as there is in the universe, God must be primordial, but Whitehead did not want to lose the further insight that God is immanent and involved in the process, especially and actively in the lives of men.

It is in the "consequent" nature of God that Whitehead conceives of him as conscious and speaks of him in personal terms. There is a conflict in Whitehead's own thought, as our investigation has disclosed. In section V of the final chapter, he re-asserts the Platonic framework of the universe as being constituted by the interaction of Creativity, God and the World, but in sections VI and VII he employs language drawn from the New Testament which cannot be made to fit into the Platonic framework of *Process and Reality*. It is indeed true, as Cobb says, that "the view that God is a living person . . . makes the doctrine of God more coherent,"[24] but this cannot be done within the framework of the System. It can become possible only after the system has been corrected and the concept of God reformulated in the light of insights which came to Whitehead after he had completed *Process and*

[21] Ibid., p. 540.
[22] Cobb, *A Christian Natural Theology*, p. 188.
[23] Gilkey, *Theology Today*, p. 542; also A. N. Whitehead, *Religion in the Making* (New York: Macmillan, 1956), p. 104.
[24] Cobb, *A Christian Natural Theology*, p. 192.

Reality. Because Cobb failed to recognize the completion which Whitehead found for his cosmology in Christ and the theological formulation of the Christian faith, his natural theology suffers from an attempt to read into the conception of God in *Process and Reality* an interpretation which it could not sustain as defined therein. Anyone familiar with Platonic philosophy will realize that while there are superficial similarities between Platonism and Christianity, there are fundamental contradictions which prevent any straightforward amalgamation of the two.

Gilkey raises a pertinent question which must be met by anyone who would utilize process philosophy in the service of theology: "How does process thought know that the aim that structures everything is an aim towards increasing value?"[25] This question does not receive a satisfactory answer in *Process and Reality*. Whitehead was fascinated by the fact of the evolution of values in the universe and this becomes the basis for his re-examination of the evidence provided by the emergence of civilization in the western world. In the *Function of Reason*, 1929, he asks the question: Why does evolution run upwards?[26] Over the period of millions of years there has been an evolution of actualities of ever greater complexity of composition and of process, issuing in the emergence of life, sentience, mind and will, arriving at man. This fact constitutes a major question in Whitehead's mind and sets him off on the search for a "counter-agency"[27] which in a universe which gives every evidence of wasting away, has yet produced these creative and evaluative actualities. He is applying the teleological principle which in his earlier studies had convinced him of the necessity for God to account for the universe. He is unwilling to believe that humanity could have evolved by mere chance. *Adventures of Ideas* is his search and he indicates this quite specifically in the first chapter. Western civilization has emerged within a particular geographical area and a specific historical period and Whitehead is here searching for those "factors in western civilization which jointly constitute a new element in the history of culture."[28] He expresses the hope that he may "discern the status of the impulses which are driving forward the world of mankind";[29] in other words, he is probing to discover an ultimate more fundamental than "creativity."

Gilkey, in his criticism of Cobb's venture, urges that "a God who represents merely the factor of order and value within process, a God without ontological transcendence over the structure of things, is hardly able to be a God whose mercy transcends the law, i.e., whose love abrogates, replaces, and thus fulfils the requirements of order,"[30] and he concludes that before Whitehead's basic vision and his categories

[25] Gilkey, *Theology Today*, p. 535.
[26] A. N. Whitehead, *The Function of Reason* (Beacon Paperback ed., 1958; Princeton: Princeton University Press, 1929), p. 7.
[27] Ibid., pp. 25f.
[28] Whitehead, *AI*, p. 9.
[29] Ibid., p. 10.
[30] Gilkey, *Theology Today*, p. 538.

can be employed as the substructure of a Christian natural theology, they must "be qualified and the philosophy as a whole subjected to transformation."[31]

A number of recent papers on Whitehead's metaphysics have focused on God and creativity and the roles of each in the creative process. Gene Reeves,[32] while agreeing that Cobb's discussion of God's role in providing the initial aims of actual occasions serves both to clarify his role as creator and to bring out its importance, yet disagrees with Cobb's claim that God is the decisive factor in creation. In the first place, he considers that Cobb confuses the issue by contrasting creativity with actual entities, as though the former were itself an entity, whereas, according to the philosophy of organism, creativity is Whitehead's way of speaking of the decision whereby actual entities are self-creative actualities. Because this act of self-creation is generic to all actual entities, Whitehead terms it "the ultimate," that most general feature which all actual entities have in common."[33] It would appear that Cobb is correct, however, in his reading of Whitehead and that creativity cannot be the decisive factor in the creation of an occasion, for it is explicitly stated by Whitehead that the decision whereby an actuality becomes is an internal process of prehending data for inclusion or exclusion from ingression. Reeve's suggestion that any one of the four formative elements is decisive, in the sense that it is necessary to the creation of an actual entity, constitutes a misuse of the word "decisive," and the arguments which follow suggest that he has not understood what Whitehead means by the phrase "initial aim." Whitehead states,

> This doctrine of the inherence of the subject in the process of its production requires that in the primary phase of the subjective process there be a conceptual feeling of subjective aim: the physical and other feelings originate as steps towards realizing this conceptual aim through their treatment of initial data.[34]

On the following page Whitehead explains further that

> each temporal entity, in one sense, originates from its mental pole, analogously to God himself. It derives from God its basic conceptual aim, relevant to its actual world, yet with indeterminations awaiting its own decisions. This subjective aim, in its successive modifications, remains the unifying factor governing the successive phases of interplay between physical and conceptual feelings.[35]

What Whitehead appears to be saying here is that God, who is present in the welter of data which comprise the past, and who orders the eternal objects to become relevant potentials for the qualification of the creativity in the ongoing process, constitutes each actual entity a pro-

[31] Ibid.
[32] Gene Reeves, "God and Creativity," *Southern Journal of Philosophy*, 7/4 (Winter, 1969), 377-86.
[33] Ibid., p. 378.
[34] Whitehead, *PR*, p. 342 (316).
[35] Ibid., p. 343 (317).

cess of becoming by giving to each the appropriate aim at definiteness for that particular situation in which it is emerging in the space-time continuum. An actual entity is initiated by God as a prehending thing, to use Whitehead's words, prehending the entities of its past through the perspective of the initial aim which constitutes it a subject in process of becoming. Because it is a subject its aim will be its own, i.e., subjective, and Whitehead suggests that this subjective aim, while it will be modified through successive decisions of the evolving actuality, none the less, remains the unifying factor governing the successive phases of the concrescence. Whitehead explicitly states that "the physical and other feelings originate as steps towards realizing this conceptual aim through their treatment of initial data,"[36] indicating that these are subsequent to the initial constitution of the actual occasion. I find myself in agreement with Cobb on this question of the decisive role of God in the initiation of the process of becoming of each new occasion; from this point on decision rests with the concrescing occasion. Its concrescene is conditioned by the other actual entities of its immediate past which determine the nature of the world to which the new actuality must conform, but the choices are those of the concrescing subject.

In an article entitled "The Viability of Whitehead's God for Christian Theology,"[37] Professor Lewis Ford makes a strong case for the contribution which Whitehead's philosophy may make towards a Christian understanding of God and the World. It is particularly distinctive, he considers, in being a philosophy of creation which does not identify creative power exclusively with God, a philosophy of pluralism in which creativity, the ultimate principle, embodies the rhythm of the one and the many whereby, in Whitehead's words, "the many become one, and are increased by one."[38] According to this view creativity is everlasting, without beginning or end, with the world contributing to God and God to the world.

Professor Ford outlines a number of what he considers to be distinct advantages for Christian theism of the non-identification of God with creativity or being-itself; each of these themes will repay careful study, as will also the replies which are made by Robert C. Neville in an accompanying paper.[39] For the present we must focus on Ford's reply to Langdom Gilkey who criticized Whitehead on the grounds that his "god is subordinate to the larger process and so to the metaphysical categories explicative of that process."[40] Ford suggests Gilkey has overlooked the fact that Whitehead initially introduced God into his philosophy as "the ground of rationality"[41] and asserts that

---

[36] Ibid., p. 342 (316).

[37] Lewis S. Ford, "The Viability of Whitehead's God for Christian Theology," *The American Catholic Philosophical Association, Proceedings for the Year 1970*, pp. 141-52.

[38] "Viability," *A.C.P.A. Proceedings, 1970*, p. 141.

[39] Robert C. Neville, "The Impossibility of Whitehead's God for Christian Theology," *A.C.P.A. Proceedings, 1970*, p. 130.

[40] Langdon Gilkey, *Naming the Whirlwind: The Renewal of God Language* (Indianapolis: Bobbs-Merrill, 1969), p. 443.

[41] A. N. Whitehead, *Science and the Modern World* (Cambridge: Cambridge University Press, 1926; cheap ed., 1933), p. 222.

"God is metaphysically intelligible because he exemplifies the metaphysical principles, yet he also creates them."[42] Whitehead does not specifically state this, but Ford arrives at his conclusion from the fact that "God as exemplifying creativity must be conceived as self-created, and the metaphysical principles which both God and the World exemplify are created in his primordial envisagement." As Whitehead expresses it: "His conceptual actuality at once exemplifies and establishes the categoreal conditions."[43]

Neville believes the doctrine set out in this quotation to be untenable, and that Whitehead was mistaken in his suggestion; that inasmuch as this is God's primordial act of self-creation it is not possible for him to be at one and the same phase of the act of his becoming bound by the metaphysical conditions which he is in process of establishing—at least not in Whiteheadian terms, for the principles would not be determinate until the concrescence had arrived at satisfaction. Neville would say that God creates the determinate metaphysical principles or categoreal conditions and he adds, "furthermore, the principles describe God in the sense he is the God who creates a world exhibiting these principles, including those articulating his created relation to the world."[44]

It is important to keep in mind also that Ford exempts "creativity" from the number of the metaphysical categories which God creates; he repeatedly re-affirms that creativity is metaphysically ultimate for Whitehead, and suggests that those who disagree with this position wish to identify God and creativity. Neville suggests an alternative in "the conception of God as creator of everything determinative, creator of things actual as well as of things possible."[45] Neville wants to distinguish between God in himself as utterly transcendent, and God as giving himself a relative nature in creating the world, and suggests we may accomplish this by recognizing two kinds of creativity. There is ontological creativity, an activity of God in creating determinate things, both unified and complex, out of nothing, and there is cosmological creativity, which is that exercised by creatures constituting the world, and which creates a one out of a previously real many. This latter kind, he declares, is the only creativity acknowledged by Whitehead, whose "God is cosmologically creative, using the simple eternal objects as initial data; I conceive God as having no initial data."[46]

Ford finds this distinction between ontological and cosmological creativity quite superfluous, ". . . since 'cosmological' creativity can account for both the being of actualities and of God, as well as the ways in which God creates the metaphysical principles, the values the world strives for, and the unity of the world."[47] If Ford here seems to be begging the question raised by Neville, this is because he is approaching

[42] "Viability," *A.C.P.A. Proceedings, 1970,* p. 147.
[43] Whitehead, *PR,* p. 522 (487).
[44] "Impossibility," *A.C.P.A. Proceedings, 1970,* p. 137.
[45] Ibid., p. 130.
[46] Ibid., p. 132.
[47] Ibid.

the situation from a point within an already established "general metaphysical character of creative advance"[48] which, following Whitehead, he accepts as simply given; in other words, Ford's and Whitehead's point of beginning for God in his primordial self-creation is from within a revised Platonic metaphysical model in which the world in some sense is considered to be eternal and God is but one of a number of factors simply given, whereas for Neville God is the creator of all, "things visible and things invisible."[49]

The issues raised in this dialogue between two Whitehead scholars bring into sharp focus the conflict which was emerging between elements of Whitehead's various thoughts about God as recorded in the final chapter of *Process and Reality*. Professor Ford provides many helpful suggestions as to how Whitehead's metaphysics may serve the needs of contemporary theological discourse, but he fails to resolve the dilemma brought about by the attempt to bring together into one statement basically Platonic and Christian points of view about ultimate reality. The solution to the problem would seem to lie somewhere between Neville and Ford. In order to assess the variety of conflicting ideas which lie behind the two points of view represented, it will be necessary to return to the sources of those ideas about God and the world which have formed the presuppositions of thought in the western world.

We will conclude this part of the essay by calling attention to developments in Whitehead's conception of God which, had his mind not been imbued with the necessity of maintaining the Platonic framework for his cosmology, might have led to a different and more coherent conclusion to *Process and Reality*.

In *Science and the Modern World*, in which Whitehead for the first time introduces God into his philosophy as necessary to account for the fact of the universe, he declares both that God is necessary to the metaphysical understanding of the situation disclosed, as a principle of limitation and of concretion, and warns of the limitations as to what metaphysics as such could say about him. "What further can be known about God," he declares, "must be sought in the region of particular experiences, and therefore rests on an empirical basis."[50] In *Religion in the Making*, the basically Platonic framework of his scheme is being indicated and God is declared to be but one of three formative elements, of which he is the ordering principle.[51] In *Process and Reality* the Platonic framework is accepted as facilitating a description of the universe as a process of creative advance into novelty, creativity is declared to be the Ultimate and God is "the aboriginal instance of this creativity, and is therefore the aboriginal condition which qualifies its action."[52] We are informed that we must learn to consider God from

[48] Whitehead, *PR*, p. 522 (487).
[49] J. N. D. Kelly, "The Creed of Nicaea," in *Early Christian Creeds* (New York: Longmans, 1950), p. 215.
[50] Whitehead, *SMW*, p. 222.
[51] A. N. Whitehead, *Religion in the Making* (New York: Macmillan, 1926), p. 90.
[52] Whitehead, *PR*, p. 344 (317-18).

two perspectives, according as we consider his primordial ordering of all things on the one hand, and consider his activity and presence as immanent and in process of becoming with the actualities of the universe on the other. In spite of the severe limitations which Whitehead has placed upon him, God becomes increasingly recognized to be playing the decisive role in the process of becoming of the universe, as the system is developed. As indicated above, the creativity which is everywhere instantiated in the actualities of the world in their process of self-creation has been primordially characterized by God. "It is the function of actuality to characterize the creativity," declares Whitehead, "and God is the eternal primordial character."[53]

Leclerc agrees that God must be the aboriginal instance of creativity, since he "is required by all other actualities as their 'principle of concretion,' as the provider of their subjective aim,"[54] but he appears unable to accept the implications of this statement, that in the beginning God was the solely existing actual entity, because to acknowledge this would, he fears, violate the ontological principle and the category of relativity, to the effect that all actual entities require "data." "Thus," he concludes, "God as an actual entity can no more be without other actual entities than they can be without God."[55] Here we meet the paradoxical situation which points up the acute dilemma for students of Whitehead when they take seriously his insistence that the metaphysical principles must apply equally to God and to all other actual entities. Whitehead is careful to emphasize tht God is *causa sui*, that he is that unique non-temporal actual entity at the base of actuality, and that he is primordial. If we take "primordial" in its dictionary sense of "the beginning" ;or "commencement" and link it with the companion statement that the primordial nature of God "is his complete envisagement of eternal objects,"[56] keeping in mind his earlier definition of "envisagement" as holding together the twin terms "vision" and "appetition" for fulfilment or a yearning after concrete fact,"[57] and link these with the final statements about the primordial nature of God as "the unconditioned actuality of conceptual feeling at the base of things; so that, by reason of this primordial actuality, there is an order in the relevance of eternal objects to the process of creation,"[58] we can only take him to be referring to the operations of God prior to the becoming of spatio-temporal actualities. It would seem that the ontological principle notwithstanding, God is here being spoken of prior to the becoming of all the other actualities of the temporal world, and that this is one of those problems which calls for clarification.

Moreover, Whitehead declares that, but for this primordial ordering by God of all the eternal objects, they would be simply "nonentity."

[53] Ibid., p. 344 (318).
[54] Ivor Leclerc, *Whitehead's Metaphysics, An Introductory Exposition* (London: George Allen & Unwin, 1958), p. 194.
[55] Ibid., p. 195.
[56] Whitehead, *PR,* p. 70 (60).
[57] Ibid., p. 50 (45-46).
[58] Ibid., p. 522 (487-88).

It becomes relevant to enquire whether they can be said to exist in any meaningful sense, otherwise than as constituting the primordial character of God, and as given by God for the concrescence of an actual world as a sharing of some aspects of his nature with transient things? The eternal objects are given as potentials for the becoming of actual entities in the actual world. Without this ordering by God, there could be no world of ordered actualities. The particularities of the evolving world presuppose this primordial ordering, declares Whitehead, but finds it necessary to explain that "it" (the primordial nature of God) "merely presupposes the general metaphysical character of creative advance,"[59] in order to maintain the Platonic shape of his system. But for this necessity, it would have seemed more rational at this point to say that God's envisagement constitutes the general metaphysical character of creative advance by his primordial characterization of creativity to be the substructure for a spatio-temporal universe for which the eternal objects constitute the potentialities for actualization in the world process in which the actualities are self-creative after having received from God their initial subjective aim at definiteness.

At this point in the summary statement God is being declared to be all in all in the origination of the process of creative advance which is the universe. "His conceptual actuality at once exemplifies and establishes the categoreal conditions,"[60] which were earlier declared to be but tentative, and awaiting validation from experience. The "subjective forms" which are exemplified in his primordial nature "are valuations determining the relative relevance of eternal objects for each successive occasion of actuality."[61] At this point Whitehead envisages God in his primordial nature as watching over the universe in its process of creative advance, and ordering the eternal objects as to their relevance for each situation.

There is a response on the part of the actualities so that God becomes also "the lure for feeling, the eternal urge of desire. His particular relevance to each creative act as it arises from its own conditioned standpoint in the world, constitutes him the initial 'object of desire' establishing the initial phase of each subjective aim."[62] Throughout this exposition, Whitehead declares, "we have been considering the primary action of God on the world," as the "principle of concretion—the principle whereby there is initiated a definite outcome from a situation otherwise riddled with ambiguity."[63]

In all these statements about the originative agency of God in his primary action on the world, Whitehead is treating God as the Ultimate reality and both creativity and the eternal objects are simply aspects or features or qualities of his nature. By the introduction of a differentiation in the nature of God according as he is considering his primordial activities, and as "consequent" in considering his active

[59] Ibid., p. 522 (487).
[60] Ibid.
[61] Ibid.
[62] Ibid.
[63] Ibid., p. 523 (488).

agency and immanence in the world, Whitehead has discovered a way of speaking about God which enables him to disclose the complexity of the creative process and the creative interaction of God and the actualities in the world in the ongoing process of the universe.

At this point it would seem more appropriate to say that the creativity which Whitehead took for the ultimate in his system and the eternal objects are *both* the result of the aboriginal creative act of God in his primordial envisagement of a universe consisting of self-creative actualities each in process of becoming. We discern them as simply there, as formative elements in the becoming of actual entities, as characterized by God in the case of creativity, as ordered by God in the case of the eternal objects, and given by him to actual entities to constitute their process of becoming by giving direction towards a specific goal. What would seem to be called for is a restructuring of the process philosophy in order to give recognition to the ultimacy of the creative activity of God in the origination of the universe. This could be undertaken, however, only if empirical evidences found in religious experience required it. Whitehead reminds us that "the transitions to new fruitfulness of understanding are achieved by recurrence to the utmost depths of intuition for the refreshment of imagination."[64] Inasmuch as Whitehead undertook such a reassessment in his later writings, it will be well to examine these to discover what further insight he is able to bring towards a resolution of the conflict in his thought about God.

[64] Whitehead, *AI*, pp. 203-04.

Part 2

Research and Discovery

Chapter VIII

The Need for a Fresh Appeal to the Philosophical, Historical and Theological Foundations

By the introduction of the conceptions of the "primordial nature" and the "consequent nature" of God in his Cosmology, Whitehead is clearly struggling with the problem of discovering a suitable terminology with which to account for aspects of reality as disclosed in mankind's experience of God and of the universe as disclosed by the scientific adventure. The attempt to differentiate aspects of the nature of God according to his operations in the world has disclosed the necessary complexity of the problems which confront those who would speak about God and the world and the severe limitations of language at our disposal for such a task. As it stands in *Process and Reality,* the account fails to provide the interpretation which was promised. The statement calls for further elucidation of the terms, and requires to be counterbalanced by insights which can come only from further disclosure if it is not to lead into error in the attempt to be overexplicit in an area of experience in which it is not possible for philosophical discourse to provide more than hints and suggestions as to the direction in which an answer might be expected to be found.

What becomes clear from our analysis is that the concept of God as immanent and at work in the world, a concept vividly portrayed in closing sections of *Process and Reality,* requires to be counterbalanced by further elucidation of God as transcendent, without losing any of his real immanence. The need for this further provision is clearly indicated in the necessity which Whitehead found himself under in Part V, Chapter II, section V, of hypostasizing "Creativity" in order to account for the creative advance in the physical process of the universe. The category of the ultimate calls for re-definition before we can proceed with the exposition of the final things as set out in the closing sections of *Process and Reality,* and Whitehead was not long in setting out upon a search to discover the empirical and metaphysical basis for such a re-formulation of the system, in other words, a search to discover "the quality of creative origination."[1]

[1] A. N. Whitehead, *Process and Reality: An Essay in Cosmology* (New York: Harper Torchbooks, 1960; first published, New York: Macmillan, 1929), p. 518 (488).

The published edition of *Process and Reality* first appeared in 1929; in March of that year, Whitehead delivered the Louis Clark Vanuxem Foundation Lectures at Princeton University, and used the opportunity offered by the occasion to investigate the function of Reason.[2] Here, clearly, Whitehead is off on another search, but, as in the case of his earlier major works, he prepares the ground by a preliminary investigation in which he isolates the central problem and fashions the linguistic tools for the speculative venture. He is searching for a clue to the solution of some of the puzzles which his system had failed to unravel. Whitehead at no time returns over the same ground again; his analyses are careful and thorough and will stand up to the tests of time; his puzzlement arises rather from deficiency of insight into the ultimate originative element in the universe, and from inadequacies of language appropriate to give unity to the variety of insights which his investigations have disclosed.

In the first lecture of the series Whitehead engages his readers in an examination of the current dogmas of biological evolution, of which he is highly critical. They fall into error, he maintains, because they put forward a partial interpretation and assert it to be the whole. Their error results from their neglect of additional aspects of the truth of the total situation—from a one-sided examination of the evidence, and from approaching it with a preconceived notion of what it was to yield. The fallacy in the dogma of the "survival of the fittest,"[3] for example, lies in the assumption that fitness for survival is identical with the best exemplification of the art of life, whereas a moment's reflection will disclose that life itself is comparatively deficient in survival power in comparison with other features of the universe, such as rocks, and that man's life is remarkably short and so vulnerable as to pose a question as to why and how complex organisms with such deficient power of survival ever evolved. The struggle for existence which is waged among organisms fails to throw any light whatsoever upon the emergence of such a general type of complex organism so deficient in survival power. The fact of the presence of such organisms in the universe calls for something more than the current evolutionary theory to explain it. What is called for is patient attention to all the empirical evidence.

One question which Whitehead suggests current evolutionary doctrines fail to grapple with is, "Why has the trend of evolution been upwards?"[4] The doctrine of adaptation to environment is incapable of explaining the fact that organic species have been produced from inorganic distributions of matter, or the fact that organic species of higher and higher types have evolved; nor can it explain the fact that animals have progressively undertaken the task of adapting their environment to their own needs. This latter is the most prominent fact in the existence of man, whose physical constitution is the most ill-

[2] A. N. Whitehead, *The Function of Reason* (Beacon Paperback ed., 1958; Princeton: Princeton University Press, 1929).

[3] Whitehead, *FR*, pp. 4f.

[4] Ibid., p. 7.

adapted of any creature to meet the onslaughts of nature. The upward movement of mankind has been made possible by the development of Reason, with the aim of a more richly diversified and satisfying life.

Attention is now turned to a consideration of the material universe, which, Whitehead maintains, "has contained in itself, and perhaps still contains, some mysterious impulse for its energy to run upwards."[5] It is not possible for us to observe this impulse, so far as its general operation goes, but there must have been some epoch, he suggests, "in which the dominant trend was the formation of protons, electrons, molecules, the stars."[6] Because we ourselves belong to the animal world, we can observe in ourselves the "appetition towards the upward trend with Reason as the selective agency,"[7] but we have no like means of direct knowledge of the sources of the energy of the physical universe. According to the findings of some scientists, it appears to be finite, and to be wasting at a finite rate. Construed solely in terms of the efficient causation of purely physical interconnections, it presents, Whitehead suggests, a sheer insoluble contradiction. This would indicate the omission from the account of some counter-agency which alone can provide the clue to fuller understanding. "But at present, as we survey the physical cosmos, there is no direct intuition of the counter-agency to which it owes its possibility of existence as a wasting finite organism."[8] In the one part of nature which we know intimately, namely, our own psycho-physical organism, we have clear evidence of activities directed by purpose, and he suggests that we should reverse the analogy by which the evolutionists have sought to interpret later developments by the earlier, and instead should "argue that some lowly, diffused form of the operations of Reason constitute the vast diffused counter-agency by which the material cosmos comes into being. This conclusion amounts to the repudiation of the radical extrusion of final causation from our cosmological theory."[9] It is the function of Reason, Whitehead points out, "to constitute, emphasize, and criticize the final causes and strength of aim directed towards them,"[10] and apart from this its primary function, the emergence of Reason is inexplicable. If the activities of Reason remain without influence on bodily actions, why should the trend of evolution have arrived at mankind? The dilemma posed by this question suggests the need for some more fundamental explanation of the origination of Reason.

In the second lecture we find an important comparison of the histories of the practical Reason and of the speculative Reason. The practical Reason may be traced back into the animal life from which man emerged and is older than man as man, "if we have regard to the faint sporadic flashes of intelligence which guided the slow elaboration

⁵ Ibid., p. 24.
⁶ Ibid.
⁷ Ibid.
⁸ Ibid., pp. 25-26.
⁹ Ibid., p. 26.
¹⁰ Ibid.

of methods."[11] The history of speculative Reason is very much shorter; if we take into account the great Asiatic civilizations it might be said to have a history of three thousand years, but the critical discovery which gave to speculation its supreme importance was made by the Greeks and has a history of a little over two thousand years. By their discovery of mathematics and logic the Greeks introduced methods into speculation and laid the foundations for the great advance in systematic knowledge which has made possible modern civilization. If we include the Asiatic civilizations, we may say that the speculative Reason has been employed by man for approximately three thousand years and during that short period the inward life of man has been transformed.[12]

But now, a remarkable disclosure; it is only in the past one hundred and fifty years that speculative Reason has been applied to technology and art; this development has resulted from the fact that the speculative and the practical Reason have at last made contact and each has corrected and strengthened the other. Whitehead suggests that there were real achievements gained by the Scholastic systems of thought. Their defects lay in their failure to bring their speculative thinking to the test by bringing their theories into contact with experience; they nonetheless made great strides forward and "formed the intellectual basis of one of the periods of quickest advance known to history."[13] Their great gift to the European world, he suggests, was "penetration in the handling of ideas."[14]

It was not until the sixteenth and seventeenth centuries that the interrelationship of speculative Reason and empirical experience became clearer; it was the men of this period who founded the various modern sciences, natural and moral, "with their first principles expressed in terms which the great scholastics would have understood at a glance";[15] this re-casting of the medieval ideas so as to form the foundations of the modern sciences, Whitehead declares, was one of the intellectual triumphs of the world.[16] Unfortunately, the understanding of the proper functions of speculative thought was hampered by the fallacy of dogmatism. In contrast to the clarity of thought of the scholastics with their clear, distinct and certain ideas as first principles, the methods of science seemed tentative and halting. But due to the triumphs of Newtonian physics science itself became settled upon a dogmatic foundation of materialistic ideas which lasted for two centuries. These two approaches, consequently, became regarded as alternative and opposite ways and sought each to cancel the other out, whereas the advancement of knowledge requires that they work together, each correcting and strengthening the other. Without recourse to metaphysics physical science is incapable of providing an interpreta-

[11] Ibid., p. 40.
[12] Ibid., p. 41.
[13] Ibid., p. 45.
[14] Ibid., p. 46.
[15] Ibid., p. 47.
[16] Ibid., p. 48.

tion of the universe. He accuses both mathematics and theology of "fostering the dogmatic habit in European thought."[17] The attempt at a truce by separating the various spheres into topics of the mind on the one hand and topics concerning matter on the other has been proven by experience to be artificial and can no longer be maintained. Man is a psychophysical organism and if he is to be understood must be studied in his wholeness. The problem facing our generation of thinkers is constituted in the fact that "the whole conception of philosophy as concerned with the discipline of the speculative Reason, to which nothing is alien, has vanished."[18] Today, however, a new situation faces both scientist and philosopher, for dogmatic finality in science has vanished and is replaced by an asymptotic approach to the truth, and Whitehead recommends that philosophers undertake the task of distinguishing between the various areas of authority, "between the authority of science in the determination of its methodology and the authority of science in the determination of the ultimate categories of explanation."[19] No one branch of scientific investigation is capable of performing this latter function and the physical scientist must, accordingly, look to cosmology to provide the metaphysical categories in terms of which he may fit the phenomena under observation into a larger pattern than his own branch of science can provide.

Whitehead is here reiterating convictions which he had expressed in the first chapter of *Process and Reality,* to the effect that the proper satisfaction to be derived from speculative thought is elucidation, and for this reason fact is supreme over thought; but even this supreme authority fails to be final because, on the one hand, there is always some remaining ambiguity in the available evidence; and secondly, if at any period of human history it had been accepted as final, all progress would have been stopped. Mankind is always building or seeking to build better; no age can achieve a "best" which will satisfy its successors. "It is of the essence of such speculation that it transcends immediate fact."[20] Its business, he points out, "is to make thought creative of the future."[21] And in this process, "the true use of history is that we extract from it general principles as to the discipline of practice and the discipline of speculation."[22]

In conclusion, Whitehead finds himself compelled to acknowledge that "cosmology shares the imperfections of all the efforts of finite intelligence."[23] The special sciences will each fall short of their aims, and cosmology equally will fail to achieve the perfect statement of the ultimate meaning of things. When a novel speculation is produced, he suggests, "Reason intervenes in the capacity of arbiter and yet with a further exercise of speculation,"[24] with the result that usually "the

[17] Ibid., p. 50.
[18] Ibid., p. 51.
[19] Ibid., p. 27.
[20] Ibid., pp. 81-82.
[21] Ibid., p. 82.
[22] Ibid.
[23] Ibid., p. 86.
[24] Ibid., p. 87.

science is modified, the cosmological outlook is modified, and the novel concept is modified."[25] The various cosmologies have "failed to achieve the generality and clarity at which they aim. They are inadequate, vague, and push special notions beyond the proper limits of their application."[26] He illustrates his point by a reference to Descartes, but might equally well have been referring to his own employment of the ultimate, "Creativity," in the closing chapter of *Process and Reality*. The intention, clearly, is to emphasize once again both the necessity and the limitations of metaphysics. The various schools of philosophy have each said something which is importantly true, but no one of them can express the whole truth, and at length each cosmology will be found to be inadequate to do justice to the full scope of experience and will call for correction by confrontation with fresh facts.

Whitehead is here, in the closing lecture of the series, laying down the principles and methods by which he will shortly re-examine the history of ideas and of their impact upon the life of individuals and of society over a period of some twelve hundred years; ideas emanating from the writings of the great prophets of Israel, the Greek philosophers, and the Christian theologians of the first five centuries of the Christian era. The series, i.e., *The Function of Reason* closes with a re-affirmation of the necessity of there being some further explanation to account for the fact of Reason and of the speculative imagination in man, both of which are matters of act. There is in man what Whitehead describes as a discrimination of appetitions according to a rule of fitness. "This reign of Reason," he confesses, "is vascillating, vague and dim. But it is there."[27] "We have thus some knowledge, in a form specialized to the special aptitudes of human beings—we have some knowledge of that counter-tendency which converts the decay of one order into the birth of its successor."[28] At this point Whitehead has isolated the goal of his search—the counter-agency; and he has identified the instrument with which he will undertake the search—Reason and the speculative imagination. We are not surprised to learn that his next major work, published in September, 1932, is entitled *Adventures of Ideas*, and that it constitutes an investigation into the effect of two or three ideas whose ferment has promoted what Whitehead describes as "the slow drift of mankind towards civilization."[29]

Whitehead makes it quite clear in the preface to *Adventures of Ideas* that he is here carrying forward the search for an explanation of the fact that civilized beings have arisen in the evolutionary process. He explains that the three books, *Science and the Modern World*, *Process and Reality*, and *Adventures of Ideas*, are "an endeavour to express a way of understanding the nature of things,"[30] and that while each may be read

---

[25] Ibid.
[26] Ibid., p. 88.
[27] Ibid., p. 90.
[28] Ibid.
[29] A. N. Whitehead, *Adventures of Ideas* (Cambridge: Cambridge University Press, 1933), Preface, p. vii.
[30] Ibid., Preface, p. vii.

separately, they do nonetheless, "supplement each other's omissions or compressions."[31] The book, as its title would indicate, is a study of the history of ideas in the development of western civilization by way of illustrating the principles of the philosophy of organism, to develop points of view introduced in the earlier works, to correct inadequacies of statement and to clarify the meaning of the final interpretation. He is hopeful that the study may enable him to "discern the status of the impulses which are driving forward the world of mankind."[32] To this end, the study is limited to the investigation of "the energizing of two or three main ideas"[33] which were introduced into Europe by the Hebrews and the Greeks, ideas "whose effective entertainment constitutes civilization."[34]

The first section of this work consists of a sociological and historical study of the growth of the sense of worth of the individual person. A serious effort is made to investigate the sources of creative change in the course of human history. Mankind throughout its slow evolution from earlier forms of life, has reacted to twin agencies which have changed the habitual patterns of living. There have been senseless agencies—natural forces, such as climate and geography, and violence in the form of attack from enemies—referred to by Plato as "compulsion" or "Necessity" (ἀνάγκη);[35] and, on the other hand, on each occasion of creative change there have been formulated aspirations which, after the senseless agencies had shaken mankind loose from established traditional structures, have issued in a re-organization on a higher level of integration by incorporating into the social structure consciously formulated ideals which had previously been prevented through the opposition of vested interests and ancestral pieties. The coincidence of such twin agencies at the great turning points of history has facilitated the advance of civilization. Whitehead suggests that two such occasions were, first, the coincidence of the barbarians and the Christians at the time of the fall of the Roman Empire, and secondly, that of steam and democracy which in the eighteenth century ushered in the Industrial Revolution. On each of these occasions we find senseless agencies and formulated aspirations co-operating "in the work of driving mankind from its old anchorage. Sometimes the period of change is an age of hope, sometimes it is an age of despair."[36]

Today these forces are most evident in the form of the constant threat of annihilation by nuclear warfare and on the other hand we have the formulated aspirations in the shape of the Charter of the United Nations with its programme of activities designed to make possible the realization of one world, and the Ecumenical Movement within the Christian Churches drawing together a divided Christendom to provide the energizing of love, both divine and human, for the

[31] Ibid.
[32] Ibid., p. 10.
[33] Ibid., p. 9.
[34] Ibid.
[35] Plato, *The Timaeus*, pp. 47E-48D; Cornford, *Plato's Cosmology*, pp. 160ff.
[36] Whitehead, *AI*, p. 7.

creative integration of men and nations into one world society. One of the interesting features of the present situation is the extent to which it is an age of hope, and that in spite of the awareness on the part of all men in our generation that our life could be snuffed out at any moment without warning, we continue to believe in and to plan for the future. There is a recognition and an acceptance of the necessity of an element of insecurity inherent in all processes of creative change; and the fact of this recognition is itself the most important feaure in the present situation, for it permits the rationality of man to triumph over and to utilize the senseless agencies creatively, in the interests, not of destruction, but for the enrichment of the life of mankind. Because ours is an age of hope, there is hope of mankind moving forward into integration and community on a world-wide scale. But the fact of this hope and its rationalization is what calls for explanation and interpretation and poses for us as for Whitehead the question of what is the ultimate meaning of this process, including the universe with its dynamic energies and man into whose hands these forces have been delivered for good or for evil, depending upon the use to which they are put. What does it all come to? and are there any clues as to its ultimate meaning disclosed in history? *Adventures of Ideas* is Whitehead's search for an answer.

In an analysis of the influence of the Platonic and the Christian doctrine of the human soul upon the sociological development of Europe, Whitehead isolates four factors which govern the fate of social groups. The first of these is the necessity for some transcendent aim to focus attention upon goals beyond purely selfish ambitions; secondly, the provision of bodily necessities of food, clothing, and shelter is essential to survival; a third factor resides in the fact that social control may be exercised by the compulsory dominion of man over man, but, if compulsion is extended beyond the barest limits necessary for social order it becomes an evil and disruptive force. There is a fourth factor, which is an alternative method of social control, and is called by Whitehead the "way of persuasion,"[37] and it is to this method that the progressive societies have decisively entrusted themselves. In any specific situation this way may give the appearance of being too slow for the advocates of reform, but it has implications which are so far-reaching as to constitute it the major factor in producing creative change.

Whitehead now calls attention to three human activities which have chiefly promoted this fourth factor, namely (i) family affections aroused in sex relations and in the nurture of offspring, eliciting a tenderness and concern for the well-being of others; (ii) intellectual curiosity, leading to the mutual exchange of ideas among scholars and research workers; and (iii) commercial activities in which the trader is personally no threat to the tribe or nation and the wares which he offers are attractive and useful. Beyond these special activities, however, there has arisen a greater bond of sympathy in

[37] Ibid., p. 109.

the growth of reverence for that power in virtue of which nature harbours ideal ends, and produces individual beings capable of conscious discrimination of such ends. This reverence is the foundation of the respect for man as man. It thereby secures that liberty of thought and action, required for the upward adventure of life on this earth.[38]

Here we find attention being focused upon "that power" which, in *The Function of Reason,* was referred to as the "counter agency"[39] required to account for the emergence of Reason. Intercourse between individuals and between societies may take one or other of two forms—either of persuasion, or of force—and the story of civilization is the history of the gradual victory of persuasion as a method of human association and action as against compulsion or force. Recourse to force, however necessary it may become on occasions, "is a disclosure of the failure of civilization, either in the general society or in a remnant of individuals."[40]

In a section on Cosmology, Whitehead introduces an important discussion of a variety of alternative doctrines of the Laws of Nature; how are we to interpret the patterns of sequences and rhythms which are everywhere present throughout the universe and but for which no purposive life would be possible for mankind. There are four main doctrines, namely, (i) the doctrine of Law as immanent, (ii) the doctrine of Law as imposed, (iii) the doctrine of Law as observed order of succession, and (iv) a fourth which is more recent in origin, the doctrine of Law as conventional interpretation.[41] Each of these ways of regarding the universe is discussed in relation to our present knowledge and as to its past history and influence on the development of thought.

The notion of Law as immanent is an attempt to express the interrelationship and interdependence of all things in nature in terms of patterns of behaviour which are the outcome of the characters of the real things in nature. As the characters and relations change, so the Laws will change, and consequently, according to this doctrine evolutionary change becomes possible; it is a rationalistic doctrine which attempts to express the fact of "some community in character pervading the things which constitute Nature."[42] Whitehead concludes that according to this doctrine a doctrine of internal relations is necessary. It is a thoroughly rationalistic doctrine which is explanatory of the possibility of understanding nature, and it involves the negation of "absolute being." Tracing the history of the doctrine, Whitehead finds it recommended by Plato in his "definition of 'being' as simply power."[43] The context in which the definition occurs makes it evident

---

[38] Ibid.
[39] Whitehead, *FR,* p. 26.
[40] Whitehead, *AI,* p. 105.
[41] Ibid., pp. 142f.
[42] Ibid., p. 142.
[43] Plato, *Sophist,* 247E, Jowett translation; cf. also Cornford, *Plato's Theory of Knowledge,* pp. 234ff. Str: "I suggest that anything has real being, that is so constituted as to possess any sort of power either to affect anything else or to be affected, in however small a degree, by the most insignificant agent, though it be only once. I am proposing as a mark to distinguish real things, that they are nothing but power."

that Plato's definition refers to the "power either to affect anything else or to be affected, in however small a degree"[44] and presupposes a doctrine of Law as immanent. Whitehead's concept of God as the principle of order, and interpreted as being the "lure for feeling,"[45] namely, a persuasive agency, appealing for decision, is his way of interpreting Law as immanent in his own system. The law as such explains the nature of things and of their impact upon one another. His position is well summed up in the following summary description of physical time: "The quantum [i.e., of time] is that standpoint in the extensive continuum which is consonant with the subjecive aim in its original derivation from God. Here 'God' is that actuality in the world, in virtue of which there is physical law.'"[46] The doctrine finds its most extreme form of exemplification in the Buddhist doctrine of the impersonal immanence of Law.

At the other extreme stands the doctrine of Law as imposition, based upon an "alternative metaphysical doctrine of External Relations between the existences which are the ultimate constituents of nature";[47] this is the ancient Semitic conception, whether Hebrew or Islamic, of a God who made the various elements in a static universe, composed of diverse items having external relations only, and upon which he imposes his Laws by fiat. On this view, no explanation can be found from examination of the nature of things as to why they behave in the way in which they do. Any interrelationship which they exhibit is simply a pattern imposed upon them from without. Newton's *Scholium* provides a good illustration of the application of this doctrine;[48] it proceeds from and in turn fosters the typical Deistic conception of God as transcendent creator; having introduced God to impose movement and order upon the world, Newton could find nothing further for him to do, except to keep the universe on its orderly path of movement.[49] Whitehead, however, makes the important point that it was this simplified notion of imposed Law from a transcendent deity that was the inspiration of those who launched the modern scientific movement. Even before the time of Descartes, he suggests, the motive force of scientific research was the implicit belief in imposed law. Indeed, apart from such belief in the imposition of order there would have been no reason for pursuing scientific research, "because the doctrine of immanence provides absolutely no reason why the universe should not be steadily lapsing into lawless chaos."[50]

Whitehead is convinced that some fusion of these two notions of Law is required in order to account for the full complexity of the

---

[44] Ibid.
[45] Whitehead, *PR*, p. 522 (487).
[46] Ibid., p. 434 (401-02).
[47] Whitehead, *AI*, p. 144.
[48] See above, pp. 31ff.
[49] See Daniel Day Williams, "How Does God Act?" in William L. Reese and Eugene Freeman, eds., *Process and Divinity* (LaSalle, Illinois: Open Court Publishing Company, 1964), p. 162.
[50] Whitehead, *AI*, pp. 146-47.

processes of the Universe: "the Universe, as understood in accordance with the doctrine of immanence, should exhibit itself as including a stable actuality whose mutual implications with the remainder of things secures an inevitable trend towards order."[51] The counter-agency is a necessary factor to account for the trend towards order and a search to discover evidence of its working is called for. Whitehead finds in Plato's Cosmology a tendency towards a fusion of the doctrines of imposition and immanence; "it includes," he says, "an ultimate creator, shadowy and undefined, imposing his design upon the Universe,"[52] but retains a measure of freedom of movement to the internal constituents so that their action and reaction are "the self-sufficient explanation of the flux."[53] Later, Whitehead suggests that The Receptacle, as discussed in the *Timaeus*, is Plato's "doctrine of the immanence of Law, derived from the mutual immanence of actualities."[54] But the real work of fusion was accomplished, he suggests by the theologians of Alexandria approximately six hundred years later. This important statement had best be given in Whitehead's own words:

> The theologians of Alexandria were greatly exercised over the immanence of God in the world. They considered the general question, how the primordial Being, who is the source of the inevitable recurrence of the world towards order, shares his nature with the world. In some sense he is a component in the natures of all fugitive things. Thus, an understanding of the nature of temporal things involves a comprehension of the immanence of the Eternal Being.[55]

This doctrine, Whitehead maintains, constitutes a reconciliation between the doctrines of Imposed Law and Immanent Law, and he proceeds to give his reasons why this is such an important step forward in our understanding of the Universe. With this new doctrine, comprised of a fusion of the ideas of imposition and immanence, "the necessity of the trend towards order does not arise from the imposed will of a transcendent God"[56] but from "the fact that the existents in nature are sharing in the nature of the immanent God."[57] Whitehead is aware that at this point he is moving out beyond the limitations inherent in the Platonic cosmology. "This doctrine, in any clear form, is not Platonic, though it is a natural modification from Plato's own doctrine."[58] He would appear at this point to be contrasting the Platonic with the Christian doctrine of creation in his remark that "in the *Timaeus*, Plato provides a soul of this world who definitely is not the ultimate creator,"[59] and that by so doing he prepared the way for the

[51] Ibid.
[52] Ibid., pp. 154-55.
[53] Ibid., p. 155.
[54] Ibid., p. 172.
[55] Ibid., p. 166.
[56] Ibid.
[57] Ibid.
[58] Ibid.
[59] Ibid.

Gnostics and the Arians. His criticism of the World-Soul as an emanation is that it fails to solve the problem which is at issue, namely that "of the relation of reality as permanent with reality as fluent."[60] The mediator, he concludes, "must be a component in common, and not a transcendent emanation."[61]

The chapter in which this statement occurs had been delivered in its main substance as a lecture in the winter of 1929-30, but was first published in *Adventures of Ideas* in September 1932.[62] It is not surprising that at this time Whitehead returned to this theme of the contribution of the Alexandrian theologians in a chapter entitled "The New Reformation"[63] in which his central theme is the nature of God.

Whitehead believes that the "way of persuasion"[64] is one of those insights which have come as a divine disclosure to mankind, but that sufficient attention has not as yet been paid to it by Christian theologians. There are, he maintains, fundamental insights into the nature of God and of his relation to the world inherent in Christian theology; but these have gone largely unnoticed by Christians in all the churches throughout most of the intervening centuries. He states it as his conviction, in 1932, that Christianity is showing all the signs of steady decay; Protestant Christianity has lost the attention of the mass of mankind and this, he believes, is because of a defect in its presentation of the essential Christian message of God and of His relation to the World. Nothing short of a re-formation of Christianity is called for, and this, if it is to be effective, will require a re-assessment of the historical period of twelve hundred years, extending from the earlier Hebrew prophets and historians to the death of Augustine in A.D. 430 (or the Council of Chalcedon, taking the period from 750 B.C. to A.D. 451).[65]

Whitehead now suggests that there are in this period three culminating phases which together constitute its threefold revelation, and that these are bound together as intellectual discovery, then exemplification, and finally metaphysical interpretation. The first phase, which he considers to be one of the greatest intellectual discoveries in the history of religion, is constituted in the conviction, to which Plato gave expression in his later Dialogues, "that the divine element in the world is to be conceived as a persuasive agency and not as a coercive agency."[66] The alternative doctrine, which was prevalent in Plato's day and is all too evident in our own, "sees either in the many gods or the one God, the final coercive force wielding the thunder."[67] Whitehead acknowledges that Plato was not always consistent, and that he wavered for a time between the two conflicting conceptions, but maintains that "he finally does enunciate without qualification the doctrine of the divine

[60] Ibid.
[61] Ibid.
[62] Ibid., Preface, p. viii. Mary Flexner Lectures, 1929-30.
[63] Ibid., Ch. 10.
[64] See above, pp. 93-94ff., and Whitehead, *AI*, pp. 205ff.
[65] Whitehead, *AI*, p. 211.
[66] Ibid., p. 213; cf. also *The Sophist, Timaeus* and *Critias* of Plato.
[67] Whitehead, *AI*, p. 213.

persuasion, by reason of which ideals are effective in the world and forms or order evolve."[68]

The second phase, which Whitehead designates "exemplification," is the supreme moment in religious history, according to the Christian religion. "The essence of Christianity," Whitehead declares, "is the appeal to the life of Christ as a revelation of the nature of God and of his agency in the world."[69] In *Religion in the Making* his attention had been focused on the teachings of early Christianity, which introduced important qualifications into the Semitic conceptions of God which they inherited from Judaism.[70] He lists at least five significant developments, all of which are pointing in the direction of a more adequate conception of God. Here, in contrast, his attention is on the person of Christ as a revelation of God and of his agency in the world. In spite of the fragmentariness of the record, he considers there can be no doubt as to those elements in the record which "have evoked a response from all that is best in human nature."[71]

> The mother, the child, and the bare manger: the lowly man, homeless and self-forgetful, with his message of peace, love and sympathy: the suffering, the agony, the tender words as life ebbed, the final despair: and the whole with the authority of supreme victory.[72]

"The whole with the authority of supreme victory!" This, it seems to me, is a new element in Whitehead's evaluation of Christ and Christianity; that a record which tells of the crucifixion of a man by his own people should be proclaimed with "the authority of supreme victory" and that it is the authority of this victory in what bore all the appearance of defeat which is the unique feature of the Christian message; not merely that this man in thus dying set a unique pattern for others to follow, but that the one who lived this life and died in this manner was and is "an exemplification of the nature of God and of his agency in the world."[73] Paul's way of putting this was that "God was in Christ, reconciling the world to himself."[74]

His recognition of this one human life as being of cosmic dimensions constitutes a forward step in Whitehead's theological understanding at this time, for the God who can be exemplified and disclosed both as to his nature and his agency only in a life lived among men must be, at least to that extent, personal both in his nature and in his relations. The Gospel portrayal of Christ going up and down the Galilean and Judaean countryside teaching and preaching and in dialogue with ordinary men and women is seen as an exemplification of the ever present divine-human dialogue taking place among men; a dialogue

---

[68] Ibid.

[69] Ibid., p. 214.

[70] A. N. Whitehead, *Religion in the Making* (New York: Macmillan, 1926), pp. 72-73.

[71] Whitehead, *AI,* p. 214.

[72] Ibid.

[73] Ibid.

[74] 2 Corinthians 5:19.

which may be rejected today as it was then by many. Whitehead concludes his introduction of this second phase with a question which removes all doubt as to the direction in which his thought is moving at this time: "Can there be any doubt that the power of Christianity lies in its revelation in act, of that which Plato divined in theory?"[75]

Whitehead speaks of three culminating phases which, in theological language, constitute the threefold revelation of Christianity, employing the word revelation here in the broad sense of disclosure of the truth. We have considered briefly two of these and now come to examine the third which he informs us was again intellectual; in fact, it is constituted in the discovery made by the Christian scholars, mainly of Alexandria and Antioch, in their efforts to solve the problem posed by Arius, who taught that the Logos was the highest of creatures, and compelled the Church to formulate its doctrine of God and of the person of Christ. The originality and value of the contribution of these scholars to the thought of the world has been underestimated, partly, he believes, because they persisted in declaring that they were only stating the faith once delivered to the saints, "whereas in fact they were groping after the solution of a fundamental metaphysical problem, although presented to them in a highly special form."[76]

In the light of the difficulties which Whitehead experienced in bringing together into one unified conception the various aspects of his thought about God in the final chapter of *Process and Reality*, it will be well to examine with care each of the statements which follow. The negative things which he now says about Plato and Platonic thought are as significant as the positive statements about the metaphysical significance of Christ and the Christian understanding of God as worked out by the theologians of Alexandria. It becomes evident in his discussion of their metaphysical discovery that through the Christian theologians Whitehead has come to a clearer understanding of the severe limitations of Platonism for an understanding of the relations of God and the World.

We noted in our earlier discussion of the Platonic background to Whitehead's thought that on occasions he appears to fail to differentiate between the Platonic Forms and the Aristotelian Universals, speaking as though these were synonymous;[77] and that this confusion of thought appeared to be at least partially traceable to the influence of A. E. Taylor, who in both his work on *Plato* and in his *Commentary* on the *Timaeus* specifically equates the "Forms" of Plato with Whitehead's "eternal objects." Here, in sharp contrast, we find a remarkable clarity in Whitehead's assessment of Plato's thought as he contrasts it with the metaphysical formulation of the Christian faith. The Christian theologians, we are now informed, "were groping after the solution of a fundamental metaphysical problem," [78] and in the answers which they

[75] Whitehead, *AI*, p. 214.
[76] Ibid.
[77] Whitehead, *PR*, p. 147 (133-34); also see above, pp. 32-33.
[78] Whitehead, *AI*, p. 214.

provided, "have the distinction of being the only thinkers who in a fundamental metaphysical doctrine have improved upon Plato."[79]

Whitehead reiterates his judgment that Platonic thought has been "the originator of the heresies, and the feeblest side of Christian theology."[80] He has now discerned that Plato is most unsatisfactory as a guide to the solution of the problem which was his primary concern in *Process and Reality*, namely, the relationship of God and the World. "When Plato is faced with the problem of expressing the relationship of God to the World, and of the relation to the World of those Ideas which it is in God's nature to contemplate, Plato's answer is invariably framed in terms of mere dramatic imitation."[81] Faced with the inevitable separation between the world of ultimate reality and the world of sensible things which is inherent in the Platonic cosmology, Whitehead must reject the Platonic interpretation as inadequate to account for the facts. "When Plato turns to the World, after considering God as giving life and motion to the ideas by the inclusion of them in the divine nature, he can find only second-rate substitutes and never the originals."[82] Most commentators would deny that Plato ever does include the Ideas in God's nature; this was a later development by the Middle Platonist and Plotinus; but Whitehead is fundamentally correct that in this world, Plato (or his successors) could find only second-rate substitutes and appearances. Whitehead now gives his final judgment on Plato's cosmology: "Thus, the World, for Plato, includes only the image of God, and imitations of his ideas, and never God and his ideas."[83]

In view of the fact that Whitehead's cosmology rested upon the Platonic conception of the ultimate, the above recognition constitutes a revolutionary change in Whitehead's outlook. It is his final rejection of Idealism; up to this point, in spite of all his attempts to transpose Bradley onto a realistic basis, he has been only partially successful because of his retention of a basically Platonic framework, with its conception of a finite God. All that has now been jettisoned and along with it Bradley's dichotomy between God and the Absolute. The central burden of Whitehead's whole philosophical venture has been an attempt to overcome the dichotomy between God and the World; now he recognizes that Platonism is incapable of accomplishing this because of its inability to provide more than an image of God and imitations of his ideas. The world, for Plato, as for his successors, is inevitably mere "appearance."

Whitehead became aware of the severe limitations of Platonism, however, only after he had discovered another and more appropriate way of speaking about God and the World. Throughout his major philosophical writings he was seeking to overcome the separation between God and the World by demonstrating the immanence of God and of the "eternal objects" in the "actual entities" which in their

[79] Ibid., pp. 214-15.
[80] Ibid.
[81] Ibid., p. 215.
[82] Ibid.
[83] Ibid.

process of concrescence comprise the world. The venture was not entirely successful and the failure became most apparent in the final chapter of *Process and Reality*, in which Whitehead found it necessary to hypostasize the Ultimate in order to save the system from incoherence. This, however, served only to accentuate the severe subordination of "God" to "Creativity"; at this point it became clear that the category of the Ultimate required to be redefined and the conception of the nature of God clarified; he had placed too great confidence in the Platonic notions about the ultimate realities and the system finally fails to explain the universe. Whitehead now discovers that the Christian theologians have provided a language more appropriate to the task of interpretation than he has been able to discover in philosophy. Their language was designed to meet the religious needs of mankind and was drawn from their experience of Christ in the Christian Church. But, when finally formulated, it is found to provide the clue to the solution of the major metaphysical puzzles which Platonism had failed to solve and his own metaphysical system had been unable to elucidate.

As background to understanding the significance of the metaphysical solution provided by the Christian theologians, Whitehead analyzes the problem with which Plato was wrestling. By retaining the gap between the transient world and the eternal nature of God, Plato was seeking to avoid implicating God in the ever-present problems of evil in all the many forms in which it impinges upon our human lives and frustrates our efforts after the just society. But the attempt has not been successful; Plato, he concludes, "only achieves the feeblest of solutions."[84] The solution, if it is to be metaphysically acceptable, must

(1) exhibit "the plurality of individuals as consistent with the unity of the Universe, . . . and the World as requiring its union with God, and God as requiring his union with the World";[85] in other words, it must not sacrifice one element of reality to another, but recognize both the reality of the individual persons and things (multiplicity) as consistent with the reality of the unity of the whole.

(2) Whitehead is insistent, moreover, that there must be genuine interrelationship between God and the World and this constitutes one of the main problems now awaiting solution. Plato and his successors have failed to achieve the goal; can an answer be found elsewhere?

(3) Whitehead introduces yet a third problem awaiting solution since the Platonic philosophy has been unable to stand the scrutiny of the facts, and that is the provision of some understanding as to "how the Ideals in God's Nature, by reason of their status in his nature, are thereby persuasive elements in the creative advance."[86] In other words, How does God work in the world? How can there be divine causal efficacy in the world while permitting to each actual entity a measure of choice in its own self-creation? How can an element of freedom be maintained for the individuals without losing the element of order

[84] Ibid.
[85] Ibid.
[86] Ibid.

necessary to the whole? Or, How can there be the possibility of change without the descent into chaos? It must be emphasized that the question for Whitehead is a factual one; he is asking a question about a matter of the utmost importance in the life of mankind. The ideals are persuasive elements in the creative advance because they have a status as included within the nature of God, and the problem is whether it is possible to give a rational interpretation of this process, or, shall we say, this initiatory aspect of the process, of concrescence of an actual entity. The complexity of the problem is now further drawn out; "Plato grounded these derivations from God upon his will,"[87] but it must rest upon some more secure base than the mere arbitrary will of a deity conceived as external to the situation. "Metaphysics requires that the relationships of God to the World should lie beyond the accidents of will, and that they be founded upon the necessities of the nature of God and the nature of the World."[88]

Here, then, are the three or four major problems which the Fourth Century theologians were compelled to face; they are fundamental metaphysical problems, though they were presented in highly special forms. The Arian heresy compelled the Church to formulate its doctrine of the nature of God. It is important to notice the variety of judgments which Whitehead is here making. "There can be no doubt," he declares, "that the Arian solution, involving a derivative Image, is orthodox Platonism, though it be heterodox Christianity."[89] In this identification of Arianism with Platonism, Whitehead is pointing up the extent to which the Fourth Century theologians, in the answers which they gave to the Arians, were framing the answers to the problems left unsolved by his own metaphysical system. The statements which follow must consequently be seen as addressed to *these* needs, and are accordingly given in the form of a metaphysical explanation. "The accepted solution of a multiplicity in the nature of God, each component being unqualifiedly divine, involves a doctrine of mutual immanence in the divine nature."[90]

In this brief statement Whitehead sums up and incorporates the insights gained through the prolonged struggle with the various Arian positions; there are at least three major questions resolved in it: (i) The acceptance of a manifoldness (threeness) within the nature of the One God; (ii) the removal of all forms of qualification and of subordination, a constant feature of the Platonic triad; (iii) and this, in turn, "involves a doctrine of mutual immanence in the divine nature."[91] Each of these is intended to assert that God is fully God in each and every one of his operations, and we must not so interpret one aspect of his operations, as to imply that the others are not also included.

Having solved the problem of the nature of God and of his relation to the world, the theologians were presented with a further and more

[87] Ibid.
[88] Ibid.
[89] Ibid., p. 216.
[90] Ibid.
[91] Ibid.

specific problem as to how the divine and the human can reside in the one person, Jesus Christ. Again, they rejected any mere association of the human individual with a divine individual, either as though he were simply another and greater prophet, or as under Adoptionism; "they decided for the direct immanence of God in the one person of Christ."[92] The great controversy between the Antiochenes and the Alexandrians about the two natures or the two persons split the Eastern Church into two sections which are only now commencing to come together to discuss the problem after fourteen hundred years of schism. But the decision of the Church at Chalcedon for "the direct immanence of God in the one person of Christ."[93] was, Whitehead believes, a triumph of Christianity over paganism, and their doctrine of the Holy Spirit, when formulated, provided for "some sort of direct immanence of God in the World generally."[94]

Whitehead disclaims any special aptitude on his part for determining the correctness of the decisions at which the Church Fathers arrived about the Trinity. This is the task of philosophical and historical theology. The whole purpose of Whitehead's discussion is to point out the fact that "in place of Plato's solution of secondary images and imitations, they demanded a direct doctrine of immanence."[95] It is this which constitutes the significance of their formulation; they have provided the terminology which enables the philosopher to speak about both the transcendence and the immanence of God without the danger of running into contradiction. "It is in this respect," Whitehead maintains, that "they made a metaphysical discovery. They pointed out the way in which Platonic metaphysics should develop, if it was to give a rational account of the role of the persuasive agency of God."[96]

Whitehead approached the final chapter of his metaphysical system in the expectation that God and the world would "embody the interpretation of the cosmological problem in terms of a fundamental metaphysical doctrine as to the quality of creative origination."[97] By introducing differentiation into our consideration of God according to whether we are thinking of his agency as "primordial" and originative of the process, or as "consequent" and implicated in it, or again, as "superjective," when we consider the manner in which he qualifies the creativity in the various temporal instances,[98] Whitehead impressed upon his readers the complexity of the problem of accounting for the universe. He was unable to provide the interpretation which he had hoped for, however, because the Platonic model which he had built into the scheme unduly limited the scope of God's activity to that of ordering a universe whose metaphysical structure was simply given, and in the end God and the World are declared to be the "contrasted oppo-

[92] Ibid.
[93] Ibid.
[94] Ibid.
[95] Ibid.
[96] Ibid.
[97] Whitehead, *PR*, p. 518 (483).
[98] Ibid., pp. 134-35 (121-22).

sites in terms of which Creativity achieves its supreme task . . . ."[99] The Platonic framework prevented Whitehead in *Process and Reality* from developing his conception of God as both primordial and consequent to their full potential and he consequently failed to provide a clear statement as to "the quality of creative origination."[100] The theologians of Alexandria, he now declares, have pointed the way in which the cosmological problems may be resolved, and recommends that 20th Century theologians should apply these insights in a reconstruction of Christian thought.[101]

Prior to undertaking this task, however, it will be well to investigate the literary and historical records of each of the three culminating phases to which Whitehead has referred us to discover the extent to which in the light of modern scholarship they may be said to provide the empirical and metaphysical grounds for the judgments which Whitehead has based upon them. We must ask what is the nature of the reality which is disclosed in Plato's concept of a persuasive God, in the life and teachings of Jesus Christ, and in the formulations of the Fourth Century Christian theologians, and apply the insights gained to our understanding of God and his relation to the Universe today.

[99] Ibid., p. 528 (492-93).
[100] Ibid., p. 518 (483).
[101] Whitehead, *AI,* pp. 217-21.

Chapter IX

Analysis of the Tradition

We must now investigate briefly each of the three culminating phases which Whitehead has identified as together constituting the threefold revelation of Christianity given in the historical period of twelve hundred years from the eighth-century prophets of Israel to the death of Augustine in A.D. 430.

The first of the three creative periods of thought which we must investigate is the notion of God as a persuasive, rather than a coercive, agency which we find in the later dialogues of Plato. Our earlier examination of the *Timaeus* has disclosed that the Demiurge as depicted in the myth is not an omnipotent creator, but rather a divine artificer who must work with materials which are provided, to bring such order as is possible into a situation considered to be to some extent chaotic. He works according to an eternal pattern, but is limited in what he can accomplish by intractable elements which are simply matter of fact, but are subject to the appeal of argument. Such order as the world displays is said to be the result of the victory of reasonable persuasion on the part of the Demiurge, depicted at this point in the myth as Reason. "Reason," he says, "over-ruled Necessity by persuading her to guide the greatest part of the things that become towards what is best."[1]

This conception of the divine as a persuasive agency was not actually a discovery of Plato, but was part of the inheritance he received in the great literature of his people. When we recall that the story of the *Timaeus* was recited in Athens on the day of the Panathanaea, and that persuasion plays a major role in the final settlement of the feud between Gods and men, there is every possibility that Plato is here commencing to take up a question which Homer left unsolved. In his writings, Zeus and the Olympians are confronted with a power called Destiny or Fate which they are unable either to control or subdue. It became the main burden of Aeschylus' *Oresteia*, a play which Cornford suggests may well have provided Plato with the theme of the divine as a persuasive agency. In the final play of this series, the *Eumenides*, Zeus and Destiny are reconciled by the intervention of divine Reason, in the person of Athena, who persuades the daughters of Necessity to co-operate with her in her beneficent purposes, to break

---

[1] Plato, *Timaeus*, 48A, cf. Cornford's trans., *Plato's Cosmology* (London: Routledge & Kegan Paul, 1937), pp. 160ff.

the vicious chain of revenge in the present for wrongs committed in the past, and so to restore peace to Athena's land.[2] Plato is therefore drawing upon the great tragedies and dramas of Homer and Aeschylus for the source of his ideas; but the myth of the *Timaeus* is the first occasion on which this idea as a metaphysical concept finds a place in the construction of a cosmology.

In all Plato's writings, his conception of the nature of God or the gods and his or their relations with the other factors in the ordering of the universe has important bearing upon his anthropology. This becomes immediately evident in the *Timaeus* in which the creation of this earth and of all the creatures in it, including man, is said to have been given over to the created gods, except that the Demiurge fashioned their souls, the immortal part of each, which was to enable them to rule the lower parts by reason and so become like the divine so far as this is possible under the limitations of their habitation in sensible bodies.

The initial command of the Demiurge to the created gods emphasizes that they are to "govern and guide the mortal creature to the best of their powers, save in so far as it should be the cause of evil to itself."[3] The created gods, in other words, are to keep order in the universe, but man is to be free to mould his own life; if he should fail to reduce the turbulent powers of his lower nature to order, the fault will be his own, and the consequences will follow in another life. This theme is continued in the *Critias*, in which it is affirmed that after the gods had each peopled their own districts they tended their nurselings as shepherds tend their flocks; "they did not use blows or bodily force, . . . but governed us like pilots from the stern of the vessel, . . . holding our souls by the rudder of persuasion according to their own pleasure."[4] Plato, moreover, regarded the orderly revolutions of the heavenly bodies as a constant reminder to mankind of the order of the universe and as constituting a pattern for all men to emulate in the ordering of their own lives. If a man becomes engrossed in appetites and ambitions, he may well become entirely mortal after passing through several successive incarnations into the lower creatures; but, "if his heart has been set on the love of learning and true wisdom and he has exercised that part of himself above all, he is surely bound to have thoughts immortal and divine . . . ."[5] The life of reason can be fully enjoyed only after death, when man will have done with things of sense, but it is our chief end here to strive to achieve to the divine perfection so far as this is possible.

Whitehead has already identified this "way of persuasion"[6] as one of the clues to the understanding of the development of a highly

---

[2] See Cornford's Epilogue, ibid., p. 362; a summary of the argument of the *Eumenides*.

[3] Plato, *Timaeus*, 42E, pp. 146-47.

[4] Plato, *Critias*, 109B and C, trans. by B. Jowett, Vol. III, p. 792.

[5] Plato, *Timaeus*, 90B; cf. Cornford, *Plato's Cosmology*, p. 353.

[6] A. N. Whitehead, *Adventures of Ideas* (Cambridge: Cambridge University Press, 1933), pp. 108-109.

civilized society; in fact, he has laid it down as a principle that only in so far as a society adopts the way of rational appeal to man as man, as a free and responsible being, in the conduct of its affairs, can it be regarded as civilized. What he does here is to locate the historic moment in the development of man in society when this became a consciously articulated principle to be pursued by man in his dealings with man because it is seen to be inherent in the understanding of and co-operation with the divine element in the World.

Plato, in his myth, portrays man as created incomplete and requiring to exercise his liberty of choice and action in order to become himself as he strives to become more like the gods. He has here divined a fundamental psychological need of man as man and has introduced it into philosophy by the medium of myth. It is an important elementary truth and the future development and enrichment of human society is dependent upon its exemplification at all levels of society and among all ages. It is a fundamentally important principle to be observed in the education of children within the family, the Church and the community, even as it is the foundation of peaceful relations among nations and peoples. It is the principle upon which all hopes of an approximation to one world will depend.

Man has finally come of age in our generation in the strict sense that there has been given into his hands—he has been charged with the responsibility for the employment of—the energy of the universe which he may develop and conserve for the enrichment of life and society for all men, or he may dissipate in the destruction of organized life on the face of the earth. In this sense, man has today come of age, and each must learn to live as an adult citizen of the earth, involving acceptance of responsibility for ensuring the employment, so far as possible, of the way of persuasion and of understanding in the ordering of the life of man in society. As the late Archbishop William Temple expressed it, "intelligent and responsible judgment is the privilege and burden of spirit or personality."[7] In other words, the exercise of free choice is the very essence of spirituality; in order to become a spiritual being man must exercise responsible choice and decision, which means decision arrived at in the light of understanding after due consideration of all the factors in the situation.

This conviction of man as responsible agent before the divine element in the universe—responsible before God—was not confined to the Greeks at the time of Plato, but had received partial exemplification in and through the faith of Abraham, Moses, and the great prophets of Israel, as a response to God conceived as actively at work in the world and in the life of the nation, moulding its history, not in myth merely, but in sober historical fact. The real contrasts in Whitehead's mind at this point are between man's humble beginnings and the potentialities of his future, between the ants and the bees on the one hand and the higher animals and man on the other; and the fundamental question

---

[7] William Temple, *Nature, Man and God*, Gifford Lectures, 1932-33 (London: Macmillan, 1934), p. 353.

with which he is concerned is whether man will rise to the full height of his potentiality in the development of free and co-operative societies on a world-wide basis, or will recoil before the dangers which beset his path and, by retrenchment, bring about that which he most fears. Plato has provided a clue in his notion of the divine as a persuasive agency. Whitehead believes this should be looked upon as "one of the greatest intellectual discoveries in the history of religion."[8] As it stands in the later works of Plato, however, it is but an idea; it was the discovery that this idea which is clearly enunciated in the later philosophical writings of Plato has received exemplification in a life that constitutes the turning point in Whitehead's thought about God, and to this we must now turn our attention.

It is surely most significant that a secular philosopher of the stature of Alfred North Whitehead should culminate a study on cosmology with an announcement that the life of an historical person, the man Jesus Christ, constitutes a disclosure of the nature of ultimate reality. That Whitehead considered this a most important discovery is evident from the fact that he declares this life to be the central empirical evidence for the threefold Christian revelation of God, and that the theologians who ultimately formulated this faith are the only thinkers who in a fundamental metaphysical doctrine have improved upon Plato. The metaphysical doctrine was based upon an interpretation of this life, and we must now examine the basic Christian documents to discover whether the evidence bears out the importance which Whitehead ascribes to the series of events which constitute and centre about this life. What is the nature of the reality which is disclosed in Jesus Christ? Can we maintain today Whitehead's thesis stated in 1932 that "the essence of Christianity is the appeal to the life of Christ as a revelation of the nature of God and of his agency in the world,"[9] and that his coming constitutes according to the Christian religion "the supreme moment in religious history"?[10]

Whitehead is here recommending the serious reconsideration of the central Christian affirmation; he is asking us to believe that at a particular moment in the history of mankind and in a specific geographic locality the Ultimate reality was disclosed in the life of a human being among contemporaries; he calls upon scholars to re-examine the evidence, and he urges that if the venture is to be successful, full attention must be paid to all of the evidence, employing the resources and methods of historical research which would be brought to bear upon any other historical investigation.

In 1932, when Whitehead issued this call, it might well have been objected that what he asks had already been undertaken and had proven to be unprofitable, for at that time it seemed as though two centuries of liberal search for the historical Jesus had ended in failure. Whitehead, however, diagnoses the inherent weakness in the old

[8] Whitehead, *AI*, p. 213.
[9] Ibid., p. 214.
[10] Ibid.

search for the historical Jesus; it was too one-sided—too narrowly conceived; the motivation of the search was the desire to be rid of dogma and they believed that the surest way to do this would be to strip away the accretions of tradition from the New Testament records and uncover the Jesus of History, the simple facts of the life, without the overlay of interpretation. In this objective their venture was doomed to failure, for at this date there are no such facts. What we have in the New Testament is a record of events which consist of occurrences plus the interpretation which was placed upon the occurrences by those who were present. The interpretation is an inextricable part of the events in question and constitutes the reason why they were recorded. The records are not written as history nor as biographies, but are given as evidence of the factuality of the message in the earliest proclamation of the Christian Gospel.

As C. H. Dodd has pointed out,[11] the fact that these are religious documents does not make them any the less historical in the sense that they are about that which happened in history. One of the significant features about the early Christian proclamation is the insistence upon witnesses to the factuality of that about which they are speaking. We do not have the facts before us today, any more than we do of any other historical event, but have evidence and sources and it is to these we must now go to discover what answers they are able to give to the questions which Whitehead has suggested we should put to them.

There is a growing consensus among New Testament scholars that the earliest proclamation of the Gospel contained six basic affirmations, consisting of five statements about Jesus followed by an interpretation of the cosmic significance of his coming, and an appeal to all men to respond to the message. According to the earliest witnesses:

(i) Jesus was descended from David, clearly linking his life with the past history of Israel and her expectations of the blessing of God upon mankind through her;

(ii) He fulfilled his Ministry among the Jews as a historical person whose life and ministry had been carried out for all to see and hear who were interested;

(iii) He was crucified, after having been handed over to the civil powers by his own Church leaders;

(iv) He was raised from the dead and exalted to God's right hand, and the evidence of this fact is to be found in the present power of healing and renewal in his name;

(v) He will come again, and his coming will be the judgment of the world.[12]

These five assertions are made within the framework of God's providential action on behalf of mankind; in other words, these historical events have happened as part of God's plan as foretold by the prophets, and because of this divine action on the part of God, the speakers are

[11] C. H. Dodd, *History and the Gospel* (London: Hodder and Stoughton, 1938), Ch. I.

[12] C. H. Dodd, *The Apostolic Preaching and its Developments* (London: Hodder and Stoughton, 1936), Ch. I.

now able to offer salvation and forgiveness to all, even to those very men who crucified Jesus, if they will change their minds and believe the good news of God's love as disclosed in Jesus. Quite clearly, there is disclosed in this earliest proclamation of the Christian message a particular view of God and of his agency in the world, and we must examine the written documents to discover the answer to our question as to what is the nature of the Ultimate reality as disclosed in Jesus?

We may next consider the record in Mark, usually considered to be the earliest Gospel to have been written and was at one time thought to be a simple ungarnished record of the life and ministry of Jesus. When we approach it without these presuppositions, however, and address to the record our question, it turns out to be a highly theological document. On examination, it is found to follow the pattern of the narrative part of the earliest *kerygma*. The author's opening words, "the beginning of the Gospel of Jesus Christ, the Son of God,"[13] recall the usual commencement of the early preaching. Even if, with some early authorities, we omit the final phrase, the intention of the author is clearly theological and the first thirteen verses are in the nature of a prologue in which the story to follow is put in its true perspective in order that the reader may appreciate the significance of the events which are being recorded. These things have happened "according to the Scriptures," and the Baptist is seen as the herald voice foretold by the prophets, who would prepare the way for the Coming One. Jesus is then introduced as coming from Nazareth in Galilee to be baptized by John in the river Jordan and this also becomes the moment for his identification as being in a special relationship with God. Mark tells it in phraseology which is dramatic and apocalyptic in imagery and intention: "At the moment when he came up out of the water, he saw the heavens torn open and the Spirit, like a dove, descending upon him. And a voice spoke from heaven: 'Thou art my Son, my Beloved; on thee my favour rests.'"[14] This brief but dramatic verse puts the record within the context of the activity of God. There is a marked similarity between this introduction in Mark's Gospel and the first eighteen verses of the Fourth Gospel. Both writers dwell on the work of John the Baptist as herald of the Coming One, both portray the mystery of the man whose life and work are about to be recounted, and indicate that he is none other than "Word" and "Son of God." Both are to record actions which are plainly those of an historical person whose life and work are to be given a theological significance. R. H. Lightfoot suggests that Mark 1:10, with its description of the heavens rent asunder, of the descent of the Holy Spirit upon Jesus, and of the voice which spoke to him declaring his divinity, is the equivalent, or counterpart in this Gospel of John 1:14, "the Word was made flesh and dwelt among us," and that Mark's chief purpose in recording this scene is to proclaim the Incarnation.[15]

[13] Mark 1:1-5.
[14] Mark 1:10-11 (New English Bible).
[15] R. H. Lightfoot, *The Gospel Message of St. Mark* (Oxford paperback ed., 1962; Oxford: Oxford University Press, 1949), pp. 18ff.

After this introduction, Mark portrays in a series of brief stories the impact of Jesus' life and ministry upon the populace. The ministry commences with the appearance of Jesus in Galilee after John's arrest, "proclaiming the Gospel of God: 'The time has come; the Kingdom of God is upon you; repent, and believe the Gospel.'"[16] The first eight chapters record Jesus' movements throughout the towns and countryside of Galilee, preaching the Gospel of the Kingdom, pronouncing the forgiveness of God upon those who came to him, healing the sick and giving sight to the blind and in every way fulfilling in his life and works the signs of the Kingdom as foretold in the prophets, yet refraining from employing any of the titles of Messiah, and referring to himself and his work under the title Son of Man. Even at Caesarea Philippi, when, in answer to a question put to the disciples, he received the reply, "You are the Messiah,"[17] Jesus neither accepted nor rejected the title, but substituted for it the title Son of Man and immediately associated this with rejection, suffering, death and resurrection, a theme which dominates the Gospel of Mark from this point on. It is Mark's intention to portray Jesus as a crucified Messiah whose identity is kept a close secret until near the end.

On his last visit to Jerusalem, Jesus performed three acts of prophetic symbolism; in the first of these, his ride into the city upon a donkey, he is openly declaring himself as in some sense Messiah coming into his own city, in fulfilment of the prophecy of Zechariah.[18] His second act was to drive from the temple precincts the money changers and their wares with the declaration, again quoting the Scriptures, "My house shall be called a house of prayer for all nations,"[19] in fulfilment of yet another prophecy of Zechariah. He is cleansing and purifying the house and opening it for all peoples. Dodd suggests that this action can have but one meaning, which is to claim Israel corporately for the spiritual worship of God now come in his Kingdom. "He has come to reveal the true Israel of God, as the centre from which His Kingdom shall be revealed to the whole world."[20] According to Mark the immediate effect of the two incidents was to unite all factions in seeking his death. "Confronted with the absolute of the Kingdom in Jesus, the world by its actions pronounced its own judgment by rejecting it and crucifying him."[21]

What, then, of the Messianic people of God and of the mission with which their destiny is bound up? The prophets had recognized that the true Israel of God would be but a remnant of an apostate nation and Jeremiah had foretold the making of a new covenant between God and Israel on the other side of a great disaster which he foresaw would sweep them away for a time for their purging and ultimate renewal.

[16] Mark 1:14.
[17] Ibid., 8:29.
[18] Zechariah 9:9.
[19] Mark 11:17, ref. Isaiah 56:7, Jer. 7:11 and Zech. 14:21.
[20] Dodd, *History and the Gospel*, pp. 133-34.
[21] Ibid.

Dodd considers that it is only in the light of this succession of prophecies that we can understand the third act of prophetic symbolism performed by Jesus at this time, in the institution of "the breaking of bread"[22] at the Last Supper. The disciples here are being treated as the nucleus of the New Israel, not because of their faithfulness, for on this very occasion he warns them that one of their number will betray him and that the others will forsake him in his hour or need. "It is by virtue of partaking of the body and blood of the Messiah that they are sealed for membership of the new Israel."[23] But before the Israel of the New Covenant can emerge into reality, Jesus as Messiah must endure the actuality of desertion by his friends, rejection and condemnation by the leaders of the nation, and the agony and death of crucifixion at the hands of the powers of this world; at that moment the whole world, the disciples included, lay under the judgment of God. Dodd concludes: "Their reunion with Him after His resurrection is the decisive instance of the forgiving grace of God. Not for their virtue or faithfulness but of His mercy, because they are His, the Lord comes to them and joins them in one body with a mission to the whole world."[24] According to the record of Luke, the Church, itself constituted by the forgiveness of the Risen Lord, in its first public proclamation, offered forgiveness to those who had crucified him, inviting them to change their minds and enter the new Israel of God as it set out upon its historic mission to the world.[25]

In the theological interpretations, which are the attempts of early Christian leaders to answer our question as to what kind of reality is disclosed in Jesus Christ, we find a remarkable concurrence. Space does not permit us to do more than make a brief analysis of the central theological teaching of the Pauline and Johannine writings.

We are brought to the central Pauline affirmation in the Second Letter to the Corinthians, in the confession that "God was in Christ, reconciling the world unto himself."[26] God has acted in and through the person and work of Jesus Christ to effect the reconciliation of the world. Having made this affirmation, the author goes on to expound the necessity and the function of the Church in such a programme of reconciliation—a programme in which Eternal Love approaches men to win them back into fellowship by an appeal in which each man's individuality must be respected because only a free response freely given can be effective in producing the restored fellowship of mutuality of love. Paul is captivated by this vision of a world restored to fellowship, and he presses on to expound the significance of the Church and its function in the world.

The central point of the Pauline appeal is that God has taken the initiative on behalf of mankind. "From first to last," he reminds his

[22] Mark 14:22-31 and 1 Cor. 11:23-25.
[23] Dodd, *History and the Gospel*, p. 137.
[24] Ibid., p. 138.
[25] Acts 2:37-42.
[26] 2 Cor. 5:19.

readers, "this has been the work of God. He has reconciled us men to himself through Christ, and he has enlisted us in this service of reconciliation."[27] The reference is clearly to the fact of the historical appearing of Jesus Christ and to his sacrificial death upon the cross. The message is so important that he repeats it in almost identical language, but so phrased as to emphasize the significance of our part in the fulfilment of this vision and work of redemption in and through the love of Christ. "What I mean is, that God was in Christ reconciling the world to himself, no longer holding men's misdeeds against them, and that he has entrusted us with the message of reconciliation."[28] There follows a re-affirmation of the persuasive activity of God, who is seeking through the lives of those who have received Christ to persuade others to respond to his gracious invitation: "We come therefore as Christ's ambassadors. It is as if God were appealing to you through us: in Christ's name, we implore you, be reconciled to God!"[29] This, furthermore, is all a part of the victory of the cross of our Lord Jesus Christ, into whose victorious triumph the apostle and his companions have entered, and are now calling upon others to enter upon their inheritance in Christ.

> Christ was innocent of sin, and yet for our sake God made him one with the sinfulness of men, so that in him we might be made one with the goodness of God himself. Sharing in God's work, we urge this appeal upon you: you have received the grace of God; do not let it go for nothing.[30]

Here we have the Pauline theology of the Cross which is further developed and carried to its logical conclusion in the Letter to the Colossians, in which Christ is set forth as "the image of the invisible God: his is the primacy over all created things ... the whole universe has been created through him and for him."[31]

In the Colossian Epistle, Christ to whom the universe owes its very existence, is portrayed as having triumphed over the cosmic powers and it is declared that through him God has reconciled not only man, but "the whole universe to himself, making peace through the shedding of his blood upon the cross—to reconcile all things, whether on earth or in heaven, through him alone."[32] We find here the source of those thoughts of Whitehead to the effect that God would turn even powers of destruction to serve his larger purpose, utilizing even "wreckage" for the service of the Kingdom. The author envisages a time when the cosmic powers, having been vanquished by our Lord, will then be reconciled to God in Him and so the whole universe will be brought into harmonious service of God.

Once again, the apostle in this letter, goes out of his way to emphasize the part which ordinary men and women must play in forward-

[27] Ibid., 5:18-6:1.
[28] Ibid., 5:19.
[29] Ibid., 5:20.
[30] Ibid., 5:21-6:1.
[31] Col. 1:15-20.
[32] Ibid.

ing the work of redemption by enduring sufferings on behalf of Christ. "It is now my happiness to suffer for you. This is my way of helping to complete, in my poor human flesh, the full tale of Christ's afflictions still to be endured, for the sake of his body which is the church."[33] Paul sees himself as carrying forward the work of Christ by this means, and urges every member of the Church, which is his body, "to continue in good heart and in the unity of love, and to come to the full wealth of conviction which understanding brings, and grasp God's secret. That secret is Christ himself; in him lie hidden all God's treasures of wisdom and knowledge."[34] Clearly, according to the Pauline interpretation, the reality which is disclosed in Christ is the ultimate reality, and it is calling for an active and thoughtful response upon the part of the hearers; in fact, it can become effective in them only as they respond with their minds as well as their hearts.

This secret of God's way of dealing with men has been hidden for long ages, but is now disclosed in Christ, and is available for all men. In Christ God has initiated a mission of persuasive love which is demonstrated in and through the ordeal of the Cross, endured by Christ on behalf of all mankind, and to the Church, as his Body, is committed the task of bearing in its own corporate body and in the lives of its individual members severally, the message of this redemptive movement and initiative of God; in this sense the Church is God's mission of persuasive love at work in the world today.

In the letter to the Romans, this theme is further developed; the divine purpose includes also the sub-human and the super-human creation, all of which will be summed up and redeemed in Christ. Paul believes that the "universe itself is to be freed from the shackles of mortality and enter upon the liberty and splendour of the children of God."[35] It was always the destiny of the cosmos that it should meet its proper end and purpose in man, when man achieves the purpose for which he was designed and takes his proper place under God as God's son. Christ, as man, has fulfilled this destiny of man so that now, in him, we are able to cry "Abba! Father!"[36] In that cry, Paul declares, "the Spirit of God joins with our spirit in testifying that we are God's children; and if children, then heirs."[37] And, as always, Paul's mind flies to the practical responsibilities which accompany such priviledged membership in the family, and he does not hesitate to give voice to the conditioning factor: "We are God's heirs and Christ's fellow-heirs, if we share his sufferings now in order to share his splendour hereafter."[38] Here, then, is Paul's description of the state of those who are "moved by the Spirit of God," which is the Spirit of Christ. They are called to a life of activity through which the purpose of God for mankind will now be fulfilled as we come to dwell in Christ, and achieve his destiny for us;

[33] Ibid., 1:24.
[34] Ibid., 2:2-3.
[35] Rom. 8:21.
[36] Ibid., 8:15.
[37] Ibid., 8:17.
[38] Ibid.

the passage which follows makes it abundantly clear that it is Paul's belief that the whole created order will benefit from our obedience: "For I reckon that the sufferings we now endure bear no comparison with the splendour, as yet to be revealed, which is in store for us. For the whole created universe waits with eager expectation for God's sons to be revealed."[39]

Paul returns to this theme, in Chapter XII of the Letter, and presses home the implications of the new life in terms of our actual daily living in the world, no longer conceived as "ours," but as members of his Body. "Therefore, my brothers, I implore you by God's mercy to offer your very selves to him: a living sacrifice, dedicated and fit for his acceptance, the worship offered by mind and heart."[40] Here, then, is a new kind of worship; the service of a life given to Christ for his service in the world. Ernst Kasemann, in an essay on "Ministry and Community in the New Testament," points out that the concept "body of Christ," as employed by Paul, may not be interpreted as signifying merely an "edifying metaphor" or as "a daring idea." "It is for the Apostle in its very corporeality the reality of the community inasmuch as the community itself, as the place of the Risen Lord's dominion, represents the new world."[41] Hence, the very great importance of Paul's further plea to his readers in Rome to adapt themselves no longer to the pattern of this world, but to allow their minds to be remade and their whole nature to be in this way transformed, in order that they may be able to "know what is good, acceptable, and perfect."[42] in the practical decisions which must be made in their day to day living. Christians are called in Christ to a holy worldliness, and it is for this reason that Paul calls for an offering of our bodies. As Kasemann puts it, "a mere communion of souls would not bear visible witness to the fact that Christ is the Cosmocrator."[43] It is in and through our bodies dedicated to him in our movements in the world that Christ will make himself known in the world today. Here we are echoing an idea which featured very prominently in the closing sections of Whitehead's final chapter in *Process and Reality*, and because Whitehead drew them from the New Testament it was not possible to synchronize the thoughts of sections VI and VII of that chapter with section V; Whitehead's Platonism at this point is face to face with his developing Christian insights which find expression throughout the final chapter in his description of the "consequent nature of God,"[44] and particularly in sections IV, VI, and VII, in which he speaks of God saving the world "as it passes into the immediacy of his own life."[45] It is possible for the world to pass into the

---

[39] Ibid., 8:18.

[40] Ibid., 12:1.

[41] Ernst Kasemann, "Ministry and Community in the New Testament," in *Essays on New Testament Themes*, English trans. by W. J. Montague (London: SCM Press, 1964), p. 68.

[42] Rom. 12:2.

[43] Kasemann, "Ministry and Community," p. 68.

[44] A. N. Whitehead, *Process and Reality: An Essay in Cosmology* (New York: Harper Torchbooks, 1960; first published, New York: Macmillan, 1929), pp. 524f. (488-89).

[45] Ibid., p. 525 (490).

immediacy of his life, however, only because God has already taken the initiative in Christ in removing the obstacles which stood in the way, and today takes the initiative in coming into the immediacy of our present experience to disclose himself and his eternal purpose as it applies to mankind today. The basis for this optimism, for which Whitehead has been criticized by many, is to be found in the New Testament documents, and particularly in the writings of Paul and the Fourth Gospel, to a consideration of which we must now turn.

If theological study is to be helpful and lead to understanding, it is important that we ask the appropriate questions. Much contemporary discussion has to do really with the problem of discovering what these questions are. What questions are evocative of thought leading to understanding? We are addressing a fundamental question to the New Testament writings, namely, What is the nature of the ultimate reality which is disclosed in Jesus Christ? When we turn to consider the Fourth Gospel we find that in the Prologue with which he prefaces his Gospel the author is providing his readers with an answer to just this question in order to deepen their understanding of the nature of the universe and of the mystery of God as a prerequisite to understanding the significance of the unique events which he is about to describe. In a record which appears to have been written to commend the Gospel to Gentile readers, the author affirms that the account which he is giving of the life, death and resurrection of a man, Jesus of Nazareth, is about the eternal and creative Word (Logos) which was in the beginning with God. The nature of this Word is such that he finds it necessary to explain that not only did the Word dwell with God, but that "what God was, the Word was."[46] Whereas the writer of Genesis invites his readers to contemplate the creative activity of God "in the beginning,"[47] the author of the Fourth Gospel, in order to interpret the significance of a particular man whose life and works are about to be recounted, carries the reader back in thought, behind the present redemptive activity which is the central theme of the Gospel, behind the creative activity of God, to a contemplation of the reality of God himself, in his inner nature, as he has been disclosed in Christ.

In the light of the disclosure about which he is to write, John finds it necessary to differentiate the Word from God at one point and to say that "the Word dwelt with God," and yet, on the other hand, to insist that "what God was the Word was," and to identify the Word with God. Whitehead, in *Religion in the Making*, calls attention to this "modification of the notion of the unequivocal personal unity of the Semitic God"[48] introduced here by the author of the Fourth Gospel as one of the important insights of Christianity in its earliest presentation. Quite clearly, we are here being invited by the author of this Gospel to contemplate a differentiation within the very being of God as a necessary move before it is possible to speak meaningfully of his creative

[46] John 1:1b (N.E.B.).
[47] Gen. 1:1.
[48] A. N. Whitehead, *Religion in the Making* (New York: Macmillan, 1926), p. 73.

activity. "When all things began, the Word already was," is the translation given by the New English Bible, with a footnote giving an alternative reading, "The Word was at the creation."[49]

Having established his meaning on this first point, the author
proceeds to call his readers to recognize that this One of whom he now
speaks is the Creative Word, the agency of God in initiating the process
of creation and bringing the world into being. "The Word, then, was
with God at the beginning, and through him all things came to be; no
single thing was created without him."[50] The meaning is unmistakable;
literally, all things came to be in the past, are coming to be in the
present, and will come to be in the future through the agency of the
creative Word, who is God. Moreover, the universe is the kind of
universe it is, because he is the kind of reality that he is. "All that came to
be was alive with his life, and that life was the light of men."[51] We may
paraphrase this verse to read, the life of the divine reality which
constituted this universe a creative process, bringing forth ever new
combinations and forms of elements and so producing living organisms with sentient bodies and mental capacities, has, in one of the
species of the animal kingdom, kindled the light of understanding,
making possible a responsive movement—"that Life was the light of
men."[52] There was a time—it must have been a very long time—before
there was any responsive light in the consciousness of men, and even
after that light dawned upon our ancestors, it was a mere flicker which
at times seemed almost to have been extinguished by the mistaken
responses of man to God and to his fellow men, and by his resigning
himself to the ever-present temptation to satisfaction with himself in
his present state and achievements.

The author of the Gospel now reminds his readers that throughout those millions of years and among the teaming multitudes of
mankind today who appear to remain in a state of virtual unknowing,
"the light shines on in the dark, and the darkness has never quenched
it."[53] The Word, throughout all those years has never abandoned his
world and his light shines on in the dark. Darkness in the consciousness
of man may prevent individuals from recognizing the light for what it is
(who he is), but, nevertheless, "the darkness has never quenched it."
This is a magnificent confession of faith in the abiding presence of God
in his world. It is a declaration about the nature of ultimate reality and it
has equally important things to say about humanity. Something has
happened within the lives of those members of the creation to whom
this inner light of freedom of thought and of action has been entrusted;
an inner darkness has enveloped them to such an extent that they are
unable to recognize the Word. Nevertheless, "the light shines on in the
dark, and the darkness has never quenched it." The powers of evil have

[49] John 1:1 (N.E.B.).
[50] Ibid., 1:2-3.
[51] Ibid., 1:4.
[52] Ibid., 1:4-6.
[53] Ibid., 1:5.

overwhelmed mankind, but the world belongs to the Creative Word, and he is actively at work within the world even though unrecognized by man.

The Word is redemptive as well as creative because he is eternal Love, and now, in a dramatic sentence, the scene changes to the contemporary situation—the world of particularity, of place and time, and of people. "There appeared a man named John, sent from God."[54] God is at work in the contemporary world, working through human lives to bring other human lives to an awareness of the presence of the light. John was not himself the light, but came to bear witness to the light. Something is happening upon the contemporary scene which is entirely unique; that which has been eternally operative and through whose agency the world and man have their very being, "the real light which enlightens every man was even then coming into the world."[55] Hence the need for a herald, lest men should fail to recognize him in his coming. But, in spite of all that the herald could do to alert mankind, "He was in the world; but the world, though it owed its being to him, did not recognize him. He entered his own realm, and his own would not receive him."[56]

This whole paragraph emphasizes the freedom and personal responsibility of men which is one of the central themes of the Fourth Gospel. The eternal and creative Word, to whom men owed their very being entered his own realm, and his own exercised their freedom of choice and "would not receive him." Because he is eternal love, he refused to compel men's allegiance; the type of response which alone could satisfy his purpose for men and women was one which must come from a free exercise of responsible choice, and there were, consequently, those who rejected the offer of his friendship. But those who did respond to him received "the right to become children of God."[57] Finally, this new aspect of the human situation, the coming of the Word to dwell among his own, is stated in unmistakable terms: "so the Word became flesh; he came to dwell among us, and we saw his glory, such glory as befits the Father's only Son, full of grace and truth."[58]

The testimony of John is now linked with a specific man who, while he came at the end of the age, was yet "before Abraham," and supersedes Moses, the founder of the nation, who gave them the Law. For, "while the Law was given through Moses, grace and truth came through Jesus Christ. No one has ever seen God; but God's own Son, he who is nearest to the Father's heart, he has made him known."[59] The Eternal Word, who was in the beginning with God and who is here identified with God in his inner nature and being, is now identified with the man Jesus, whose life and works are about to be recorded. In a

[54] Ibid., 1:6.
[55] Ibid., 1:9.
[56] Ibid., 1:10-11 (N.E.B.).
[57] Ibid., 1:12.
[58] Ibid., 1:14.
[59] Ibid., 1:17-18.

life lived among men, in a particular part of the world, and at a specific time, he is declared by this author to have made the Father "known."

In a carefully structured theological document, the author presents the account of Jesus, an historical person, preaching and teaching and performing miraculous cures, each of which is declared to be a sign to those whose eyes are open to receive the truth. Each sign produces a twofold reaction; on the one hand, those who received his message saw in it a confirmation of their faith and these were led into a deepening understanding; but, on the other hand, there were those who rejected both him and his message; in these we are presented with an increasing antagonism and indignation amounting to bitter hatred and opposition. Men judge themselves by their response to Jesus.[60] Meanwhile, the author reminds the reader that the central figure in the drama, Jesus, whether at Capernaum, in Bethany, or at Jerusalem is always abiding in the Father's love, so that he is able to say "I and the Father are one,"[61] and "if ye have known me ye have known my Father also,"[62] when addressing his disciples, and when his enemies challenge his authority he replies "before Abraham was born, I am."[63]

This Gospel is divided into two parts which Dodd suggests should be regarded as two acts of a drama.[64] Throughout the first act the union between the Eternal Logos and the man Jesus Christ is being demonstrated by a series of episodes each containing accounts of the works of Jesus accompanied by instruction which the narrative illustrates. The Logos or Word takes the flesh of the man Christ Jesus—becomes embodied, or "enfleshed," as the Fathers were later to describe it. According to the author, the whole purpose of the ministry of Jesus up to the raising of Lazarus is to demonstrate that this Incarnation of the Word has taken place. What is not so obvious, but which is pointed out by Dodd, is that these are all Christological themes, illustrating the union between the man Jesus and the Eternal Logos. The glory which is manifested throughout is the glory of the Only-begotten of the Father. The Logos possessed the divine glory fully and was shown forth in the acts of the life, and so we read that "Jesus manifested his glory and his disciples believed on him."[65] The whole succession of the signs is employed to illustrate the fact that the Logos has become flesh, and is making known the Father's presence. He can do this because he is dwelling "in the bosom of the Father."[66]

Each of these incidents, however, must also be looked at from the human point of view; John is equally emphatic that Jesus' manhood is real and is fully disclosed in the obedience of Jesus, which also discloses that he is the abode of God. "I can do nothing of myself; as I hear, I judge; and my judgment is just, because I seek not my own will but the

[60] Ibid., 3:18-21.
[61] Ibid., 10:30.
[62] Ibid., 14:7.
[63] Ibid., 8:58.
[64] C. H. Dodd, *The Interpretation of the Fourth Gospel* (Cambridge: Cambridge University Press, 1953).
[65] John 2:11.
[66] Ibid., 1:18.

will of him who sent me."[67] The Jews simply cannot understand him, because they seek their glory from men: only those who are willing to do God's will can perceive that God is in Christ. His coming was judgment. The world's salvation, however, depends upon the second act in which Jesus identifies himself with sinful mankind under judgment in order that they also may be caught up with him into eternal life. This is the great theme from John 12:23 ff "The hour has come for the Son of man to be glorified . . . ." and is summed up in the graphic picture, "I, when I am lifted up from the earth, will draw all men into union with myself."[68] Because of their sins, men are unable to come into God's presence; if they are to be brought into communion with the holy God, God must cross the barrier and be where they are, and the judgment on this world is the point at which Jesus descends to make common cause with men in order that by His being united with them in their sin and judgment, they may be united with and identified with Him in his glory with the Father.

Throughout the Fourth Gospel, the glory is continually breaking through, disclosing the deeper issues of the encounter between light and darkness, good and evil, love and hatred, and always both forces are incarnated in the lives of men—eternal light and goodness and truth and love in the life and ministry of Jesus, and the opposites in a variety of persons all of whom finally co-operate in a final effort to be rid of him. Here, more clearly than in any other part of the New Testament, we have a portrayal of Ultimate Reality, in the Person of Jesus, exemplifying God as persuasive love, appealing to men by every means at his disposal, to change their minds and believe the Gospel of the Kingdom. Refusing to compel their allegiance, he offered himself on their behalf in an offering which can only be understood as including the whole story of his incarnate life; as expressed in the First Epistle of John, "it is by this that we know what love is: that Christ laid down his life for us."[69] God's love, the author reiterates, was disclosed in this "that he sent his only Son into the world to bring us life."[70] The becoming incarnate of the only Son is the great new thing, and it has issued from the love which God has for his creation. Lest his readers should fail to get the point, he explains further that "the love I speak of is not our love for God,"[71] it is not the Platonic Eros, the striving of the human soul for God, but on the contrary, he is writing about the divine movement of love towards mankind. It is in this assurance that the Christian finds victory, even as in the Fourth Gospel, it is the figure of the crucified, praying for forgiveness upon those who nailed him to the cross, who discloses the real victory; "It is accomplished."[72] For this evangelist, the cross is the victory, a victory which is disclosed in the various scenes of Easter Day and after.

[67] Ibid., 5:30ff.; 12:23ff.
[68] Ibid., 12:32.
[69] 1 John 3:16.
[70] Ibid., 4:9 (N.E.B.).
[71] Ibid., 4:10 (N.E.B.).
[72] John 19:30 (N.E.B.).

We conclude that for this evangelist, the ultimate reality is disclosed in Jesus to be creative and redemptive love, eternally at work for man's salvation, always respecting the creative freedom which has been bestowed upon man, always seeking by persuasive love to win men to himself that he may unite their lives with God and with God's purposes for all men; that through them he may initiate a movement of redemption in which men will discern God at work among them. In Jesus the eternal has entered into the limitations of the temporal in order that the temporal may be incorporated into the eternal.

We find that in the New Testament God has been disclosed as personal, and in some respects as manifold in his essential being. He is clearly declared by all the writers we have examined to be actively at work in the world and in particular in the life and work of Jesus Christ, in his ministry and teaching, in his death and resurrection, and in the gift of the Spirit and the Church as the body of Christ. In and through the ongoing life of the Church and in the activity of the Spirit through the lives of believers, God is, in and through Christ, gathering out a people who are indwelt by him, and who are sent into the world to be witnesses to each successive generation. We have located here in the early transmission of the Christian faith the insights which will enable us to understand Whitehead's language in those sections of *Process and Reality*[73] in which he seeks to speak of the consequent nature of God, but this can be done only after we have followed Whitehead in his discovery of the metaphysical interpretation of this faith.

[73] Whitehead, *PR*, Part V, Ch. II, secs. 4, 6, and 7.

Chapter X

Problems in the Metaphysical Interpretation of the Tradition: The Fourth-Century Climate of Opinion and Whitehead

His recognition of the uniqueness of Jesus Christ as a revelation of God in and through the life of a historical person, and of the fact of the emergence of the Christian Church and the interpretation which it placed upon his life and death from the very beginning of the Christian movement, constituted for Whitehead fresh empirical data which must be taken into account by the philosopher if he would be true to his own principles and procedure; eventually it must call for a re-examination of the metaphysical scheme. It was therefore only natural that Whitehead, having made this discovery of one unique individual who stood out above founders and leaders of religions throughout the world as being in himself a revelation of the nature of God and of his agency in the world, should now focus attention upon this life and upon the interpretation which it received in the Christian Church as the next stage of his search. If ultimate Reality has been disclosed in Jesus Christ, then it is important to discover the meaning of God as disclosed in him. A whole cluster of questions centre around Jesus Christ and the answers to these questions, Whitehead finds, have been provided by the Christian theologians in their refutation of the assertions of the Arians in the fourth century.

Inasmuch as Whitehead discovered the clue to the inadequacies of the Platonic system in the answers given by the Christian theologians in replying to the Arian heresy, it will be important to investigate both the problems and the answers given, paying particular attention to those phases of the problem which have contributed towards Whitehead's discovery. First, a brief look at the intellectual climate of the fourth-century Roman world. Platonism was the dominant philosophy of the period and exercised an unconscious influence upon the minds of men and women both within and without the Church. It was a form of Platonism which had undergone a considerable process of transformation during the early centuries of the Christian era in which elements of Stoicism and of Aristotelian thought were incorporated into a basically Platonic system.

Of the two leading exponents of Middle Platonism, Atticus and Albinus, the former identified the Demiurge of Plato's *Timaeus* with the Good, a move which enabled him to treat the Platonic Forms as thoughts in the mind of God. Albinus, who was influenced extensively by Aristotelian thought, appears to have been the first to have transferred the Forms as ideas of God to the First Intellect conceived as the Prime Mover of Aristotle's Metaphysics. He next posited a Second Mind or World Intellect, through which the First Mind works, and which is set in motion by desire for the First. This Second God, or "Universal Intellect," identical with its Ideas, is really the creator of the universe and is intimately linked with the World Soul or Third Principle, which emanates from the Second. The distinctions between the three spheres are somewhat blurred for Albinus; not only is his Primary Intellect conceived as thought and object of thought, but it is also act, as it is for Aristotle.

There are important similarities between the system of Albinus and that of Whitehead in that for Whitehead the ultimate is "creativity" or creative activity, and his primordial nature of God is comprised of the full multiplicity of the eternal objects and envisages the universe as a creative process. In his conception of God's envisagement of the world Whitehead is near to Albinus who makes the statement that God has filled all things with himself according to his own will, meaning not that the Supreme God is immanent in the world, but that the universe participates in him, inasmuch as the Cosmic Intelligence has him as the object of thought and of desire.[1] According to Albinus, God willed that the Cosmic Soul should awaken and turn towards him, "and that they should be brought into order or 'created,' and that the intelligence should thenceforward preserve the established order throughout the Universe."[2] What is particularly noticeable here, however, is the twofold tendency in Platonic thought towards extreme transcendence of the supreme principle on the one hand, and the clear development of three Hypostases in the divine nature on the other.

Plotinus and His System of Neo-Platonism

The twofold tendency which we have noticed as taking place within Platonism, moving towards extreme transcendentalism on the one hand, and to the development of a triad in the divine nature on the other, was carried to its full development in the work of Plotinus, who flourished in Alexandria from the middle of the third century. By incorporating into what was basically a Platonic approach to reality elements of Aristotelian, Stoic, and Oriental mystical thought, Plotinus produced a monistic system in which reality is conceived as a vast hierarchical structure with grades descending from what is beyond Being to what falls below it and can be described only in negative terms.

[1] R. E. Witt, *Albinus and Middle Platonism* (Cambridge: Cambridge University Press, 1937), p. 129, ref. to Albinus, *Didaskalikos*, 65, 1.
[2] Ibid.

He enunciates with great care the interrelationships of the various grades of reality, each an emanation from that which is higher, and all owing their existence to the One to which all seek to reutrn. Following Plato, his master, Plotinus maintained the distinction and the opposition between the "intelligible" world and the "sensible" world, and insisted that the soul, being immaterial, and belonging to the divine world, is immortal.

The divinity of Plotinus is a graded triad in which the highest principle or "Hypostasis," God, is utterly transcendent. Variously spoken of as simply "The First," or "The Good," but more properly designated "The One," this First Hypostasis is strictly unknowable, supra-existent and beyond Being. Whereas Aristotle's Unmoved Mover was a "thinking thought," Plotinus' "One," The Transcendent, "neither knows itself nor is known in itself."[3] It is, nevertheless, the source of all Being,[4] and with it all existences whatsoever seek union as their true goal. Plotinus always speaks of it in impersonal terms by employing the neuter gender.

Below the One, as an emanation from it, is the Second Hypostasis, which is at one and the same time, the Intellectual-Principle and Being, as the primal act of generation from the fulness of the One. This product, he suggests, has turned again to its begetter and been filled, and has become its contemplator, and so an Intellectual-Principle. It is, moreover, the Divine Mind, whose "knowing is not by search but by possession, its blessedness inherent, not acquired."[5] It contains all the Forms in their perfection and is pure being in eternal actuality. "All its content, thus, is perfect, that itself may be perfect throughout, as holding nothing that is less than divine, nothing that is less than intellective."[6] Whereas Soul deals with one thing after another and with a multitude of individuals each in its own time, now Socrates, now a horse, always some one entity from among beings, the Intellectual-Principle is all, and its entire content is simultaneously present in an eternal now. There is for it no future nor past; it is the authentic existence.

Below the Intellectual-Principle, and emanating from it, is Soul, the Third Hypostasis in the Plotinian hierarchy. Whereas the Second appears to be patterned after Aristotle's Mover, as a "thinking thought" whose total activity is intellective, and as comprising the entire multiplicity of Plato's Forms, the Third Hypostasis, the Soul, is the active agency in bringing into being the whole universe. It has breathed life

---

[3] Plotinus, *Enneads*, trans. by Stephen MacKenna (3rd ed.; London: Faber & Faber, 1962), V. 3,13; p. 396.

[4] Paul Tillich, *Religious Experience and Truth*, ed. by Sydney Hook (Edinburgh: Oliver and Boyd, 1962), pp. 313-15, defines "God" in one of its connotations as "the unconditioned transcendent, the Ultimate." He suggests that "the thing referred to in the mythical symbol is the unconditioned transcendent, the source of both existence and meaning, which transcends being-in-itself. . . ." Tillich's thought would appear to be identical with that of Plotinus at this point in his system.

[5] Plotinus, *Enneads*, V. 1,4; p. 372.

[6] Ibid.

into all living things; "it is the maker of the sun; itself formed and ordered this vast heaven and conducts all that rhythmic motion."[7] At this point, Plotinus' Soul is very much like the immanent God of the Stoics, but he is careful to remind the reader that, while it is operative in all things whatsoever, Soul is, nonetheless, "a principle distinct from all these to which it gives law and movement and life, and it must necessarily be more honourable than they,"[8] for, whereas they gather and dissolve as Soul brings them life or abandons them, Soul, since it never can abandon itself, is of eternal being. It is nonetheless, according to Plotinus, a secondary being, an image of the Intellectual-Principle. It is actually the total of the activity of the Intellectual-Principle, "the entire stream of life sent forth by that Principle to the production of further being; it is the forthgoing heat of a fire which has also heat essentially inherent."[9]

There are, according to Plotinus, two parts to Soul; sprung, as it is, from the Intellectual-Principle, soul is intellective, but with an intellection operating by the method of reasonings. To bring this rational nature to maturity it must look continually towards the Divine Mind; when it does so, it becomes its true self. But, whereas the operation of the Intellectual-Principle is motionless, the Soul's operation is by motion, and its image is generated from its movement in a downward direction, and this image is Sense and Nature, the vegetal principle, and so produces "another hypostasis or form of being, just as its prior (the loftier phase of the Soul) is produced from the Intellectual-Principle which yet remains in untroubled self-possession."[10] Plotinus repeatedly emphasizes the inter-relatedness of the whole hierarchy: "there is from the first principle to ultimate an outgoing in which unfailingly each principle retains its own seat while its offshoot takes another rank, a lower, though on the other hand every being is in identity with its prior as long as it holds that contact."[11]

By identifying the Good of the *Republic*,[12] which Plato situates "beyond being," with the absolute One of the first hypothesis of the *Parmenides*,[13] in which all multiplicity is denied to the One, Plotinus carries the doctrine of the absolute transcendence of God to its final limit. Paul Henry, S.J.,[14] suggests that another innovation introduced by Plotinus is the move by which he makes the Forms or "Ideas" states of being of the Intellectual-Principle and no longer distinct objects, "the notion of bringing the very subject of thought into the intelligible world, and of considering the hypostases less as entities than as spiritual attitudes."[15] On the other hand, it is to Aristotle, and not to Plato that

[7] Ibid., V. 1,2; p. 370.
[8] Ibid.
[9] Ibid., V. 1,3; p. 371.
[10] Ibid., V. 2,1; p. 380.
[11] Ibid., V. 2,2; p. 381.
[12] Plato, *The Republic*, sections 508e-509b inclusive.
[13] Plato, *The Parmenides*, sections 137-142 inclusive.
[14] Paul Henry, S.J., Introduction to the *Enneads*, p. xliii.
[15] Ibid.

Plotinus owes the fundamental principle that "the thought *par excellence* is self-thought, in which intelligence and intelligible coincide";[16] and his Third Hypostasis, the Soul of the world, bears unmistakable marks of the central doctrine of Stoicism. Dr. Henry suggests that we may roughly compare the three Plotinian Hypostases to the three Gods, or Absolutes, of the three philosophies which had preceded him, namely, Platonism, Aristotelianism, and Stoicism, though always transposed by Plotinus into a Platonic key and connected, rightly or wrongly, with entities in the Dialogues.

The Arian Creed and the Nicean Crisis

Such was the dominant expression of Platonic philosophy in Alexandria in the fourth century. It must not, however, be forgotten that Plato's Dialogues were for the most part available and were familiar ground to both Christians and pagans alike. The *Timaeus*, the *Phaedrus*, and the *Politics*[17] were evidently as well-known to Athanasius as to the Arian party. Add to this Christian and non-Christian writings strongly influenced by the Middle Platonists, such as Origen's extant writings which were the earliest attempts at a fusion of Platonic and Christian thought into a systematic statement and were common ground to theologians on both sides of the dispute, and we have the setting for the problem which came to a head in the controversy with Arius and his friends.

It is unfortunate that, in his zeal to banish heresy from his realms, Constantine destroyed all the writings of Arius and we are dependent for the most part upon quotations from his writings which are included in works written in refutation of his views. It is, consequently, impossible to obtain information about his opinions prior to the controversy and on other matters which might throw light upon his particular interpretation of the doctrine of God. There are, however, a number of clues in contemporary documents; for example, Porphyry, the biographer of Plotinus, who in A.D. 301 had brought out the definitive edition of *The Enneads*,[18] had attacked Christianity in his polemical writings and his works had been proscribed; is it merely coincidence that in the document in which he proscribes Arius's writing, Constantine links their author with the name of Porphyry? The letter of the Emperor, addressed to the bishops and people, declares, "So now it seems fit both that Arius and such as hold his sentiments should be denominated Porphyrians, that they may take their appellation from those whose conduct they have imitated."[19] Moreover, Photius, in his Epitome of the Ecclesiastical History of Philostorgius, states that,

[16] Ibid., p. xlvi, and Aristotle's *Metaphysics*, L7, 1072b, pp. 20-22.

[17] For references to the *Phaedrus*, see Athanasius' *contra Gentes*, 5, 2 and 33.2; to the *Republic*, 10, 4; to the *Timaeus*, 41, 2; to the *Politics*, 41, 3 and inc. 43, 7.

[18] Henry, *Enneads*, p. xxxv, and ref. to R. Harder.

[19] Constantine, Letter to the Bishops and People, as in Socrates, H.E.I.9.30-31, cf. J. Stevenson, *A New Eusebius. Early Christian Writings in Translation* (London: S.P.C.K., 1960), p. 384.

though Philostorgius was a supporter of the Arian cause and praised Arius for his rejection of the divinity of the Son, he criticized him for becoming involved in the most absurd errors, "because he everywhere affirms that God cannot be known, or comprehended, or conceived by the human mind; and not only by men, (which perhaps were an evil more easy to endure), but also not even by His own only-begotten Son."[20] This report of Philostorgius is borne out by the records of other contemporary Church historians and is confirmed in the text of a letter which was drawn up by Arius and his friends at Alexandria and addressed to their bishop at the time of their condemnation by the Synod of Egypt. The letter, which served for some time as a formal Arian confession, is so quoted by Hilary of Poitiers and the text is preserved by Athanasius and by Epiphanius. In it the signatories confess their faith in the absolute uniqueness and transcendence of God, which they profess to have received from their forefathers and to have learned from their bishop: "We acknowledge One God, *alone* Ingenerate, *alone* Everlasting, *alone* Unoriginate, *alone* True, *alone* having Immortality, *alone* Wise, *alone* Good, *alone* Sovereign, Judge, Governor, and Providence of all, unalterable and unchangeable."[21] The word *monos*, "alone," is repeated eight times in this brief statement, indicating their desire to exalt the transcendence of God as far as is possible to do by the employment of language. Moreover, it becomes evident in the next sentence of the letter that this statement of extreme transcendentalism is about God the Father alone, with the deliberate intention of the signatories to eliminate the Son from participation in these attributes and qualities, except in a secondary sense. They state that before everlasting ages God "begot his unique Son, through whom he made the ages and all things."[22] This, they explain elsewhere, was necessary because the world of contingency could not bear the weight of direct contact with the Divine; the Son was therefore brought into being first as a kind of under-worker, or instrument of God. The letter makes quite clear that it was "by the will of God he was created before times and before ages and received life and being and glories from the Father, the Father so constituting him."[23] The Son is a perfect creature, and must not be simply equated with the rest of creation; he is unique in the sense that he is the first of created beings and is himself the agent in the creation of all else. The letter, in unmistakable terms, marks off the distance between the Father and the Son.

> God being the cause of all things is without beginning and most unique, while the Son, begotten timelessly by the Father and created before ages

---

[20] Photius, *Epitome of the Ecclesiastical History of Philostorgius*, trans. by Edward Walford, incl. in Sozomen's *Ecclesiastical History* (London: Henry G. Bohn, 1855), p. 434.

[21] Arius, Letter to Alexander, bishop of Alexandria, c. 320, contained in Athanasius, *On the Synods of Ariminum and Seleucis*, 16, in Stevenson, *A New Eusebius*, p. 346 (italics mine).

[22] Arius, The Confession of the Arians, ibid., p. 346, but quoted here from *The Library of the Christian Classics*, ed. by Edward Rochie Hardy, Vol. III (London: SCM Press, 1954), pp. 332-33.

[23] Ibid.

and established, was not before he was begotten—but, begotten timelessly before all things, he alone was constituted by the Father.[24]

The language employed here is similar to that which is used by Plato in the myth of the *Timaeus* in which it is declared that the Demiurge made only the created gods and the souls of men and then assigned the task of creating the visible universe to the created gods.

In a letter addressed to Eusebius, the bishop of Nicomedia, shortly after the controversy broke out in the Church at Alexandria, Arius complains that "we are persecuted because we say, 'The Son has a beginning, but God is without beginning.' For this we are persecuted, and because we say, 'He is made out of things that were not.'"[25] He agrees with Alexander, his bishop, that there are three hypostases, but for Arius they are arranged in a graded hierarchy and the distance between the Father and the Son is the difference between Creator and creature, the Infinite and the finite. The Son, the letter to his bishop asserts, "is neither eternal nor co-eternal nor co-unbegotten with the Father, nor does he have his being together with the Father."[26] According to the Arian premises, the Father must be prior in all things to the Son, otherwise you would be admitting "two unbegotten sources"[27] and would fall into polytheism. To suggest that the Son was consubstantial with the Father was tantamount to saying that God "is compound and divisible and alterable and a body";[28] this passage clearly harks back to Origen's *First Principles*, in the first book of which he argued that God is not to be thought of as being a body, but is a simple intellectual existence.[29] Origen, however, was prepared to recognize distinctions within eternity and within deity, which the Arians appear unable to do; their sense of the utter transcendence of God is more akin to that of Plotinus than of Origen. They appear to be unaware of the necessity for qualification of all language employed to speak about God; they were consequently rigid in their adherence to terminology, and in their insistence upon pressing each term to its logical conclusions, they fell into serious error.

The implications of the Arian creed were further drawn out and propagated in popular songs, and epigrams, exerpts from which are preserved in the writings of Athanasius. Though the Son is called God, this, says Arius, is merely a courtesy title; for he is not really God, but

---

[24] Ibid.

[25] Arius, Letter to Eusebius of Nicomedia, cf. *Library of Christian Classics,* Vol. III, pp. 329-31.

[26] Arius, The Confessions of the Arians, p. 333.

[27] Ibid.

[28] Ibid., p. 334.

[29] The language of Origen is similar to that which Plotinus employs later, cf. Origen, *First Principles,* trans. by G. W. Butterworth (London: S.P.C.K., 1936), Bk. I, Ch. I. On p. 10, Origen states: "God therefore must not be thought to be any kind of a body, nor to exist in a body, but to be a simple intellectual existence, admitting in himself of no addition whatever, so that he cannot be believed to have in himself a more or a less, but is Unity, or if I may so say, Oneness throughout, and the mind and fount from which originates all intellectual existence or mind."

simply by participation in grace. As to his real nature and substance, it belongs to things generated and created. Moreover, as a creature, "the Word cannot perfectly and exactly either see or know His own Father";[30] but what he knows and what he sees, he knows and sees according to our own power. And though we speak of him as Word and Wisdom of God, this also is merely a courtesy title according to grace; God has many powers, of which the Word is one. But he is by nature, as all others, alterable, and remains good by his own free will and of his own choice. Arius always hastened to add that as a matter of fact, God foreknew that the Son would remain virtuous and bestowed upon him, by anticipation, glory which afterwards, as man, he attained from virtue.[31]

In the light of this brief survey of the main clauses of the Arian creed and its implications as drawn out by the authors themselves, it is now possible for us to arrive at an estimation of the significance of the Arian challenge to the Church in the fourth century, and, even more important, to discover some of the implications of this way of speaking about God for the future of Christianity. Was the difference a mere matter of words, as Constantine at first considered it to be, as indicated in his letter addressed to Alexander and Arius, written in 324,[32] urging them not to allow a mere trifle of a difference of words to become a cause of dissention in the Church? It very soon became apparent to Hosius, Constantine's commissioner, that Arius had no intention of changing his mode of expression, and, furthermore, that he had obtained the backing of a considerable body of opinion throughout the East. The contents of his letters and the reports of his conduct in meetings of clergy at Alexandria indicate that Arius was more interested in demonstating the superior quality of his powers of argument than any concern for the welfare of the Church. The Arian approach to the problems under discussion is fundamentally rationalistic and, while they made a point of quoting Scripture proof-texts to back up their conclusions, they made no attempt to correct the contradictions of their rationalized conclusions by an appeal to the sense of Scripture. The whole movement would appear to be as much a philosophy as a religion. Protagonists on both sides of the dispute were Platonic as regards philosophical outlook and were Origenistic in theological terminology; superficially considered, the Platonic triad appeared to have much in common with the Christian conception of God as taught in the Church; the Arian crisis represents a confrontation within the minds of men of these two views of God and the World which, while superficially similar, are fundamentally opposed in other respects.

The Arian conception of God as utterly transcendent, and a graded hierarchy of three hypostases, is typically Platonic. Much of the

[30] Arius, in the "Thalia," as quoted by Athanasius, in *contra Arianos*, Discourse I, section 6.
[31] Athanasius, *contra Arianos*, Discourse 1.5 and 6.
[32] See Stevenson, ed., *A New Eusebius*, pp. 352-53.

terminology employed by them is similar, if not identical at points, with that of Neo-Platonism, though at no point does the one set of terms fit exactly the other. The emphasis on the unity, "monos," is typical not only of Arius, but also of Eusebius of Caesarea in his *Demonstratio*, and both display the same dread of the thought of ascribing equality of status to Father and Son. This, they felt, would be to fall into the error against which Plato had warned in the *Parmenides*, of introducing multiplicity into the First Principle. The One must be absolutely one— "the Alone." But, whereas Plotinus had conceived of the same reality existing at different levels by a process of emanations from the higher to the lower, the Arians, employing the creation language of Christian theology, having placed the Father in the category of the utterly tran- scendent, were led to deny divinity to the Son. They were ready at times to employ the language of Plotinus and to speak of the generation of the Son, as Origen had done, but in obedience to their logic went on to define this as having an equivalence to "creation" or "making," and to declare the Son to be a "perfect creature of God." Later, when they were working out the implications of their system, the Arians did not hesitate to take the extreme view of the Neo-Platonists, that God is utterly unknowable by man and that the Son, being a creature, had no knowledge of him either; in fact, that he did not even know his own essence, let alone that of his Father.[33] It would appear, therefore, that while there is every evidence that Arianism was a forthright attempt to equate the Christian doctrine of God as a Triad with the Platonic triad in its contemporary forms, the attempt was not successful, and the Arian position was, consequently, riddled with contradictions which disabled them from formulating a creed upon which even their own members could agree, during a period of almost fifty years throughout which, by political maneouvering, they were able to obtain the backing of the Imperial power.

Plotinus, Arius and Whitehead Compared

We are investigating the background to the Arian dispute in the Christian Church in the fourth century, with a view to discovering the source of the insights which convinced Whitehead of the superiority of the Christian formulation over the Platonic cosmology, and it may help to clarify the problems inherent in the various attempts at interpreta- tion of the universe to compare the concept of God enunciated by Whitehead in *Process and Reality* with the hierarchy of Plotinus on the one hand and the Arian creed on the other. As noted above, the ultimate in Plotinus' system is designated "The One" and is declared to be utterly transcendent; even to assert that it is "One" is false since it is beyond being or essence: "It is precisely because there is nothing within the One that all things are from it; in order that Being may be brought about, the source must be no Being but Being's generator, in what is to be thought of as the primal act of generation."[34] The One is therefore

[33] Excerpts from the "Thalia" as given by Athanasius, in his *Epistle Concerning the Council held at Ariminum in Italy and at Seleucia in Isauria*, section 15.
[34] Plotinus, *Enneads*, V. 2,1; p. 380.

beyond all statement, except to assert that it is the source of all Being and of the Intellectual-Principle. In spite, however, of the statement that we can have no knowledge of the One, Plotinus is able to state that it is an Hypostasis, in fact, to depict it as the highest Reality and as the Good of Plato and the cause of all. Whitehead's ultimate, "Creativity" is clearly not an hypostasis at the commencement of his system, but becomes progressively more akin to Plotinus' One as the scheme develops. It is declared to be without a character of its own, yet it is the dynamic activity which is the ground of all reality in the universe. The primordial nature of God is declared by Whitehead to be the "creature of creativity" and to be "the primordial created fact," whereas Plotinus' Intellectual-Principle is said to be produced by emanation from the One in some strange way which he finds difficulty in explaining. In discussing the origin and order of the Beings following on the First, Plotinus reiterates that all things run back to it as their source: not only the Intellectual-Principle (which is also Being) and Soul which is brought forth in turn by the Intellectual-Principle by a further emanation, but in a sense the One is "this in which each particular entity participates, the author of being to the universe and to each item of the total."[35] Plotinus proceeds with further explanation to the effect that the multiplicity in each thing is converted into a self-sufficing existence by this presence of the One, which is thus the author of all the Being that any entity has and must, therefore, itself be beyond Being.

Both the One of Plotinus and the ultimate in Whitehead's system are regarded as impersonal; Whitehead refers to "creativity" simply as "it," whereas Plotinus speaks of "It" with a capital because the One in his system is definitely the First Hypostasis, God. Whitehead describes "creativity" as "that ultimate notion of the highest generality at the base of actuality. It cannot be characterized, because all characters are more special than itself."[36] And yet again, creativity is described as "the principle of novelty";[37] the whole process is an exemplification of the ultimate. In Whitehead's system, creativity is denied actuality in itself; it acquires actuality in its instances (actual occasions) in which it acquires a character and is conditioned for future novelty, in contrast to Plotinus' One, which remains completely unconditioned by any of its emanations, being entirely self-sufficient. As we have noted, however, Whitehead introduces a subtle change in the status of creativity in section V of the final chapter of *Process and Reality*, where we are informed that "Creativity achieves its supreme task"[38] of the reconciliation of permanence and flux. At this point Whitehead's ultimate is fully hypostasized and the resemblance to the One of Plotinus is Close.

There are affinities between Whitehead's primordial nature of God and the Second Hypostasis in Plotinus' *Enneads*. The multiplicity of all the Forms of Plato's philosophy are seen as comprising the nature

[35] Ibid., V. 3,17; p. 399.
[36] Whitehead, *PR*, p. 47 (43).
[37] Ibid., p. 31 (28).
[38] Ibid., p. 528 (493).

of Plotinus' Intellectual-Principle even as Whitehead declares that God in his primordial nature comprises the full multiplicity of all "eternal objects" and is declared to be "the unlimited conceptual realization of the absolute wealth of potentiality."[39] Moreover each (the Second Hypostasis of Plotinus and the primordial nature of God for Whitehead) is said to be the architect of the world process. One basic difference is found in the derivation of God for Whitehead's system; God is declared to be derivative, but his derivation is by creation rather than by emanation from the First. In this respect Whitehead's primordial nature of God is very like the created gods of the Platonic myth, and has clear metaphysical affinities with the Arian conception of the Son as the first of the creatures and the agent in the creation of all else. Our investigation of the Arian documents has disclosed that, while the Christian terminology of "Fatherhood" is employed, the description is that of the One of the Neo-Platonic triad of three unequal hypostases."[40] A corollary to this declaration of the utter aloneness and unknowability of the Father is a doctrine of the subordination of the Son or Word of God, who is explicitly declared by them to be derivative, and to belong to the created order. He is the first in that order, and in this sense, is primordial and unique, but nonetheless, belongs to the created order of existence. What we have, consequently, is a demi-god, typical of the created gods of the Platonic myth, to bridge the gap between God and the world, to whom the world owes its existence, because he is "the primordial created fact,"[41] to borrow Whitehead's terminology. God, as primordial, in Whitehead's system, is declared to be "the outcome of creativity,"[42] and the "primordial creature"[43] of creativity, and resembles in many respects this Arian conception of the Son of God, so called. Whitehead, in borrowing from Plato, had unwittingly incorporated into his system a number of ideas which would not fit well with those elements of Christianity which he endeavoured to introduce in the final sections of the work.

One major contrast of Whitehead's primordial nature of God with Plotinus' Intellectual-Principle is constituted in the fact that the movement of the Intellectual-Principle, like that of all Platonic realities, is upwards only, in the direction of the Transcendent One with which it seeks union, whereas for Whitehead, God's envisagement of the world constitutes an urge towards realization; and the process of the universe, as of that of each actual entity, receives from God its initial subjective aim. Whitehead's philosophy, in contrast to Plotinus', is world affirming; for Whitehead, God is clearly immanent and at work in the world and he (Whitehead) is searching for a form of language adequate to give expression to this aspect of experience. Such order as there is in the universe is given to it by God; it is, Whitehead says, by reason of this primordial actuality that there is "an order in the relevance of eternal objects to the process of creation."[44] It is the reason why there is a universe, and why it is the kind of universe that it is.

We have noted[45] that the third Hypostasis in the system of Plotinus is the Soul, described by him as "an image of the Intellectual-Principle,"[46] and again, as being "even the total of its activity, the entire stream of life sent forth by that Principle to the production of further being";[47] it is, in other words, a further emanation. While the Soul is intellective, its intellection operates by the method of reasonings. It becomes its true self when it contemplates the Supreme Intelligence. According to Plotinus, Soul is the author of all living things, to which it gives law and movement and life and "guides all to its purposes; for it has bestowed itself upon all that huge expanse so that every interval, small and great alike, has been ensouled."[48]

The World Soul is the active agent of becoming in the system of Plotinus, much as the consequent nature of God is, in Whitehead's scheme, "the weaving of God's physical feelings upon his primordial concepts,"[49] or, alternatively, "it is the realization of the actual world in the unity of his nature, and through the transformation of his wisdom."[50] Moreover, God, as consequent, is in process of becoming with every other creative act. "He shares with every new creation its actual world; and the concrescent creature is objectified in God as a novel element in God's objectification of that actual world."[51] The aim which directs the creatures in their striving to enter into God is itself derived from "his all-inclusive primordial valuation."[52] In this process, God's primordial nature is unchanged, according to Whitehead, but his derivative nature is consequent to the creative advance of the world. There is a similarity in the thought of Whitehead and of Plotinus at this point in the development of their systems. In discussing the work of the Soul, Plotinus states that "within the Supreme we must see energy not as an overflow but in the double aspect of integral inherence with the establishment of a new being";[53] he suggests, moreover, that Soul, sprung from the Intellectual-Principle, must, for its perfecting, "look to that Divine Mind, which may be thought of as a father watching over the development of his child born imperfect in comparison with himself,"[54] indicating clearly that the World Soul is conceived to be in process of formation. Both philosophers are attempting to speak of the same aspects of experience.

[44] Ibid., p. 522 (486-87).
[45] See above, pp. 124ff.
[46] Plotinus, *Enneads*, V. 1,3; p. 371.
[47] Ibid.
[48] Ibid., V. 1,2; p. 370.
[49] Whitehead, *PR*, p. 524 (488).
[50] Ibid.
[51] Ibid., pp. 523-24 (488).
[52] Ibid., p. 523 (488).
[53] Plotinus, *Enneads*, V. 1,3; p. 371.
[54] Ibid.

Whitehead's conception of the consequent nature of God may not, however, be exactly equated with Plotinus' Soul. In contrast to Plotinus' system, in which the Second Hypostasis, the Intellectual-Principle, is the fulness of Being and the World Soul attains fulness of Being by striving upward and becoming increasingly more intellectual, in Whitehead's system, there is no sharp demarcation between the intellectual and the physical, but on the contrary, the nature of God acquires a fulness of Being and completeness only in and through the completion of the physical and mental advance of the creative process, and the universe itself is to be gathered up into the nature of God; this condition Whitehead describes as "everlastingness—the Apotheosis of the World."[55] Whitehead has, moreover, incorporated into his conception of the consequent nature of God what he has understood to be the metaphysical implications of the records of the New Testament, and in particular, of the teaching of Jesus as recorded in the Gospels; "the consequent nature of God," he states, "is the judgment of a tenderness which loses nothing that can be saved"[56] the exposition of this, and the two final sections, is virtually a cosmic interpretation of Christ. In the concluding sections of *Process and Reality*, accordingly, we detected a fundamental contradiction in Whitehead's presentation of God. On the one hand, he is stated to be simply the one arm of the two "contrasted opposites in terms of which Creativity achieves its supreme task of transforming disjoined multiplicity . . . into concrescent unity, . . ."[57] and all this without any further definition of "creativity," which has been specifically defined as an impersonal ultimate; on the other hand, in the two closing sections, God is being spoken of as ultimate and as personal—to speak of "the kingdom of heaven"[58] implies a King, and at this point Whitehead's Platonism is being challenged by his deepening appreciation of the cosmic significance of Christ. Whitehead's Platonism is at war with his emerging Christian faith; he has not yet discovered the metaphysical solution to the problem as to "the quality of creative origination"[59] and until he has made this discovery it is not possible for him clearly to enunciate the relationship between God and the World.

Whitehead was attracted to the solution proposed by the theologians of Alexandria because in responding to the questions raised by the Arians, they had pointed the way to the solution of dilemmas with which he had unsuccessfully struggled in his twentieth century cosmology. He had, with important qualifications, based his system upon that of Plato because he found that it was more favourable to interpretation in terms of process than was the cosmology which had dominated the scientific world since the days of Newton. Recognizing that some form of process philosophy was required to give a rational account of the

[55] Whitehead, *PR*, p. 529 (493).
[56] Ibid., p. 525 (490).
[57] Ibid., p. 528 (492-93).
[58] Ibid., pp. 531-32 (496-97).
[59] Ibid., p. 518 (483).

universe as disclosed in the findings of the various sciences, Whitehead undertook to provide it by utilizing such elements of former cosmologies as would be helpful in providing the interpretation called for in the twentieth century. Our exposition has disclosed that the cosmology which he developed was basically Platonic in framework, but with important qualifications. Whitehead is an empiricist who maintains that the real is the actual which, in his system, means the activity of becoming. He is concerned to interpret the real world which is investigated by the sciences, the world of experience including man and the universe, and he adopts as the principle of the ultimate a feature of the universe, namely the "creativity," which is everywhere disclosed to be a component in actualities. He explains that "creativity" takes the place of "prime matter" in Aristotle's system, and the "Receptacle" of Plato's cosmology. In this way he seeks to account for the universe as a creative process.

It is a fundamental principle of Plato's philosophy that God is good and must not therefore be made responsible for the evil in the world; this involved, however, a conception of God as merely one of a number of elements which together go to make up the universe as known to us and resulted in a dualism between God and the world which Plato was unable to resolve. The fully developed Platonic scheme failed to bridge this gap between God and the World; in fact, in the final development through the *Enneads* of Plotinus, the One or the Good, which is equated with God, is utterly transcendent, so much so that it is impossible to say anything positive about it. All reality is an emanation from the One through a hierarchy of Hypostases extending downward to include the universe and man, all of which are, at best, but images of that which is higher in the scale. While Plotinus calls his One the Good, it has lost all the qualities usually implied in the title; it is specifically declared to be beyond thinking and in this respect is a stage beyond the Unmoved Mover of Aristotle, Who is declared by him to be a thinking thought. Plotnius' One is beyond all description, and the search of the soul for union with God is the "flight of the alone to the alone," a flight in which there can be no movement from the Higher to the Lower.

The Platonic Framework, nevertheless, seeks to provide a language by means of which to account for the complexity of the universe, and Whitehead found it attractive and helpful up to a point. He rejected the extreme transcendence which he felt was implied in the Semitic conception of God, and by setting up an impersonal ultimate, "creativity," which it was, by definition, impossible to hypostasize, he sought to safeguard his system against the dangers, while employing much of the terminology of the Platonic system. Our comparison of the final interpretation given in *Process and Reality* with the Plotinian system has disclosed many similarities in terminology, and when it became necessary in section V of the final chapter of *Process and Reality*[60] for Whitehead to hypostasize "Creativity" in order to deliver the system from the charge of pantheism, the parallelism was very close, between

---

[60] Ibid., p. 528 (492-93).

the One, the Intellectual-Principle, and the Soul of the Plotinian system and Creativity, God and the World of Whitehead's cosmology. There are important exceptions; whereas Plotinus speaks of "emanations" and of generation from the highest to the lowest, Whitehead speaks of "creative activity" and, whereas for Plotinus all movement must be in an upward direction alone, and the lower, while participating in some way in reality, are but imitations of the higher, for Whitehead the universe is declared to be the product of creativity and the order in it to be the result of the envisagement and activity of God in a process in which there is interrelationship and co-operation between God and the World. Our analysis of the final two sections of *Process and Reality* disclosed that his thought at this point is deeply influenced by New Testament conceptions, even to speaking of the Kingdom of heaven and of the love of God for the World, but that the system provides no grounds upon which to base these statements which really constitute the introduction of new elements calling for interpretation, and of such significance as to transform the system when fully intepreted. The doctrine of an impersonal ultimate principle as the substructure of the universe does not fit well with the proclamation of the Kingdom of God, and the announcement that the action of the fourth phase of the creative process is the love of God for the world will call for a re-definition of what we mean by God in a doctrine which permits the employment of language implying personality.

It is not surprising, therefore, that in his re-investigation of the evolutionary process and of the history of ideas in the formation of civilization, Whitehead's search is for empirical evidence for what he describes as "the counter-agency" by means of which to account for the emergence of life and mind and value and social organization, with the increasing focus of attention on the intrinsic worth of the human person and of the supreme importance of the element of rational persuasion in the emergence and advance of civilization. In the light of these disclosures, resulting from his re-investigation of the empirical evidence, Whitehead concludes that Plato's idea of the divine element in the world as a persuasive agency rather than a coercive agency is "one of the greatest intellectual discoveries in the history of religion."[61] That Plato should have made this discovery in his old age is itself a logical development from his conviction of the goodness of God; that it should be clearly set forth in the *Timaeus* which is the nearest that a Greek philosopher could come to a myth of Creation is further evidence of the direction in which Plato's mind was moving in his attempt to interpret the universe and man in society.

Whitehead found this idea particularly attractive because it fits in with the findings of psychology, sociology and the history of civilization about the nature of man in society and because it enunciates a principle which is of fundamental importance in the development of man as a spiritual being. If there are to be personal relations between man and

[61] A. N. Whitehead, *Adventures of Ideas* (Cambridge: Cambridge University Press, 1933), p. 213.

the divine, these can only become possible where the divine is conceived as an agency of rational persuasion, whose presence is disclosed in works of love and service, an agency of friendship and of concern for man's real good, and as working with him to the defeat of the forces of tyranny and chaos which ever threaten to overwhelm human life and society. It is this insight of Plato, clearly enunciated in his later Dialogues, that Whitehead hails as a great advance in religious thought and one urgently needed in our own generation. At best, however, it was but an idea, an idea embodied in a myth and therefore potent in its influence on succeeding generations of thinkers.

It was Whitehead's discovery that this idea had received embodiment—exemplification—in a life lived out under all the limitations of human existence in a particular community during a specific historical epoch which convinced him that in Christ he had found a clue to the understanding of the nature of God and of his relation to the World. This was by no means Whitehead's first contact with Jesus Christ and the New Testament. He states in his memoirs that while at Cambridge he had engaged in the study of theology for a period of eight years, but that he had failed to find the study helpful and had given it up and sold his books. Our investigations have disclosed that at the time of writing *Religion in the Making* Whitehead had identified five major themes which play an increasingly important part in his conception of the nature of ultimate reality as his thought develops.[62] Now, however, he is saying something much more specific in his declaration that "the essence of Christianity is the appeal to the life of Christ as a revelation of the nature of God and of his agency in the world."[63] This change of emphasis is in accord with the focus of attention throughout *Adventures of Ideas* upon human freedom and worth, and on the persuasive agency of God which finds its most significant illustration in the interaction between persons, and will lead in the direction of the conception of God as personal.

The acceptance of Jesus Christ as in himself a disclosure of the nature of ultimate reality will call for a re-examination of Whitehead's conception of God and the Ultimate as expressed in *Process and Reality*. The Incarnate Christ has demonstrated what Plato and his followers, including Plotinus, were incapable of conceiving, namely, the immanence of God in his creation. Whitehead had been convinced of the necessity for recognizing the immanence of God in order to account for the processes of the universe, but had rcognized that in some way he must also be conceived as transcendent to the world, even though he denied final transcendence in the account in *Process and Reality*, in which he maintained that the process is the reality. In *Adventures of Ideas*, however, in the discussion of the reconciliation effected by the Alexandrian theologians between the doctrines of Imposed Law and Immanent Law, he rejects both of the Platonic theories, that of Plato's

---

[62] See above, pp. 21-22; also A. N. Whitehead, *Religion in the Making* (New York: Macmillan, 1926), pp. 72-73.

[63] Whitehead, *AI*, p. 214.

Timaeus, in which he "provides a soul of this world who definitely is not the ultimate creator,"[64] and the "World-Soul as an emanation," which was Plotinus' attempt to account for the emergence of the universe. It becomes clear at this point that Whitehead has discovered that he requires a more clearly articulated doctrine of Creation if he would understand, and provide an interpretation of, the relations between God and the World. This he found in the writings of Athanasius of Alexandria, who in face of the challenge of Arianism, set about the task of formulating the arguments by which the Church might safeguard the faith against interpretations which, while they seemed superficially to be very similar, were in reality diametrically opposed to the Christian faith. As Whitehead states the problem, "they considered the general question, how the primordial Being, who is the source of the inevitable recurrence of the world towards order, shares his nature with the world."[65]

Whitehead has, at this point, discovered that the problems with which he has wrestled in the construction of his twentieth-century cosmology are those with which these theologians were confronted at Alexandria in the fourth century by the Arian interpretation of the Christian faith. It is evident that the questions which were before the Church at Nicaea are those which he is now raising in connection with the person of Jesus Christ, namely, What kind of reality is disclosed in Jesus Christ? And, if he is ultimate reality, What must be the nature of ultimate reality that it can be adequately disclosed only in and through the life of a man? And a further question is equally fundamental, namely, What must be the nature of the universe and of its relation to the Ultimate Being, to render possible the events of the Incarnation?

Whitehead discovered that the Christian theologians, in their reply to the Arian challenge, had formulated a number of metaphysical doctrines which, taken together, provide the answers which he needed for the completion of his philosophy of organism and we must investigate now some of the basic documents of the period to find the source of those discoveries.

The problem came before the Church in the form of a question about the nature of Jesus Christ, who was declared by the Arians to belong to the created order of existence.

The formal reply of the Council of Nicaea to the Arian challenge was incorporated in a creed of the type of baptismal creed used throughout Palestine and Syria at the time. Into this the Nicaean Fathers interpolated a number of key clauses designed to rule out the Arian interpretation by declaring formally that the Son is "true God from true God," that he is "begotten not made,"[66] "begotten from the Father, only-begotten, that is, from the Substance of the Father," and finally, a reaffirmation of this same point, insisting that the Son is "of One Substance with the Father." By such phraseology they sought to

---

[64] Ibid., p. 166.
[65] Ibid.
[66] J. N. D. Kelly, *Early Christian Creeds* (London: Longman's, 1950), p. 215.

establish that it is the faith of the Christian Church that the Son shares the very being and essence of the Father, and is therefore fully divine in every sense of that word. They now press on to emphasize the agency of the Son in both Creation and Redemption, in the clause:

> ... through whom all things came into being, things in heaven and things on earth, Who because of us men and because of our salvation came down and became incarnate, becoming man, suffered and rose again on the third day, Ascended to the heavens, and will come to judge the living and the dead; And in the Holy Spirit.[67]

It is one thing, however, to formulate accurate statement of what the Church holds to be the faith, but it is quite another thing to convince the minds of men of the truth and adequacy of the statements so agreed upon by a few. For this there is required a form of argument by which the truths so set out may be seen to be indeed the truth. The problem was particularly acute at the time of Nicaea and during succeeding years because, with the conversion of the Emperor to the Christian faith and the removal of the stigma against being Christian, people were crowding into the Christian churches and requesting baptism, bringing with them their contemporary world view which was largely at this time Neo-Platonic. The conflict which heretofore had been between different persons each holding his own viewpoint was now being faced within the minds of the same people and consequently there was an urgent need for a clear formulation of arguments by which the faith as set out at Nicaea might be defended. This task fell to the lot of Athanasius, bishop of Alexandria from 328 until his death in 373.

[67] Ibid., pp. 215-16.

Chapter XI

The Formulation of the Christian Doctrine of the Trinity: Athanasius, the Nicaean Formula and Whitehead

Whitehead provides a number of clues to the source of the arguments which convinced him of the superiority of the Christian formulation over the Platonic cosmology which had, up to this time, dominated his thought about the nature of ultimate reality. In a discussion of Law as Immanent he remarks that after Plato, "the next important landmark in the history of this doctrine is provided by the theological Alexandrians, some five or six hundred years later";[1] these men, he explains, "were greatly exercised over the immanence of God in the world."[2] Later, in a chapter entitled "The New Reformation,"[3] he states that the third phase in the "threefold revelation"[4] of Christianity "is the first period in the formation of Christian theology by the schools of thought mainly associated with Alexandria and Antioch."[5] These men, he explains, "were groping after the solution of a fundamental metaphysical problem, although presented to them in a highly special form."[6] "They had to consider the nature of God,"[7] a topic on which Whitehead gives it as his judgment that "the Arian solution, involving a derivative Image, is orthodox Platonism, though it be heterodox Christianity."[8]

In other words, the problem with which these Alexandrian theologians were faced was identical with that which Whitehead declared in 1926 to be the "one religious dogma in debate," namely, "What do you mean by 'God'?"[9] This has been the fundamental ques-

[1] A. N. Whitehead, *Adventures of Ideas* (Cambridge: Cambridge University Press, 1933), p. 165.
[2] Ibid., p. 166.
[3] Ibid., p. 205.
Ibid., p. 213.
[5] Ibid., p. 214.
[6] Ibid.
[7] Ibid., p. 216.
[8] Ibid.
[9] A. N. Whitehead, *Religion in the Making* (New York: Macmillan, 1926), p. 67.

tion behind his whole philosophical venture. As indicated earlier, it is the central problem in contemporary theological debate.[10] It was considered to be of paramount importance by Bonhoeffer, as indicated in the outline of a book which he proposed to write had he survived the ordeal of the concentration camp. "What do we mean by 'God'?"[11] is the ultimate question to which he is led by consideration of the question which he raises earlier in the *Letters,* namely, "How do we speak . . . in a secular fashion of God?"[12] and interjects in parentheses, "but perhaps we are no longer capable of speaking of such things as we used to."[13] Bonhoeffer's question has been reiterated in subsequent theological debate in England and America and it is becoming increasingly clear to ordinary members in the Christian Churches that this is the fundamentally important question at the heart of contemporary theological discussion. All problems of faith and practice among Christians must ultimately come to focus in this question and will be decided in the light of such answers as can be found to Whitehead's question, "What do you mean by 'God'?"[14]

The question before our generation of Christians is identical with that which was asked in the fourth century; and because it is asked in a Christian context, the answers now as then must centre around the person and work of Jesus Christ, whose historical appearing constituted the beginning of Christianity, and whose life and death have been declared by Christians to constitute "the supreme moment in religious history."[15] In all discussion of the subject of God, the question finally arrives back at this question as central, "What do you think of Jesus Christ?" and from this proceeds a second, namely, "What kind of reality is disclosed in him?" It is significant that Whitehead, in an investigation of the history of ideas, and in a section of his report on that investigation in which he is dealing with cosmologies, finally returns to this question, and declares that "the essence of Christianity is the appeal to the life of Christ as a revelation of the nature of God and of his agency in the world."[16] This judgment, as we might expect, leads him into a further investigation to discover the answers to the question of the nature of ultimate reality as disclosed in Jesus. If Jesus Christ is a revelation of the nature of God and of his agency in the world, it is important that we should discern the full significance of the disclosure which has been made in him, and this is the burden of the third phase of Whitehead's search.

For answers to these questions, Whitehead takes us to the fourth century, to the Arian controversy about the person of Jesus Christ who, the Arians maintain, is the first of the creatures. Whitehead declares

---

[10] See above, pp. 10-11.
[11] Dietrich Bonhoeffer, *Letters and Papers from Prison,* ed. by Eberhard Bethge, trans. by Reginald H. Fuller (London: SCM Press, 1953), p. 179.
[12] Ibid., p. 123.
[13] Ibid.
[14] Whitehead, *RM,* p. 67.
[15] Whitehead, *AI,* p. 214.
[16] Ibid.

that in the formulation of answers to this challenge "these Christian theologians have the distinction of being the only thinkers who in a fundamental metaphysical doctrine have improved upon Plato."[17] In this Christian doctrine Whitehead locates a metaphysical formulation of "that ultimate theme of the divine immanence, as a completion required by our cosmological outlook."[18] The questions with which these Alexandrians dealt are so central and the answers formulated so fundamentally important to the contemporary debate that an investigation of their sources is in order at this time.

Investigation of the history of the Arian controversy discloses that it was Athanasius, bishop of Alexandria from A.D. 328 to 373, who finally formulated the theological rationalization of the faith and won the support of the whole Church for the Nicaean formula. His achievements are recognized by no less significant successors than the Cappadocian Fathers, who carried the debate forward from where Athanasius had left it.[19] An examination of his writings discloses the soundness of their judgment. We have reason to believe, therefore, that Whitehead found in the writings of Athanasius the arguments which convinced him of the superiority of the Christian conception of God and of his relation to the world over the Platonic cosmology which had dominated his own philosophical writings up to this time.

There are a number of reasons why Whitehead would be particularly attracted to the writings of Athanasius. His practical concern about God and the world is identical with that which inspires Whitehead's works. The two writers lived in very different times and their ways of stating things are coloured by their respective understandings of what the specific situation calls for. Both men, however, write in a period when world leadership is searching for a formula of unity, some cohesive agency to hold society together. Athanasius writes in the midst of turmoil, during an episcopacy of forty-five years, seventeen of which were spent in exile in France, Italy, or the North African desert because he differed in matters of faith from the ruling coterie. His letters and treatises are addressed to specific situations and groups of people and always with the one objective of removing error and increasing understanding of the Common Faith of Christians. He writes as a pastor of pastors, with a deep concern for the redemption which is in Christ, and his real stature is disclosed in his later writings when, having won his arguments against the Arians, he is moving in the direction of winning the Easterns behind the Nicaean formula as the one basis upon which all Christians could agree.

Whitehead writes as a philosopher who has witnessed the ordeal of the ages in the greatest bloodbath mankind had up to that time perpetrated upon man; his own family has been involved and the younger

[17] Ibid., pp. 214-15.
[18] Ibid., p. 206.
[19] Basil of Caesarea, as a deacon accompanying his bishop to Constantinople in 359, read and welcomed Athanasius' *De Synodis*, and writing a few months later, adopted the words of Athanasius as his own, "One God we confess, etc.," from *De Synodis*, sec. 53.

son was killed in action near the end of the War. There is an urgency in his appeal to his readers which comes from his realization that Christianity, which according to its own principles should be the one force which might lead the world into peace, has lost its leadership in the world, and the Churches in their divided state are fighting rear-guard actions and losing ground.[20] Seen from this perspective, the problems facing Athanasius and Whitehead are identical. The major difference in the two situations is constituted in the fact that in Athanasius' day the world ruler (the Emperor) was looking to the Church and expecting from it the leadership to maintain unity in the Empire, whereas in Whitehead's day the Church has lost the leadership and is being increasingly ignored by a world which includes the whole human race. The apparent advantage in Athanasius' day, however, was negated by the internal discord over matters of faith so that the actual situations addressed by the two writers are remarkably similar.

Athanasius' empirical approach to problems would also appeal to Whitehead. He is concerned about man in his relations with God in the real world of human experience, and has familiarized himself with such scientific knowledge as was available about the universe. In handling questions about the faith his method is to investigate the sources in the Scriptures, and here he lays down rules for the guidance of the student who would seek to discover the truth from the study of the Scriptures: he must expound faithfully (1) the time of which the author wrote, (2) and the person, (3) and the point—"lest the reader, from ignorance missing either these or any similar particular, may be wide of the true sense."[21] In his polemical works, Athanasius spends much of his time examining the Arian interpretation of Scripture proof texts and demonstrating from the Scriptures that they have misinterpreted them. Having investigated the Scriptural sources, he next examines the *use* of the Church in its major services such as baptism and the Eucharist, in its instruction of catechumens and in the language employed in worship; finally, he considers what effect the Arian proposals, if accepted, would have upon the availability of salvation for mankind today. The real argument for the truth of Christianity, for Athanasius, is always to be found in the evidence of the present power of the Gospel, when faithfully proclaimed, to convert and to transform the lives of men and women. This practical concern for the welfare of mankind dominates all his polemical writings as well as the two-volume apologetic treatise on the faith. It will be important, for purposes of this essay, to examine some of the major writings of Athanasius and, inasmuch as we are concerned with the metaphysical foundations of his thinking, it would seem reasonable to commence with his early works in

[20] Whitehead's concern finds expression in all his major works: cf. *Science and the Modern World*, Ch. XII, and especially pp. 224-25; *Religion in the Making*, Ch. IV, especially pp. 143-47; *Process and Reality*, Part V, Ch. II, "God and the World"; and *Adventures of Ideas*, pp. 18-20, 41, 105-109, and Ch. X.

[21] Athanasius, *Four Discourses against the Arians*, I, sec. 54 (Oxford: James Parker and Company, 1877).

the hope of discovering some clues as to the presuppositions of his thought.

Whitehead may have discovered some of the answers to his problem in the short treatise, *contra Gentes,* the first part of a two-volume treatise written as an apologetic for the faith. The *contra Gentes* might equally well have been entitled "About the God of the Universe," for its subject is the Christian doctrine of creation. The phrase "the God of the Universe"[22] is Athanasius' favourite designation for God in this treatise, and appears to have been also favoured by Whitehead in his later years. Many years after writing *Adventures of Ideas,* during a conversation with the journalist, Lucien Price, in a discussion about a passage in Plato's *Timaeus,* Whitehead states that "Plato's God is a God of this world. . . . Since then our concept of this world has enlarged to that of the universe. I have envisioned a union of Plato's God with a God of the universe."[23]

There are many features of the *contra Gentes,* in addition to its recognition of the necessity for seriously considering the relation of God and the world, which would prove attractive to Whitehead. It is the most Platonic of all Athanasius' writings; many of the arguments are drawn from the *Timaeus.* It contains references to the *Phaedrus,* the *Republic* and the *Politics,*[24] and some of the language is reminiscent of Plotinus in those sections of the *Enneads* in which he is describing the origination of the earth.

The purpose of the *contra Gentes* is to set out clearly the radical difference between the Christian conception of the world as created by God out of nothing and the wide variety of contemporary pagan attempts to account for the world by a series of emanations or of graded hierarchies. In Part I varying forms of pantheism, dualism, idolatry and polytheism are refuted in detail. We meet here what might be called Athanasius' demythologization of the universe by the assertion of the Christian doctrine of creation. The arguments for the existence of God are all teleological, a feature which would be particularly attractive to Whitehead; the universe is described as an orderly process of interrelated parts all dependent upon the creative and sustaining activity of God, who is here portrayed as immanent and as having given to the creation something of himself, so that the creation itself manifests the order and harmony which is in God.

Part II carries the argument forward in an analysis of the human soul which is declared to be a road to bring us to God. The soul is rational by nature and immortal, and is that part of us by which alone God can be perceived.[25] For the soul is made after the image and likeness of God, and each man has, therefore, a kind of mirror of the

    [22] Athanasius, *contra Gentes,* sec. 40,4.
    [23] Lucien Price, *The Dialogues of Alfred North Whitehead* (London: Max Reinhardt, 1954), p. 214.
    [24] References in *contra Gentes* to *The Phaedrus* (246C, 248A, 253E, 254) in *contra Gentes* 5.2; 245C in ibid., 33.2; *The Republic,* I in ibid., 10,4; *The Timaeus,* 29E, in ibid., 41,2; *The Politics,* in ibid., 41,3.
    [25] Athanasius, *contra Gentes,* sec. 30.

Image of the Father within him so long as he remains in contemplation of God. The argument of this section recalls the theme of Whitehead's *Function of Reason*. Athanasius argues that the rational soul differentiates man from the irrational creatures; he alone thinks of things external to himself, and reasons about things not actually present; he exercises reflection and he chooses by judgment the better or alternative reasonings. He judges by thought those things which he apprehends by the senses and often overrules his impulses by his intelligence, which is a faculty different and distinct from the bodily senses and acts as judge over them. The body, with its senses, is likened to a well-fashioned musical instrument; when skilled intelligence presides over the body there is a harmony, as when a skilled musician plucks the lyre.[26]

The rationality and the order of the Universe, Athanasius argues, proves that it is the work of the Reason or Word of God. "Who then might this Maker be?"[27] he asks, and proceeds to affirm that "the God we worship and preach is the only true One, Who is Lord of Creation and Maker of all existence."[28] At this point Athanasius is very much a modern, insisting that we must first clarify what we mean by God before we can proceed with significant discourse about the relations between God and the world. Notice that "the only true One"[29] is not the utterly transcendent and unknowable One of Plotinus, but is the "Lord of Creation and Maker of all existence,"[30] who has disclosed something of himself in his Creation. Further identification follows which makes quite clear that it is an interpretation of the universe in the light of the Christian revelation which is being given: "Who then is this, save the Father of Christ, most holy and above all created existence, Who like an excellent pilot, by His own Wisdom and His own Word, our Lord and Saviour Christ, steers and preserves and orders all things, and does as seems to Him best?"[31] Having identified the Incarnate Lord, Christ, with the Creative Word, Athanasius proceeds to a further differentiation of the Reason or Word of God from the Stoical conception of the seminal ($\sigma\pi\epsilon\rho\mu\alpha\tau\iota\kappa\acute{o}\varsigma$)[32] principle, which is without soul and has no power of reason or thought on the one hand, and from the Jewish ideas of such words as belong to rational beings and which consist of syllables and require the breath as the vehicle of transmission, "but I mean the living and powerful Word of the good God, the God of the Universe, the very Word which is God, Who while different from things that are made, and from all Creation, is the One own Word of the good Father, Who by His own providence ordered and illumines this Universe."[33] In this brief passage we find the improvement upon Platonism in all its forms which the Christian theologians were able to effect by drawing

[26] Ibid., secs. 31-32.
[27] Ibid., sec. 40.
[28] Ibid.
[29] Ibid.
[30] Ibid.
[31] Ibid., sec. 40,2.
[32] Ibid., sec. 40,4.
[33] Ibid.

upon and applying to their understanding of the universe the insights received from the revelation of God in Christ. Here is everything which Plato was able to say about God, and more; here is God as portrayed in Whitehead's philosophy, and more. It is important to note that Athanasius is here speaking about the operations of "the Word of the good God, the God of the Universe,"[34] and insisting that he, the Word, is different from things made and from all creation. Without mentioning the Arians by name, he is countering their central assertion that the Son is a creature.

It is this operation of the Word of God, "Who by his own providence ordered and illumines this universe,"[35] which Whitehead ascribes to God in his primordial nature. In this connection, Whitehead declares that God is "the unconditioned actuality of conceptual feeling at the base of things,"[36] and that by reason of this primordial actuality, "there is an order in the relevance of eternal objects to the process of creation."[37] In terms of his "primordial nature" Whitehead is able to speak of the providence of God in his ordering of the possibilities for becoming in the universe. And, on the other hand, in terms of the "consequent nature" of God, he speaks of him as "saving the world as it passes into the immediacy of his presence."[38] But he provides no explanation of the origin of "creativity" itself and of the fact of "the general metaphysical character of the creative advance"[39] of which God is said to be "the primordial exemplification";[40] neither does he provide any satisfactory account of the union of the two natures in God, and because God as "the outcome of creativity"[41] is finite, the system suffers from elements of incoherence which it is not possible, within the terms of the categories of *Process and Reality,* to eliminate.

Athanasius achieves coherence where Whitehead fails because he has learned from revelation that God is the creator of everything that is, both the visible and the invisible; creation ἐξ οὐκ ὄντων overcomes the dichotomy which Whitehead is unable to transcend in his system. Here and elsewhere throughout his writings Athanasius is able to assert, in consequence, that the "One own Word of the good Father,"[42] who by his own providence ordered the universe, is the same One who, as immanent within all things, illumines and sustains the universe. The discovery of this formula is good news to Whitehead, because it has been one of the central objectives of his metaphysical undertaking to provide a rational account of the immanence of God. Athanasius, by his application of the truth of God as disclosed in Christ, is able to point the

[34] Ibid.

[35] Ibid.

[36] A. N. Whitehead, *Process and Reality: An Essay in Cosmology* (New York: Harper Torchbooks, 1960; first published, New York: Macmillan, 1929), p. 522 (486).

[37] Ibid., p. 522 (486-87).

[38] Ibid., p. 525 (490).

[39] Ibid., p. 522 (487).

[40] Ibid.

[41] Ibid., p. 135 (122).

[42] Athanasius, *contra Gentes,* sec. 40,4.

way to coherence and unity in our metaphysical understanding of the universe.

Athanasius employs a wealth of similes to illustrate his point and to qualify his terms. The Word, he declares, is the unchanging Image of the Father. Men are composed of parts and are made out of nothing, and they consequently have their discourse composite and divisible, but God possesses true existence and is not composite—this in reply to the charge of the Arians against their bishop Alexander of Alexandria and against the Homoousios—wherefore his Word also has true Existence and is not composite, but is the one and only begotten God, "Who proceeds in his goodness from the Father as from a good fountain, and orders all things and holds them together."[43] The Word is, according to the theology of Athanasius, the present sustaining power of all created things; "there is nothing that is and takes place but has been made and stands by Him and through Him."[44]

Whitehead, in *Adventures of Ideas,* states that he has learned from the Alexandrian theologians that the necessity of the trend towards order in nature does not arise from the imposed will of a transcendent God. "It arises from the fact that the existents in nature are sharing in the nature of the immanent God."[45] This, as we have noted, is fully enunciated in *contra Gentes* by Athanasius who declares that because God is good he guides and settles the whole creation by his own Word in order that by the governance and providence and ordering of the Word, Creation may have light, and be enabled to abide always securely. "For it partakes of the Word Who derives true existence from the Father."[46] This uniting action of the Word is described in great detail, and the action of the Word is now likened to that of a musician who has tuned his lyre and adjusted the various notes one to another, so as to produce out of the many and various sounds one complete harmony; so also, he declares, the Wisdom of God handles the universe as an instrument in his hands. Three further similes or models are now employed to illustrate the relation of God to the universe, in such a manner that no one of them may be taken as applying descriptively. In a great chorus there are many members, each of whom utters sound according to the ability of his voice, but all interwoven by the skill of the one conductor produce together one harmony; or, even as the soul moves the many senses and instincts according to the proper function of each and maintains an inward harmony; or, as a very great city, built and administered by its king and ruler who has built it, in like manner must we conceive of the whole universe, even though each of the examples or all of them taken together are quite inadequate to do more than indicate the relationship in which the world stands to God.[47]

Athanasius here and throughout the *contra Gentes* employs the teleological approach to an understanding of the nature of the uni-

[43] Ibid., sec. 41,1.
[44] Ibid., sec. 42,2.
[45] Whitehead, *AI,* p. 166.
[46] Athanasius, *contra Gentes,* sec. 41,3.
[47] Ibid., sec. 43.

verse and man, an approach which Whitehead is led to adopt as the only way in which to account for the order, structure, pattern and interrelatedness of all things throughout the universe, as disclosed in the findings of modern science.[48] In *The Function of Reason,* Whitehead argues that the emergence of creatures with the power of mental activity, and possessing a measure of self-direction of their lives in a universe which appears to be physically wasting away, calls for some further explanation than mechanistic evolutionary theories are able to provide. He is convinced of the need for some counter-agency at work in the world to account for the fact of the emergence of creatures possessed of mental powers. In the conception of God as a persuasive agency, as enunciated by Plato in his later Dialogues and in the discovery of the uniqueness of Jesus Christ as a revelation of the nature of God, Whitehead has located important clues to the problems which are confronting him; here, in Athanasius we find the insights which enable him to recognize the severe limitations of Platonism. In *contra Gentes* Athanasius is laying the foundation for his later polemical writings against the Arians by distinguishing terminology which is appropriate when speaking of the relationship between God and the world from that by means of which to speak of God, the Father, and his relationship with his Word.

The method employed by Athanasius is instructive for theologians who would help to solve some of the puzzlement which is represented in the present theological ferment. Before attempting to speak of the Incarnation of the Word of God, Athanasius sets down in unmistakable

---

[48] This fact of the order, structure and apparently built-in plan is part of the continuing mystery of the universe as disclosed in modern science and which deepens as the various sciences penetrate to an identification of the elementary particles or elements of the composition of the universe. To give but two examples from contemporary thinkers:

i) Fred Hoyle, after explaining that science is a model of the real world which we construct inside our own heads, proceeds to comment on the uncanny ability of science to foresee wholly new phenomena, and concludes that "it seems as if in our thinking we follow the same logical pattern that is inherent in the external world itself," as if in our brains we are able to reflect something of the structure of the universe. He ascribes the amazing success of science in predicting the future to the fact of our "having learned to be guided in the most effective manner by the external world itself' (cf. Mervin Stockwood, ed., *Religion and the Scientists* [London: SCM Press, 1959], pp. 56-57). This is Fred Hoyle in 1957;

ii) In the remarks quoted above, Hoyle is reiterating something which Austin Farrer had suggested in 1943. Farrer agrees with Kant up to a point, that we construct our orderly picture of the world on principles which emanate from within the mind, but suggests that the fact this construction of ours is found to be applicable when applied to the external world would suggest that the mind may well have evolved these principles because it has been faced since its origin with a causally-ordered world and that the mind has the power of apprehending the order that is there. He concludes: "If causality is the law of the mind, it may be so because it is the law of existence, and the mind knows existence. If the nature of mind as such is to be an apprehension of what is then 'to be intelligible' is not a character of things, but a relation between them and some mind whose particular finitude does not act as a filter straining out the things in question." Farrer concludes that to find the order in the world "is to find the starting point of metaphysics" (Austin Farrer, *Finite and Infinite* [2nd ed.; Westminster: Dacre Press, 1959], p. 19).

terms the Christian doctrine of creation by God out of nothing, explicitly contrasting this to the Epicurean doctrine of emergence by Chance, on the one hand, or the Platonic doctrine of creation by an artificer, on the other. The Platonic doctrine, he points out, constitutes too great a limitation upon God and must be rejected. If we would avoid contradictions, God must be clearly differentiated from the world which he has made and which he sustains as its Maker and Creator. He justifies this procedure as necessary in order that men may realize that "the renewal of creation has been the work of the self-same Word that made it at the beginning. For it will appear not inconsonant for the Father to have wrought its salvation in him by whose means He made it."[49]

The implications of acceptance of the Incarnation of the Word were such as to call for a clarification of what Christians mean by Creation. If God became incarnate in Jesus of Nazareth, then this fact tells us something very important about God and also about the world into which he came as a human being. We are compelled to raise the question of the relationship between God and the world and before we can hope to formulate a satisfactory doctrine of the Incarnation, it is necessary to clarify the meaning of Creation as disclosed in the revelation of God's love for the world which is made known in Christ. Athanasius does this by drawing upon all that both Old and New Testament have to say about the world, how it came into being, its contingency, and its function in the eternal purpose of God. He makes much use of the conception of the Word as developed in St. John's Gospel, in which the Word is clearly identified with God.

It is important to notice further that, while Athanasius' doctrine of Creation was formulated only gradually and as weaknesses in the Church position, or erroneous interpretations by others, necessitated that he re-think various aspects of the faith, yet, once clearly formulated, this was seen to be self-evident, and the new formulation to be but a drawing out of that which had been implied in the faith and practice of the Church from the beginning. On the other hand, as fully formulated, the Church's faith represents a clear advance upon all expressions of the faith up until that moment and there are important philosophical implications in the Christian formulation which were not sufficiently drawn out at the time, nor adequately since. The present climate of opinion is such as to call for just this philosophical exercise to provide the Christian answers to questions posed by the universe and the human condition as disclosed in scientific laboratories and in human experience.

The Incarnation of the Word of God

Throughout the treatise *On the Incarnation of the Word,* but particularly in the central sections, Athanasius avoids the dangers of overstatement of some aspect of the operation of the Son and of understating others, by insisting upon speaking of all his manifold operations

[49] Athanasius, *On the Incarnation of the Word*, sec. 1 (LCC,III, p. 56).

and relationships within the compass of a single sentence. He keeps carefully in view at all times the twofold purpose of the Word's becoming man, both of which operations are works of love. First he has come to put away death from us and to renew us, and secondly, by his coming among us incognito, "being unseen and invisible, in manifesting and making himself known by his works to be the Word of the Father and the ruler and king of the universe."[50]

It is customary in Christian circles to interpret the life and work of Jesus Christ as "both a sacrifice for sin, and also an example of godly life";[51] but there is a third aspect of his coming among us which is fundamentally important for our understanding of God and of his way of working in the world, and the failure of Christian theology to develop this is declared by Whitehead to be a major defect in our understanding of the message of Christianity, namely, that Jesus Christ is a revelation of the nature of God and of his agency in the world. A brief glance at Christian history will disclose the extent to which this aspect of the revelation has been neglected by the Church, yet it is clearly present in the interpretation of the Incarnation of the Word as given by Athanasius, who insists that he came incognito in order that as man he might so live and work among men as to manifest the love that the Father has for all men and might win men to himself by the persuasive power of his own personality and the inherent truth of his life; the aim of drawing men to himself was, furthermore, that they might come to know the Father and to realize that he, to whom they come in his incarnate life, is indeed "not man only, but also God, and the Word and Wisdom of the true God."[52]

Section 17 describes in great detail the ubiquity of the Word so as to leave no possibility of misunderstanding in the mind of the reader as to who he is whose human life and works are being described. Athanasius enunciates here with great clarity a doctrine of the immanence of God the Word, who, while present in the whole of creation, is at once distinct in being from the universe and present in all things by his own power. It was this metaphysical analysis of the various operations of God in the world which convinced Whitehead that the Alexandrians had provided answers to questions which his investigations had led him to ask but for which he had been unable to frame suitable answers. "They considered the general question, how the primordial Being, who is the source of the inevitable recurrence of the world towards order, shares his nature with the world."[53] Athanasius, in the following passage, seeks to interpret the relationship and the operations of God in the world in terminology which would be particularly acceptable to Whitehead and to all who are interested in discovering some way to speak of the creative process of the universe in Christian terms.

[50] Ibid., sec. 16 (LCC,III, p. 70).
[51] Collect for the Second Sunday after Easter, *Book of Common Prayer*.
[52] Athanasius, *On the Incarnation*, sec. 16.
[53] Whitehead, *AI*, p. 166.

Athanasius explains with the utmost care that it is the creative Word, who gives order to all things and whose providence is revealed "over all and in all"

> ... and giving life to each thing and all things, including the whole without being included, but being in his own Father alone wholly and in every respect—thus, even while present in a human body and himself quickening it, he was, without inconsistency, quickening the universe as well, and was in every process of nature, and was outside the whole, and while known from the body by his works, he was none the less manifest from the working of the universe as well.[54]

It is important to note the distinctions which are made here; the Word is declared to be in the Father in his full being. Athanasius is drawing upon the Johannine doctrine that the Son dwells in the Father's bosom, even while he is living out his incarnate life on earth.[55] The Word, Athanasius maintains, was both transcendent and immanent at one and the same time, and the fact of the Incarnation, while it was a new initiative on God's part on behalf of mankind, did not in any way disturb or alter the fact of the transcendence of the Word in his immanence. The Word, he declares, was in the process of nature, yet outside the whole, and while manifest in the body by his works, was, nonetheless, "dwelling in the bosom of the Father," implying that the Father himself is working in the world in and through all his works. Athanasius is able to say these things now without fear of being misunderstood, because of his prior insistence upon the recognition of the Creative activity of the Word in bringing the world into being. He is the world's creator and sustainer, who in his incarnate life has become its redeemer.

Because he is the world's creator, the Word is able to be three things all at the same time; the limitations accepted in his humanity do not in any way interfere with his other spheres of operation. Athanasius is well aware of the mystery of that of which he speaks; he simply re-affirms that which has been disclosed in revelation and which must be maintained in the mind as simultaneously fact if we would avoid falling into error; he concludes, ". . . this was the wonderful thing that he was at once walking as man, and as Word was quickening all things, and as the Son was dwelling with the Father."[56] By insisting that the primordial Being who has given existence and order to the universe now dwells as man among men, Athanasius is able to avoid the dilemma in which Whitehead became involved in *Process and Reality* by defining God as less than ultimate; Whitehead, we will recall, ended up with God and the world as the contrasted opposites in terms of which Creativity is said to be achieving its supreme task, God being conceived as the conceptual pole in the twin polarities which constitute the process,[57] the ultimate nature and meaning of which remains unexplained.

[54] Athanasius, *On the Incarnation*, sec. 17 (LCC,III, p. 71).
[55] John 1:18.
[56] Athanasius, *On the Incarnation*, sec. 17.
[57] Whitehead, *PR*, pp. 528-29 (492-94).

Whitehead's problem here stems from the fact that his system is based upon an inadequate evaluation of the "creativity" which he has declared to be the ultimate in the philosophy of organism; he has not pushed far enough back in arriving at his category of the ultimate. The creativity, which he observes to be everywhere operative throughout the universe, is evidence of something more fundamental lying behind it and causing the universe to become in this manner; the creativity is an expression of that which is truly ultimate, and without which no explanation can be complete. Through revelation this ultimate has been disclosed to mankind as creative Love, the love of a personal God who while transcendent, is at the same time immanent and actively at work in the world. Athanasius is able to understand and to speak of the creation by the Word of God because he has received the revelation of God in Christ; he is able to speak of the creation by the Word because he has clearly identified the Word as the Word of the Father and the only begotten Son. By his insistence that even while in his Incarnate life the Word was "without inconsistency, quickening the universe as well, and was in every process of nature,"[58] Athanasius is laying the foundations for the Christian understanding of the universe as disclosed in contemporary scientific investigation, and is overcoming the contradictions into which Whitehead's attempt led him. The Creative Love by whose agency the world came into existence is himself personal and is operative within the world in both creation and re-creation.

Our investigation of the Plotinian hierarchy[59] disclosed that neither the One nor the Intellectual-Principle of his system has any commerce with the world, except through the Soul which is described by Plotinus as an image of the Intellectual-Principle and is the active agent in bringing the world into being. We noted, in our comparison of Plotinus with Whitehead[60] that, while there is a certain similarity between the World Soul of Plotinus and the "consequent nature" of God in *Process and Reality,* inasmuch as each is said to be imperfect and to be in process of becoming, yet there is an evident contrast insofar as for Plotinus the Soul attains reality only as it separates itself from sense and process and presses upward in contemplation of the One, whereas for Whitehead, God is conceived as immanent and his "consequent nature" is in process of becoming with the actualization of the world in the temporal process. Whitehead envisages the time when the creative process will itself be gathered up into God, and only when this is accomplished will God be fully expressed in and through the process of the universe. Our study of Athanasius' doctrine of the Incarnation discloses that it is just at the point at which the contrast between Athanasius and Plotinus is most acute that Whitehead discovered the superiority of the Christian doctrine of the immanence of God over the Platonic. His criticism of the Platonic explanation is that "Plato's answer is invariably framed in terms of mere dramatic imitation,"[61] with the

[58] Athanasius, *On the Incarnation,* sec. 17.
[59] See above, pp. 123ff.
[60] See above, pp. 130ff.
[61] Whitehead, *AI,* p. 215.

consequence that "the World, for Plato, includes only the image of God, and imitations of his ideas, and never God and his ideas."[62] Whitehead's philosophy requires a doctrine of the immanence of God in a world which is conceived as real, inasmuch as it is the outcome of his creative activity and possesses that reality which is given to it by God, its creator and sustainer.

The Victory of the Cross

Recalling that the second phase of Whitehead's discovery is constituted in his recognition of the uniqueness of Jesus Christ as a "revelation in act, of that which Plato had divined in theory,"[63] and that, in the life of Jesus as portrayed in the New Testament, he has been impressed by the stark reality of the suffering and agony of the Cross and the manner in which the account is recorded "with the authority of supreme victory,"[64] it will be important for purposes of our study to examine briefly Athanasius' explanation of the meaning of the crucifixion. Athanasius clearly adopts the great theme of the Fourth Gospel that the Cross is the victory. By his death, Christ wrought a twofold redemption in which death is thought of in one aspect as a debt which had to be paid on behalf of the whole human race, and on the other is viewed as a process which had to be effected by God, by which the process of corruption which resulted from human sin might be reversed and man might be started on the way of redemption. Christ, says Athanasius, accepted on the Cross and endured a death inflicted by his enemies, in order that he himself might be believed to be the life, and death be brought utterly to nought. The death which they thought to inflict as a disgrace was actually a monument to victory against death itself; and, moreover, the resurrection was on the third day in order that the very people who had witnessed his death upon the Cross might be witnesses of his resurrection also.[65]

The focus of the argument here, as in other aspects of Athanasius' theology, is essentially practical; the historical facts of the events of the life and death of Jesus receive further corroboration and their interpretation is confirmed by the effects in the lives of those who come to put their trust in him. That death is destroyed is evident from the fact that it is despised by all Christ's disciples who choose rather to die than to deny their faith in him. They are quite willing to die, he suggests, because they know that through death they begin to live and to become incorruptible through the resurrection, and he asks the question: "Who is so incredulous... as not to see and infer that Christ, to whom the martyrs witness, himself supplies and gives to each the victory over death, depriving him [i.e., death] of all his power in each one of them that hold his faith and bear the sign of the Cross?"[66] At this

---

[62] Ibid.
[63] Ibid., p. 214.
[64] Ibid.
[65] Athanasius, *On the Incarnation*, secs. 24 and 25 (LCC,III, pp. 78-79).
[66] Ibid., sec. 29 (LCC,III, p. 83).

point Athanasius is applying his interpretation of the Incarnation and the Cross to the present experience of the Church in its life of witness; the present power of Christ to sustain men throughout the ordeal of persecution is itself a principal proof of the reality of the resurrection, because it is a demonstration that God who was operative in and through his life is presently at work in the lives of the martyrs. A further evidence is found in the power of the Saviour in persuading so great a multitude from every side, from Greece and from foreign parts, to come over to his faith and obey his teaching. In the face of such evidence of the present influence of Christ, Athanasius asks, ". . . will anyone still hold his mind in doubt whether a resurrection has been accomplished by the Saviour, and whether Christ is alive, or rather is himself the life?"[67]

The whole point of the arguments of this section is to bring home to his readers that Christ works by persuading the minds of men of the truth of the Gospel, and that he does this, demonstrating that he is alive and present just as truly as he was throughout his ministry on earth, with the additional achievement that through the Cross he has won the victory on behalf of all men, and that his victory becomes theirs as they put their faith in him and become his servants in the work of reconciliation. Athanasius spells out the variety of the works which Christ is invisibly performing in the lives of men, drawing them "to religion, persuading to virtue, teaching of immortality, leading on to a desire for heavenly things, revealing the knowledge of the Father, inspiring strength to meet death, showing himself to each one";[68] he piles up the evidences of the power of Christ in the community in the cessation of magic, the end of witchcraft, the desertion of idols and the departure of men from evil ways. Throughout these sections of the work Athanasius is reiterating the twin themes which constitute the first two phases of Whitehead's discovery, namely, the revelation of God as a persuasive agency, as disclosed in the life and works of Christ and the portrayal of the Cross as the victory.

This theme is carried forward in an appeal to Jewish readers, to whom he speaks of Christ as "the King of Creation"[69] and declares that his death has a cosmic significance. "He it is that was crucified before the sun and all creation as witnesses, and before those who put him to death: and by his death has salvation come to all, and all creation been ransomed."[70] A final appeal addressed to Greeks calls upon them to observe that Christ has in fact persuaded the whole world "to worship one and the same Lord, and through him God, even his Father."[71] He contrasts the failure of the philosophers to win support for their theories with the amazing success of Christ in persuading men to his ways. The wonder, he says, is before the eyes of all that

[67] Ibid., sec. 30 (LCC,III, p. 84).
[68] Ibid., sec. 31 (LCC, III, p. 85).
[69] Ibid., sec. 37 (LCC,III, p. 91).
[70] Ibid.
[71] Ibid., sec. 46 (LCC,III, p. 101).

... while the wise among the Greeks had written so much, and were unable to persuade even a few from their own neighbourhood, concerning immortality and a virtuous life, Christ alone, by ordinary language and by men not clever with the tongue, has throughout all the world persuaded whole churches [assemblies] full of men to despise death, and to mind the things of immortality . . . .[72]

The transforming power of Christ is further illustrated by the fact that when men have come over to his school they "no longer mind the things of war; but all is peace with them, and from henceforth what makes for friendship is to their liking."[73] What Athanasius is maintaining throughout this section of the work on the Incarnation would be particularly to Whitehead's liking, for this is virtually what he is attempting to express in section IV of the final chapter of *Process and Reality*, in his description of the "consequent" nature of God. Whitehead seeks to speak of the present creative and redemptive activity of God in the world under the image of "the patience of God"[74] who, he declares, is "tenderly saving the turmoil of the intermediate world by the completion of his own nature,"[75] in which God functions as a persuasive agency at work in the world. There is much in Athanasius' doctrine of the Incarnation which would appeal to Whitehead, but there are aspects of Whitehead's language about God in *Process and Reality* which will come under question when we consider Athanasius' arguments against the Arians. To these we must now turn, but space does not permit us to do more than analyze those aspects of the argument which have a particular bearing upon problems with which Whitehead became involved in *Process and Reality*. For this purpose we will investigate briefly the *Discourses against the Arians*.

Athanasius' Arguments against the Arians

Concern for the redemption wrought in Christ as the central message of the Church, and as giving meaning and purpose to all aspects of its life, worship and service, is the guiding principle in all the polemical writings of Athanasius. "He had not been thus worshipped, nor been thus spoken of, were he a creature merely,"[76] he declares, and reminds his readers that when Scripture speaks of the Word, "it does not understand Him as being in the number of *all*, but places Him with the Father, as Him in whom providence and salvation for *all* are wrought and effected by the Father."[77] Athanasius attacks the Arian suggestion that the Son "was not before his generation,"[78] and that "once he was not."[79] If Arius is right in his opinion, then the Eternal

[72] Ibid., sec. 47 (LCC,III, p. 102).
[73] Ibid., sec. 51 (LCC,III, p. 106).
[74] Whitehead, *PR*, p. 525 (490).
[75] Ibid.
[76] Athanasius, *Four Discourses*, II, xvi, 24.
[77] Ibid., II, xvii, 24.
[78] Ibid., I, ii, 5.
[79] Ibid.

God is found to be not eternal inasmuch as the Son and Holy Spirit are added to him, and so, while once there was not a Trinity, now there is one, and God is declared to be "deficient, before the Son was generated, and complete when he had come to be."[80]

Furthermore, according to the Arians, the Son is a creature and so "the Three is discovered to be unlike Itself, consisting of strange and alien natures and substances."[81] This, Athanasius points out, is to destroy the Triad and to fall into the worst form of polytheism. "What sort of a worship is this, which is not even like itself, but is in process of completion as time goes on?"[82] If you admit two additions to God, there is no logical reason why there should not be a whole succession of acquisitions to his nature. But this is not the Christian interpretation of God; for them "there is an eternal and one Godhead in a Three, and there is one Glory of the Holy Three."[83] It belongs to Greeks, Athanasius suggests, "to introduce a general Trinity, and to level it with things generate; for these do admit of deficiencies and additions,"[84] deliberately contrasting the Christian Trinity with that of Plotinus, in which each successive emanation out from the One is a lesser reality than that above it, in a scale descending to the material world, and in which Plotinus describes the World Soul as a "child born imperfect in comparison with"[85] the Intellectual-Principle, and that it must for its perfecting look to the Divine Mind.

This whole series of arguments of Athanasius against the Arians exposes the foundational weaknesses of Whitehead's definitions of the nature of God in *Process and Reality*, in which God is declared to be the creature of "creativity" and his "consequent" nature is said to be in process of becoming. In spite of the attempts of interpreters to minimize the implications of this suggestion that God is a creature,[86] a careful reading of *Process and Reality* leaves no room for doubt that Whitehead intended to allow God only such reality as reduces him to a status less than the ultimate in the system, for he explicitly states that God is the "outcome of creativity."[87] This would seem to be one major area in which Athanasius helped Whitehead to discern inadequacies in the Platonic conception of God as finite. Athanasius is equally emphatic on the unsuitability of any conception of God as in process of becoming and it is evident that the whole area of experience which Whitehead was endeavouring to describe by his designation of God as "consequent" will require reconsideration. Metaphysically, Whitehead's conception of God in *Process and Reality* resembles that of the Arians; Whitehead, indeed, sought to avoid the conception of utter transcen-

[80] Ibid., I, vi, 17.
[81] Ibid.
[82] Ibid.
[83] Ibid., I, vi, 18.
[84] Ibid.
[85] Plotinus, *Enneads*, V. 1,3 (MacKenna trans., p. 371); also see above, p. 133.
[86] John B. Cobb, Jr., *A Christian Natural Theology* (Philadelphia: Westminster Press, 1965), pp. 206f.
[87] Whitehead, *PR*, p. 135 (122).

dence of God which was a feature of the Arian creed, but in the final issue, when it became necessary to hypostasize "Creativity," and that without any further definition, we have an ultimate which is as unknowable as the Arian God. Against all such attempts at dividing up the nature of God, Athanasius asserts that "the Triad is not originated; but there is an eternal and one Godhead in a Triad, and there is one glory of the Holy Triad."[88]

Athanasius solves the problem by considering the three Persons of Father, Son and Holy Spirit as internal relations within the Divine Unity, and he develops a variety of arguments in defence of his statement. In the life and worship of the Church, the Spirit and the Son are glorified, together with the Father and have been so from Apostolic times. The Arian teaching renders all such worship blasphemous. Why, asks Athanasius, is the Son named together with the Father in the baptismal consecration, unless he is of one Substance with the Father,[89] and finally, the Arian doctrine undermines the Christian conception of Salvation. If the Son is a mere creature, and does not know the Father, as the Arians say, how can he reveal the Father? The whole conception of our union with God through Christ becomes impossible if Christ is conceived as a mere creature.

Athanasius, however, was concerned with much more than merely countering the arguments of the Arians; what was called for was a clear statement, in terms of contemporary thought, of what the Christian Church understood its faith to mean, and this Athanasius proceeded to formulate. The problem was extremely complicated by the fact that three conflicting triadic conceptions of the divine nature were contending for the minds of men at this time:
  (i) The Neo-Platonic triad:
        The One, utterly transcendent and beyond Being, is also called the Good, but is beyond mind; it is strictly impossible to speak of the One, yet it is declared to be the source of all reality, to It all seek to return;
        The Intellectual-Principle, Being, and Mind, is also the World of the Platonic Forms; is the causal principle, an emanation from the One; is equivalent to Plato's Demiurge;
        Soul is an emanation from the Intellectual-Principle, is the active agent in the world of process; is divided into two parts: (a) a higher Soul, akin to Mind and (b) a lower Soul, Nature, the Soul of the phenomenal world.
        A Triad of three unequal hypostases in descending order or priority by emanation from the One.
  (ii) The Arian triad:
        God is absolutely unique and utterly transcendent, the unoriginate source of all; is incomprehensible and utterly unknowable.

---

[88] Athanasius, *Four Discourses,* I, vi, 18.
[89] Ibid., II, xviii, 41.

The Word or Son is declared to be a creature or thing made; had a beginning; can have no direct communion with, no direct knowledge of, the Father; is liable to change and to sin; is not truly God, but merely so by courtesy; yet, is creator of all else.

The Holy Spirit is a created being, under the Son.

A Triad of three persons, each of different essence, in descending order of priority, the First alone being truly God.

(iii) The Christian doctrine of Father, Son and Holy Spirit, Three persons in one God, as disclosed in the person and work of Jesus Christ and as held by the Church from the earliest times.

Obviously, these three diverse views as to the nature of ultimate reality cannot all be true and if Christianity is to claim the attention of men's minds, it must be clearly differentiated from both of these alternative schemes.

Athanasius had inherited from Origen a train of thought according to which the Logos, begotten everlastingly from the Father, is his Son eternally existing, and distinct personally from the Father. In the Second *Discourse* against the Arians, Athanasius draws out the implications of this doctrine in a series of similes designed to refute the Arian arguments as to the creatureliness of the Son. God, he states, can never be without his Word, any more than the light can cease to shine or the river source to flow. The Son must, therefore, exist eternally alongside the Father.[90] This point is pressed home in the Third *Discourse,* by a further implication to the effect that "just as the Father is always good by nature, so He is by nature always generative" (ἀεὶ γεννητικός).[91] The language of generation employed here by Athanasius has some similarity to the language of Plotinus, who compares the generation of the Intellectual-Principle from the One to "the brilliant light encircling the sun and ceaselessly generated from that unchanging substance";[92] but at this point all similarity ceases. The Platonist, in consistency to his principles, proceeds with the cautionary note: "At the same time, the offspring is always minor";[93] that which is generated is always, with Plotinus, subordinate to the Hypostasis from which it emanates. The thought of the First and the Second Hypostases in the divine hierarchy being identical in essence or importance was unthinkable for Plotinus even as it was for the Arians. Arius, in the *Thalia,* had urged his readers, "Understand that the One was; but the Two was not, before it was in existence."[94] Plotinus, in speaking of that which is generated from the One, explains that "this greatest, later than the divine unity, must be the Divine Mind, and it must be the second of all existence, for it is that which sees the One on which alone it leans while the First has no need whatever of it."[95] In the Plotinian system the One must be

[90] Ibid., II, xviii, 32, 33.
[91] Ibid., III, xxx, 66.
[92] Plotinus, *Enneads,* V. 1,6 (Mackenna trans., p. 374).
[93] Ibid.
[94] Arius, in the *Thalia,* as quoted by Athanasius, in *De Synodis,* II:15.
[95] Plotinus, *Enneads,* V. 1,6 (MacKenna trans., p. 374).

entirely self-sufficient, and there must be no movement of the One in the direction of that which comes after it; the movement of love for the Platonist is always from the begotten to the begetter—"the offspring must seek and love the begetter."[96]

We have here arrived at the point of extreme contrast between the Platonic and the Christian world views; there is no possibility in the Plotinian hierarchy for an affirmation such as "the Father loveth the Son";[97] the whole Johannine theology of the coinherence of the Father and the Son was unthinkable for Plotinus. Athanasius' solution to the deficiencies in the Plotinian hierarchy is also the solution to the similar problem faced by Whitehead in *Process and Reality*. Whitehead's attempt to bridge the gap and account for the universe failed in spite of his efforts in selecting an impersonal ultimate and developing his conception of the "consequent" nature of God. The Christian solution of insisting upon the same reality existing in each of the three Hypostases of the One God is the answer to the problems posed by both Plotinus and Whitehead. The secret of Athanasius' success is in his insistence upon retention of personality in God as disclosed in and through Jesus Christ. Plotinus' One is beyond Being and utterly unknowable, does not even know Itself, yet is declared to be the source of all being; Whitehead's "creativity" is without a character of its own, and yet is exemplified in everything that is; it does not initiate action any more than does Plotinus' One because it is an impersonal principle and is always referred to by Whitehead as "it" even as Plotinus refers to the One as "It."

Athanasius' answer that the Father, Son and Holy Spirit are One God overcomes the problem of the separation of God and the World by declaring that God is fully involved in every operation of all Three. He is insistent that the generation of the Son is an eternal process inherent in God's very nature and that the Son, as the Father's offspring, must be really distinct from him, and also eternal. "Two they are because the Father is Father and not the Son and the Son is Son and not the Father."[98] The basic thought here is that God can never be without his Son—the very term "father" implies "son" as simultaneously being—but as Son he is begotten of the Father and since God is without change, the begetting of the Son must be an eternal act. The Father is everlastingly generative by nature. Athanasius is here calling upon what he had learned from Origen and is echoing his predecessor, Alexander of Alexandria. He refrains from using the word hypostasis with its possibility of misinterpretation to imply tri-theism, and simply states that the Son is distinct from the Father.

Athanasius presses on to draw the logical implications from the doctrine of the eternal generation, that the Son who is begotten from the nature of the Father is of the same essence with the Father, and consequently, is different in nature from creatures and other in sub-

[96] Ibid.
[97] John 5:20.
[98] Athanasius, *Four Discourses*, III, xxiii, 4.

stance (οὐσία). He belongs to the Essence of the Father; (at this stage in the discussion, Athanasius employs the phrase "Homophyes" rather than "Homoosios";) as a result, in so far as the Father and the Son are distinct, they are like each other; the Son is the Image of the Father; he is the stream and the Father is the source; he is the brightness and the Father is the Light. "Nor is this Form of the Godhead partial merely, but the fulness of the Father's Godhead is the Being of the Son."[99] Athanasius is here working out his doctrine of the περιχώρησις or "coinherence" of the Persons in "identity of Godhead and the unity of Essence,"[100] and arriving at the logical implications of the Nicaean formula. In so far as we speak of the Godhead and apply Homoousios to the relation of the Son to the Father, our language involves the conclusion of the identity of Essence; there is a Oneness of nature between the Two, and so we have the paradoxical doctrine of the clear distinction between the Father and the Son and, at the same time, the assertion of an indivisible stuff of Godhead eternally existing as Father and as Son.

Athanasius on the Holy Spirit

Athanasius' doctrine of the Trinity is not complete until, faced with a situation in which a group of people who, while they accept the Homoousion of the Son, insist on speaking of the Holy Spirit as a thing made and a creature, and in response to an appeal from Serapion, bishop of Thmuis, he formulates, in a series of *Letters*, the Christian doctrine of the Holy Spirit.[101] His method here is once again to appeal to the Scriptures, to the constant practice and usage of the Church, and finally to the logical implications of the Arian assertion of the creatureliness of the Spirit. The Holy Spirit, he argues, is unique in the strict sense of the word, while, by their very nature, creatures are multiple. There can be only one Holy Spirit, even as the Father is One and the Son is One. There can, moreover, be only one Sanctification which is operated by the Father, through the Son, with or in the Spirit. He is the Spirit of whom Christ spoke, whom he promised, and whom he gives. Inasmuch as the Spirit comes from the Son and the Son is unique, therefore, the grace which comes from him must also be perfect and unique. The Spirit is immutable, invariable, and unchanging, while creatures, by their very nature, are constantly changing. The Spirit shares the immutability of the Son, as the Son shares the immutability of the Father.

The creatures, moreover, are limited each to their own locality, whereas the Holy Spirit is Infinite, fills the world, and is omnipotent. The Holy Spirit is eternal, while the creatures did not exist before they were brought into existence in this world. His argument is that the Holy Triad is eternal, and the Spirit, therefore, cannot be a creature. In-

[99] Ibid., III, xxiii, 6.
[100] Ibid., III, xxiii, 3.
[101] Athanasius, *The Letters of Saint Athanasius Concerning the Holy Spirit*, trans. by C. R. B. Shapland (London: Epworth Press, 1951).

deed, so far from being contingent, and from having been brought into existence like the creatures, the Holy Spirit partakes in the act of creation. According to the Scriptures, the Son is as much a creator as the Father, and the Spirit collaborates with him. This point is argued in the First Letter, "But if the Father, through the Word, in the Holy Spirit, creates and renews all things, what likeness or kinship is there between the Creator and the creatures? How could he possibly be a creature, in whom all things are created?"[102] This full cooperation of the Three Persons in every creative work is reiterated again in the Third *Letter,* in which Athanasius states: "The Father creates all things through the Word in the Spirit; for where the Word is, there is the Spirit also, and the things which are created through the Word have their vital strength out of the Spirit from the Word."[103] We meet here, quite clearly, an extension of Athanasius' conception of the mode of God's operations in the world. In the treatise on the Incarnation, the works of creation and of sanctification were all ascribed to the Word and to the Incarnate and glorified Lord; the Church had not at this time clarified its doctrine of the Holy Spirit, and Athanasius is hesitant to go beyond the definition in a positive statement, but is here working out the arguments which emphasize the Oneness of the Holy Three and will enter into the vocabulary of the Church in speaking about the Holy Spirit. Here the Spirit, the Third member of the holy Triad, is said to be the mode of God's operation in both creation and sanctification, and Athanasius' doctrine of the Trinity is complete. As summarized in the latter part of the First Letter, it is an affirmation of the mutual immanence of the Father, Son and Holy Spirit, in the One Divine Reality,

> For the Holy and blessed Triad is indivisible and one in itself. When mention is made of the Father, there is included also His Word, and the Spirit who is in the Son. If the Son is named, the Father is in the Son, and the Spirit is not outside the Word. For there is from the Father one grace which is fulfilled through the Son in the Holy Spirit; and there is one divine nature, and one God "who is over all and through all and in all" (Ephes. 4:6).[104]

Here we have the fully developed doctrine of the Trinity in which there is declared to be an equality of nature and of operations of all three divine Persons.

"There is from the Father one grace which is fulfilled through the Son in the Holy Spirit."[105] Athanasius develops this theme; the Spirit, he says, is called unction and he is seal and pertains to the Word who anoints and seals. For the unction has the fragrance and odour of him who anoints; he quotes Paul, in the Second Letter to the Corinthians, to the effect that Christians are "the fragrance of Christ."[106] The argu-

[102] Ibid., Letter I,24, p. 126.
[103] Ibid., III,4, p. 173.
[104] Ibid., I, 14, pp. 93-94.
[105] Ibid.
[106] 2 Cor. 2:15.

ment of the "seal" is developed; the seal has the form of Christ who seals, and those who are sealed partake of it, being conformed to it; as the apostle says: "My little children, for whom I am again in travail until Christ be formed in you."[107] Being thus sealed, we are duly made, as Peter puts it, "sharers in the divine nature";[108] and thus, Athanasius concludes, all creation partakes of the Word in the Spirit. Moreover, it is through the Spirit that we are all said to be partakers of God. For the Apostle says, "Know ye not that ye are a temple of God and that the Spirit of God dwelleth in you?"[109] In the Spirit the Word makes glorious the creation, and, by bestowing upon it divine life and sonship, draws it to the Father. But that which joins creation to the Word cannot belong to the creatures; and that which bestows sonship upon the creation could not be alien from the Son. The Spirit, therefore, does not belong to things originated; he pertains to the Godhead of the Father, and in him the Word makes things originated divine. But he in whom creation is made divine cannot be outside the Godhead of the Father, and so the Spirit must be equally divine. There is one divine energy at work in the world, and consequently,

> when the Spirit comes to us, the Son will come and the Father, and they will make their abode within us. For the Triad is indivisible, and its Godhead is one; and there is one God, "over all and through all and in all" (Eph. 4:6). This is the faith of the Catholic Church.[110]

Athanasius has formulated the language by means of which it will be possible to speak of the sanctification of all of life by the mutual indwelling of the Three in One, who "make their abode within us." He is bringing together the insights of the Johannine and the Pauline theology and showing that they are in agreement. The *Letters* all dwell on the relation which the Spirit has to the other divine Persons. To Athanasius, the distinctions between the Father and the Son and the Spirit are real distinctions. He recognizes and affirms a relation of substantial identity—numerical unity—the One *Ousia* of the Three divine Persons; the unity is a necessary conclusion from his teaching on the Homoousios. The Holy Trinity is one God, and a corollary of this is the unity of substance in the Three divine Persons—the περιχώρησις.[111] The clear formulation of the doctrine of the Holy Spirit as the mode of God's operations in the world will have important insights to bring to the problems which Whitehead endeavoured to interpret by introducing the conception of the "consequent" nature of God in his system.

Athanasius' doctrine of the Trinity is now complete, and we find him, in the *Tome to the Antiochenes*, reiterating much of the thought of these *Letters*, in a document in which he seeks to win support from the Eastern part of the Church for the Nicaean formula; he is aware that at

[107] Gal. 4:19.
[108] 2 Peter 1:4.
[109] 1 Cor. 3:16-17.
[110] Athanasius, *Letters* (Shapland trans.), III,6, p. 176.
[111] See above, pp. 159-60.

this time, in A.D. 362, the differences between East and West are largely a matter of language and terminology. He accepts as satisfactory the confession of the Easterns that "they believed in a Holy Trinity, not a trinity in name only, but existing and subsisting in truth, 'both a Father truly existing and subsisting, and a Son truly substantial and subsisting, and a Holy Spirit subsisting and really existing do we acknowledge.'"[112] During discussion of these matters at the Council of Alexandria, Athanasius had heard from their own lips their interpretation of the meaning of these words, and they had assured him that at no time had they said there were three Gods or three beginnings, and that they would not tolerate any such opinions among their number, "but that they acknowledged a Holy Trinity but One Godhead, and one Beginning, and that the Son is coessential with the Father."[113] There is at this time a growing movement of the whole Church in the direction of accepting the implications of the formulary of Nicaea, namely, that the manifoldness in the nature of God, disclosed by the Incarnation of the Word, must be recognized to be within the Being of God, so that while we speak of the Three, this is not to speak of three Gods, but there is one Godhead and one worship. The Easterns have now affirmed Athanasius' faith, not only in the doctrine of the relations of the Father and the Son, but also in the Holy Spirit, affirming that "the Holy Spirit is not a creature, nor external, but proper to and inseparable from the Essence of the Father and the Son,"[114] recalling the language of the *Letters to Serapion.*

Summary of Athanasius' Contribution to Theology

We may briefly summarize the contribution of Athanasius to our understanding of the nature of God and of his relation to the world as follows:

1. God is both transcendent and immanent. He is the world's creator, who is immanent and at work in the world, without losing his transcendence. The creation is portrayed as a continuing process (activity), itself a disclosure of God in his works. An important insight as to procedure in the formulation of doctrine is found in Athanasius' insistence upon a clear formulation of the Christian doctrine of the Creation of the World by the Word of God "out of nothing" (drawing upon the insights of Christian faith to differentiate clearly what Christians understand about the relations of God and the created universe from all other contemporary views), as prerequisite to an understanding of the Incarnation.

2. The Christian message of the Incarnation of the Word of God has disclosed a manifoldness in the nature of God which is here recognized to be within the Being of God and so, while we speak of the Three and insist on the real distinctions of the Persons (Hypostases), this is not to speak of three Gods, but there is One Godhead and one worship;

---

[112] Athanasius, *Tomus Ad Antiochenos*, 5.
[113] Ibid.
[114] Ibid.

there is an identity of Essence and a mutual immanence and coinherence of the Three in every operation of God.

3. Having formulated the Christian doctrine of Creation, Athanasius was able to enunciate the conception of the Creator who is also the Redeemer. In the Incarnation, God is acting to redeem mankind by love; the transcendent Logos, who is the agent in Creation, himself pervading and sustaining the whole universe, alone could become the redeemer, because in coming into the world, he was coming to his own. In the Incarnation he is three things simultaneously: he who is the Transcendent Word, who pervades and sustains the whole universe, while continuing to fulfil these roles, now becomes particularized in his humanity, becoming fully man. The Incarnate Lord exemplified in his relations with men the outgoing love and forbearance of God, engaging in persuasive activity; having submitted himself to the conditions of man in society, he accepted the consequences in rejection and death upon the Cross. By accepting death at the hands of men, he triumphed over both sin and death, and won for mankind the offer of a deathless life. He also demonstrated in his own person what God intends for man, living a human life as God would have it lived. By living out a life under human conditions he has shown the way in which we too may respond to God and find fulfilment in him.

4. Man is declared to be a created being, created in the image of God, and able to share in the life of God without losing his creaturehood; the significance of "in his own image and likeness" is seen as the ability to become a person, involving freedom of choice and of action within a limited sphere. This is the essence of man's spirituality, and its safeguard necessitates that redemption must be an internal process, involving personal response to God on the part of free agents. It was this peculiar destiny of man which necessitated the Incarnation, life, and death of Christ to redeem him and to reverse the process of destruction which is at work within the life of mankind through their having rejected the light which was given to them.

5. All the manifold operations of God are from the Father, through the Word, and with or in the Holy Spirit. Consequent upon the Incarnation, the knowledge of God and of his salvation in Christ is made available to all men in and through the Church.

6. In and through the Incarnation, mankind has received new knowledge of God, so that God is no longer "ineffable, unknowable, incomprehensible," but is disclosed as eternally "Father," "Son" and "Holy Spirit"—three distinct Hypostases—in intimate relationship within the nature of the One God, and all of equal status and fully God. This is now seen as the essential contrast between the Christian and the Platonic conceptions of God.

Through the work of Athanasius and those who succeeded him, the Church emerged from the Arian struggle with a clearly formulated Christian doctrine of God. There followed a prolonged controversy on the problem as to how the Word, if fully divine, can become incarnate in the life of a man. This is the specifically Christological problem which emerged and was felt acutely only after the theologians had settled the problem of God. An examination of this question would take us outside the subject of this essay. Whitehead is aware of the significance of this problem and gives it as his judgment that the decision of the Church at Chalcedon for "the direct immanence of God in the one person of Christ" was a triumph of Christianity over paganism.[115] Metaphysically, this constituted a significant advance upon the Platonic categories of thought which had hitherto dominated the minds of men, and gave to Christianity an opportunity for its leaders to take the initiative in formulating a specifically Christian philosophy, and we must examine some of the insights which Whitehead discovered in the theology of Athanasius.

The Christian Solutions to Whitehead's Problems

Three important insights emerge from our investigation of the theology of Athanasius, in each of which the fully formulated Christian doctrine stands out as inherently superior to either of the Arian or the Plotinian alternatives. Whitehead acknowledges these as being turning points in his own recognition of the important contribution of the Christian theologians to thought.

On the one hand, he is impressed with the importance of the περιχώρησις, "a doctrine of mutual immanence in the divine nature,"[116] as a solution to the problem of speaking of the "multiplicity" in the nature of God without falling into contradiction. Those who deny that there is any significant development in Whitehead's concept of God beyond *Process and Reality* would do well to read again this significant chapter in *Adventures of Ideas*.[117] In the section in which the passage quoted above occurs, Whitehead is specifically contrasting the Platonic conception of God with the fully formulated Christian doctrine and rejecting the former in favour of the latter. Our analysis of the various attempts to speak about God has disclosed that at the very point at which both Plotinus and Arius contrast the extreme transcendence of the One with the clear subordination of the Second Hypostasis or Son as the case may be, Athanasius, drawing upon the disclosure of God's nature given in and through the revelation in Christ, is able to insist upon the Oneness of Essence of Father, Son and Holy Spirit. In the case of the relationship between the Father and the Son, he claims the reported words of Jesus in support of his formulation: "I and the Father are one,"[118] "I am in my Father and the Father in me,"[119] and "He that hath seen Me hath seen the Father,"[120] and concludes that "the fulness of the Father's Godhead is the Being of the Son, and the Son is whole God."[121]

---

[115] Whitehead, *AI*, p. 216; also see above, pp. 102-03.
[116] Ibid.; also see above, pp. 160 and 162.
[117] Ibid., Ch. X, "The New Reformation."
[118] John 10:30.
[119] John 14:10.
[120] John 14:9.
[121] Athanasius, *Four Discourses*, III, xxiii, 6.

Plotinus, by contrast, is at great pains to explain that "what comes from the Supreme cannot be identical with it and . . . the emanation, then, must be less good, that is to say, less self-sufficing."[122] His efforts to safeguard the uniqueness of the One by insisting that the emanation must be "single"[123] and that it must be "less good," because less self-sufficing, serve only to point up the contrast between God as portrayed in Plotinus' *Enneads* and God as disclosed in Christ.

Athanasius was able to press on beyond Plotinus at this point and to assert the identity of nature of the Second Person and the Third with the First in the Christian Triad, and to eliminate all traces of subordinationism within the divine nature. By drawing out the implications of the Christian Gospel of redemption through the Incarnation of the Word of God, he was able to demonstrate the error and contradiction in the Arian attempts to speak of God the Father as utterly transcendent and of the Son as a derivative Image. Athanasius realizes that, in speaking about the nature of God, the distinctions must be seen to be internal to the nature of the One God. He recommends that the terminology by which God has been disclosed in history is more appropriate and reiterates his argument that the Father is Father and not the Son; the Son is Son and not the Father; the Holy Spirit is proceeding from the Father and the Son; and that these are eternal relations in which the Three are mutually immanent each in the other so that all the operations of God are one. Whitehead recognizes this doctrine as the first step towards the solution of the problem of God and the world, which had been a major concern of the final chapter of *Process and Reality*.

There is, on the other hand, a sense in which the distinctions and the names by which we speak of God have reference to the operations of God, and it is in this aspect of the doctrine that we meet the second major contrast between the formulated Christian doctrine and opposing views. We only know God in and through his operations, through his disclosure of himself in the universe and within history, and in so far as we can see a distinction, we must find it in the activity of the Father, the Son and Holy Spirit. The Christian divine Persons are always in real relations with the world and man, and the doctrine of the mutual immanence of the Persons in each operation of God means that God as God is actively at work in the world. Once this has been established, it follows that the Incarnation was clearly the initiative of God undertaken "for us men and for our salvation."[124] In contrast, the Arian insistence upon the extreme transcendence of God precludes any real contact of God with the world, and their introduction of a created demigod fails to bridge the gap. Whitehead could not fail to notice the similarity, metaphysically, between his own system and that of Arius; an ultimate which is by definition "without a character of its own"[125] is

---

[122] Plotinus, *Enneads*, V. 3,15 (MacKenna trans., p. 396).
[123] Ibid.
[124] The Nicaean Creed.
[125] Whitehead, *PR*, p. 47 (42).

unsatisfactory as a principle of interpretation. The Plotinian triad was equally unsatisfactory in this respect, for Plotinus' One "neither knows itself nor is known in itself,"[126] and his Second Hypostasis, the Intellectual-Principle, gazes only upward towards the One. The Soul (declared to be but an image of the Intellectual-Principle) alone has contact with the phenomenal world.

In direct contrast to this extreme transcendentalism, the Christian formula of faith confesses that the Father is the creator of heaven and earth—of things visible and invisible. Athanasius insists upon this as the foundation upon which our understanding of God and Man and the relations between them must rest. Secondly, the Nicaean formula affirms and Athanasius argues that the creation was effected by the Word, incorporating the full implications of the Johannine doctrine of the Logos Incarnate. In his *Letters* to Serapion, this is further developed to include the operation of the Holy Spirit as the mode of God's operations in the world. The Father creates all things through the Son and in the Holy Spirit. The Son is the redeemer of the world who "for us men and for our salvation, came down, becoming enfleshed (ἐνανθρωπήσαντα),"[127] "and was crucified also for us, under Pontius Pilate."[128] The creator became the redeemer and the revealer of the Father and accepted death for himself, in order that he might cancel out its power over men and that he might re-create them. The Holy Spirit is the Creator Spirit, the mode of God's operations in the world, who spoke by the prophets and who indwells the lives of the members of the Church, revealing to them what is the mind of Christ. What the Christian theologians affirm here is diametrically opposite to what Plotinus was able to say about the relations between the Three Hypostases in his system, in which the One alone is properly called God. This doctrine of the Creator and sustainer who himself became the redeemer (by entering into and becoming a part of that which he has created in order that he might bring men into a relationship of reconciliation) provides the basis for an interpretation of the major problems which remained unsolved at the conclusion of *Process and Reality*.

Behind the specific questions which Whitehead was seeking to resolve was his search for a way of speaking of God as immanent without denying his transcendence, the question as to "how the primordial Being, who is the source of the inevitable recurrence of the world towards order, shares his nature with the world."[129] He is convinced that "in some sense he is a component in the nature of all fugitive things."[130] His own attempts to speak of these various functions by introducing the conceptions of God as "primordial" and as "conse-

---

[126] Plotinus, *Enneads*, V. 3,13 (MacKenna trans., p. 396).

[127] The Creed of Nicaea, as quoted in the Letter of Eusebius of Caesarea, cf. H. M. Gwatkin, *Selections from Early Writers Illustrative of Church History to the Time of Constantine* (London: Macmillan, 1911; first edition, 1893), pp. 180ff.

[128] The Old Roman Creed, cf. J. N. D. Kelly, *Early Christian Creeds* (London: Longman's, 1950), p. 102.

[129] Whitehead, *AI*, p. 166.

[130] Ibid.

quent" helped to call attention to the complexity of the problem, but in the end failed to provide a wholly satisfactory interpretation of the activity of God in the world. The language of emanations as employed by Plotinus, is equally unsatisfactory, because it leaves the material world without real significance. Athanasius, by insisting upon the creation of the world by God out of nothing, was able to differentiate clearly between God and the world, and to speak of God as actively at work in the world "in every process of nature,"[131] quickening and sustaining it throughout, yet without being himself tied to the universe, otherwise than by the love which led to its creation. In every operation he remains God, the creator, and the world is his created universe.

Athanasius makes much of the fact that even human sin and rebellion did not prevent God from acting in the world on our behalf, but, on the contrary, "the reason of his coming down was because of us, and that our transgression called forth the loving-kindness of the Word, that the Lord should both make haste to help us and appear among men."[132] He shared our nature and became one of us in order that he might bring us to God. The theme receives its full development when Athanasius comes to speak of the work of the Spirit in sanctification of the soul. Having already insisted, in his earlier work, the *contra Gentes,* that all creation, in the very fact of its existence, partakes of the Word,[133] and having reiterated this in the treatise on the Incarnation,[134] he carries the doctrine of creation forward to the full Christian conception that "the Father creates all things through the Word in the Spirit."[135] It is through the Spirit, he urges, quoting Paul, that we are all said to be partakers of God.

Whitehead discerns in this fully developed Christian doctrine, according to which "the existents in nature are sharing in the nature of the immanent God,"[136] "an important reconciliation between the doctrines of Imposed Law and Immanent Law."[137] In his chapter on "Laws of Nature"[138] he argues for the necessity for some doctrine of Imposed Law to provide the metaphysical structure which makes possible a universe. On the other hand, scientific investigation discloses a situation which convinces him of the necessity for some doctrine of Law as Immanent to account for the interrelatedness of all things. Approaching the study of the universe empirically, the scientist uncovers everywhere order, structure, pattern in nature, whether with powerful telescope he is surveying the vastness of the universe of stellar systems and spiral nebulae, or with the microscope is looking into the minute particles formed into variegated crystals. As he passes from the study of the inorganic to the organic the pattern becomes more clearly evident

---

[131] Athanasius, *On the Incarnation,* sec. 17 (LCC,III, p. 71).
[132] Ibid., sec. 4 (LCC,III, p. 59).
[133] Athanasius, *contra Gentes,* 41.
[134] Ibid.
[135] Athanasius, *Letters,* III,4.
[136] Whitehead, *AI,* p. 166.
[137] Ibid.
[138] Ibid., pp. 131ff.

and, in the life of man that which is inherent in every facet of nature comes to consciousness of itself, and we have the gradual emergence of free yet circumscribed personality and the purposeful activity which enables man to unlock many of the mysteries of nature and so to transform his world.

Everywhere there is structure, pattern, order, but everywhere there is also an element of spontaneity in the process of development. So far as the astronomers have been able to perceive, no two stellar systems are exactly alike; and this fact becomes immediately apparent in crystallography. No two patterns of frost crystals are identical. In man this element of spontaneity becomes a conscious valuation, leading to meaningful choice among alternatives and resulting in a life of purposeful activity with a view to changing his environment and adjusting himself to tensions inherent in the interrelationships of individuals in a highly structured society. Whitehead seeks to interpret this aspect of experience by suggesting that it constitutes the weaving of God's physical feelings upon his primordial conceptualization of the universe. He suggests that, inasmuch as there is emerging that which is novel, therefore, God, in the process of the universe, is acquiring a new nature and in this sense is himself in process of becoming. Our examination of the formulation of the Christian theology has shown this to be an unsatisfactory way in which to speak about God. Yet, there is the feature of the creative advance throughout the universe which must be accounted for. The evidence afforded by the sciences, physics, astronomy, chemistry, biology and in particular the recent advances in molecular biology have, as one exponent puts it, "heightened our realization that the universe is all of a piece, from the primeval 'gas' of fundamental particles to the brain of man . . . ."[139]

Christianity affirms that the universe is the result of the creative action of God—"no single thing was created without him,"[140] and that all the mysteries which are yet to be disclosed by scientific investigation will be found on examination to be further evidence of that creative purpose which initiated and sustains the self-creative process which we call the world and which has issued in the psycho-physical, self-conscious, spiritual being, man. The Christian doctrine of God has provided an answer to the problem of whence and why and to what end. Its designation of God the Father, the source of all, as creative love, and of his Word as the agency of God in bringing the universe into being, is completed by the doctrine of the Holy Spirit as the mode of God's operation in the world. Whether we speak of the Three as source and act and motion, the fact that God is conceived in personal terms introduces a new element of understanding and the doctrine of the immanence of God becomes meaningful in all consideration of the interrelationship of the manifoldness of the elements of the universe and the life of mankind. As Archbishop William Temple points out,

[139] A. R. Peacocke, "The Molecular Organization of Life," being Ch. III of I. T. Ramsey, ed., *Biology and Personality* (Oxford: Basil Blackwell, 1965), p. 36.
[140] John 1:3.

"personality, whether human or divine, is, in so far as it is immanent, a principle of variation,"[141] and he concludes that "if the immanent principle is personal, we must not only see the whole universe as the expression and utterance of His activity, but must expect to find in its course special characteristic and revealing acts, which are no more truly His than the rest, but do more fully express Him than the rest."[142] In the doctrine of the Trinity, the Christian theologians have provided an interpretation of the metaphysical structure, of the creative origination and sustaining power of the universe, and of the redemptive and recreative presence within and at all times operative, by which the world is being guided into the fulfilment of an eternal purpose of love embracing all mankind, and including all the ages.

[141] William Temple, *Nature, Man and God*, Gifford Lectures, 1932-33 (London: Macmillan, 1934), p. 295.
[142] Ibid., p. 296.

Chapter XII

The Completion of Whitehead's Ideas in the Christian Understanding of God, and the Re-formulation of the Cosmological Framework as the Basis for a Reconstruction in Theology

We are now in a position to evaluate Whitehead's employment of theological language and arrive at some conclusions as to the significance of his philosophical undertakings for the future of theological expression in the final quarter of the twentieth century. To this end it will be important to recapitulate, however briefly, the process of the development of Whitehead's thought about God and the world as indicated in his philosophical writings.

In an early work, *An Enquiry Concerning the Principles of Natural Knowledge*, published in 1919, Whitehead gives no indication of his awareness of the importance of the religious insights of mankind. He informs the reader that his aim is to bring three main streams of thought, the scientific, the mathematical and the philosophical to bear upon the problem of discovering a more adequate language for the interpretation of the universe as disclosed in scientific investigation. The religious stream of thought has not at this time been recognized formally as having a significant contribution to make towards a solution to the problem. Six years later, in the development of his metaphysical undertaking, he discovers the need for God as the principle of concretion, to account for the fact of there being a universe; God is here described as an attribute of the "substantial activity"[1] (later identified as "creativity"). In *Religion in the Making* God is said to be the principle of order making possible the visible world in a process in which the schematic background is basically Platonic and his study of World

---

[1] A. N. Whitehead, *Science and the Modern World* (reprint ed., 1933; Cambridge: Cambridge University Press, 1926), p. 216.

Religions has convinced Whitehead that the metaphysical sub-structure of the universe must be impersonal.

In his developed cosmology, *Process and Reality*, Whitehead elects to follow the framework of Plato's *Timaeus*, in which God or the gods are given a limited role in the ordering of a creative process. Because he was convinced of the necessity of an impersonal sub-structure for the universe, he was led to believe that the "substantial activity," now designated "creativity," would serve as a suitable ultimate principle for a dynamic universe in which process is ultimate. Our analysis has disclosed that this is one of the fundamental weaknesses of the system in that "creativity," as defined by Whitehead, is unable to carry the full extent of origination which the universe requires for its interpretation. Furthermore, we discovered that God, defined by Whitehead as the creature of creativity, is discovered in the final chapter to be involved in enclosure within the universe which as the principle of concretion and of order and limitation he has brought about. To extricate himself from the charge of pantheism, Whitehead now finds it necessary to hypostasize "Creativity,"[2] and to give to it all the qualities of purposive activity usually ascribed to a transcendent Creator. We were led to the conclusion that the ultimate categories of the System called for further elucidation before the system could meet the test of coherence and provide the interpretation of the universe for which it was designed.

Our analysis of the concluding sections of the final chapter of *Process and Reality* disclosed a twofold development in Whitehead's thought about God; he is being increasingly influenced by later developments in Platonism, and moving in the direction of a triadic hierarchy somewhat after the pattern of Plotinus; and on the other hand, ideas whose origin must be traced to the life and ministry of Jesus Christ and to the New Testament documents are coming more clearly into focus. At this point in Whitehead's development two conflicting cosmologies are confronting the one mind and call for further clarification of the thought of the philosopher and ultimately for decision as to which is more suitable to provide the final interpretation of the metaphysical scheme and of the universe whose description it was designed to elucidate.

Part Two of our investigation has disclosed that Whitehead continued his search for a more adequate way of speaking about ultimate reality beyond the confines of *Process and Reality*. In the Louis Clark Vanuxem Foundation Lectures which Whitehead delivered in March of 1929,[3] his examination of biological theories of evolution convinced him of the need for some counter-agency to account for the fact that in a universe which appears physically to be wasting away, the trend of evolution has been upwards, issuing in the development of reason in

[2] A. N. Whitehead, *Process and Reality: An Essay in Cosmology* (New York: Harper Torchbooks, 1960; first published, New York: Macmillan, 1929), p. 528 (492-93).

[3] A. N. Whitehead, *The Function of Reason* (Beacon Paperback ed., 1958; Princeton: Princeton University Press, 1929), pp. 24-27.

one species, particularly the emergence of speculative imagination, creative of the future. We were not surprised to find that his next major philosophical publication was entitled *Adventures of Ideas*, and constituted an investigation into the effect of two or three ideas whose ferment has promoted the drift of mankind towards civilization. Published in September 1932, this document contains series of lectures which had been delivered during the intervening three years, including the four Mary Flexner Lectures delivered during the academic year 1929-30.[4]

In a study on Laws of Nature and on Cosmologies, Whitehead calls for a fusion of the doctrines of Imposed Law and Immanent Law which, he declares, had been proposed by Plato in his later Dialogues, and was the great achievement of the theologians of Alexandria[5] four to six hundred years later, and he concludes that the reconciliation which they effected between Imposed Law and Immanent Law "arises from the fact that the existents in nature are sharing in the nature of the immanent God."[6] At this point in time, in the year 1929-30 Whitehead is commencing his critical comparison of the Platonic with the Christian conception of God, an examination which is carried forward in a discussion which is introduced for the first time in *Adventures of Ideas*, in 1932, in which Whitehead submits to a devastating criticism the Platonic conception of the relationship between God and the World, as quite unsuitable for the solution of the problems before the metaphysician. "The World, for Plato, includes only the image of God, and imitations of his ideas, and never God and his ideas,"[7] whereas Whitehead was seeking validation of his conviction of the necessity for recognizing the immanence of God in the world. One aspect of his conviction of the importance of Plato's thought received re-inforcement, however, namely, the insight that God is to be conceived as a persuasive agency rather than a coercive agency in the world.

Our examination of the writings of Plato, the New Testament, and the theologians of the fourth century has upheld Whitehead's conclusions regarding each of the three culminating phases which he declares constitute the threefold Christian revelation of God. Plato does propose that we conceive of God as a persuasive agency in his relations with the universe and man; the Gospel writers and a number of other New Testament documents which we examined portray Jesus Christ as an exemplification of the nature of God and of his agency in the world, and for the most part, he is portrayed as a persuasive agency, pre-eminently in the life and death of Jesus Christ; it must be acknowledged, however, that there are other conceptions of God, in more primitive imagery, portrayed throughout both Old and New Testaments.

----

[4] A. N. Whitehead, *Adventures of Ideas* (Cambridge: Cambridge University Press, 1933), Preface, p. viii.
    [5] Ibid., pp. 165-66.
    [6] Ibid., p. 166.
    [7] Ibid., p. 215.

In the writings of the theologians of Alexandria Whitehead became aware of a more appropriate way of speaking about God than Plato had been able to offer: "The accepted solution of a multiplicity in the nature of God, each component being unqualifiedly divine, involves a doctrine of mutual immanence in the divine nature."[8] At least three major questions are resolved in this brief statement:

   (i) a multiplicity in the nature of God, in which Whitehead receives support for his move in the direction of introducing differentiation in the nature of God according as he is considering the variety and complexity of his agency in the world;

  (ii) the removal of all forms of qualification and of subordination, a constant feature of the Platonic triad. God as portrayed by the Christian theologians is divine without qualification, and is creator of all things, visible and invisible;

 (iii) a doctrine of mutual immanence in the divine nature; the Christian theologians insist that God is God in all his manifold operations in the world.

Again, when the theologians were faced with the problem as to how the divine and the human could reside in the one person, Jesus Christ, "they decided for the direct immanence of God in the one person of Christ," says Whitehead, and their doctrine of the Holy Spirit provided for "some sort of direct immanence of God in the World generally."[9] In order to remove all misunderstanding, he presses home the argument:

> my point is that in the place of Plato's solution of secondary images and imitations, they demanded a direct doctrine of immanence. It is in this respect that they made a metaphysical discovery. They pointed out the way in which the Platonic metaphysics should develop, if it was to give a rational account of the role of the persuasive agency of God.[10]

The findings from our research into the works of Athanasius of Alexandria, the chief spokesman for the Church in framing its reply to the various Arian positions, supports the interpretation which Whitehead has placed upon them. While he at no time refers back to the problems experienced in the final chapter of *Process and Reality*, our examination of the documents has disclosed that the metaphysical position which he is criticizing in the Arians and in Platonism resembles in many respects the position at which Whitehead had arrived in the concluding chapter of his cosmology, and that the accepted solution in the fourth century, providing as it did, for "a multiplicity in the nature of God, each component being unqualifiedly divine" end involving a "doctrine of mutual immanence in the divine nature"[11] and insisting on the direct immanence of God in the world, is the solution after which he was groping at that time, but lacked an adequate language to describe.

---

[8] Ibid., p. 216.
[9] Ibid.
[10] Ibid.
[11] Ibid.

At this point Whitehead, realizing that what is now called for is a theological undertaking for which he possesses no special aptitude, calls upon Christian theologians today to re-investigate the whole field and to apply the insights in a philosophical theology "to show how the world is founded on something beyond mere transient fact, and how it issues in something beyond the perishing of occasions."[12] Since Whitehead issued this invitation more than forty years ago we have experienced a world-wide economic depression and a second devastating world war, followed by thirty years of feverish search for formulas for peace in one part of the world or another. They have been years of triumph and of tragedy for many in the western world; man has conquered space and has walked on the moon, and the mystery of the universe remains, as vast beyond the grasp of the human imagination. We have witnessed twenty years of tragic fruitless war in Vietnam which have demonstrated the limitations of coercion in bringing peace to developing nations. As we enter the final quarter of the twentieth century, aware that the tools for the destruction of civilization have been fashioned and are in the hands of men today, perhaps we are now ready to consider seriously adopting the way of persuasion as a deliberate policy? As Whitehead put it in 1932:

> There stand in the public view the persuasiveness of the eternal ideals, the same today as when realized in the Founder of Christianity, and the compulsoriness of physical nature, which passes and yet remains, and the compulsoriness of that realized urge toward social union, such as the Roman Empire, which was then, and is now, as it were a dream.[13]

We are under constant pressure today to make that dream a reality while there is still time.

Our analysis of the concept of God in *Process and Reality* and our examination of the theological debates of the fourth century of the Christian era have together disclosed a wealth of insight into the complexity of the problems and the difficulty of speaking about God and the world in any meaningful sense. The exercise is one in which we engage only because we have been convinced on empirical grounds of both the reality and the goodness of God, and believe ourselves called into life as rational creatures who must seek for the meaning of life—an understanding of the purpose and end of living as disclosed to us in God. This will involve, as Whitehead continuously reminds us and the fourth century theologians have affirmed, some comprehension of the immanence of God in the world. Can we now bring together the insights of the fourth century theologians on the one hand and the process philosophy on the other and speak about God in language which will be meaningful to our contemporaries and lead to a deeper understanding? The history of theological debate reminds us of the extreme difficulty of doing so without falling into error from the perspecive of some particular viewpoint, but perhaps the hoped for gains are worth the risk and so we must undertake the adventure.

[12] Ibid., p. 221.
[13] Ibid., p. 218.

In his chapter on "Cosmologies" Whitehead declares that "Plato's cosmology includes an ultimate creator, shadowy and undefined, imposing his design upon the Universe."[14] It is this ultimate creator whose relationship to the world was clarified and defined by Athanasius as the first step in overcoming the confusing statements which were being made by the Arians, and it is this problem of ultimacy which came under question in the final chapter of Whitehead's cosmology.

Whitehead's system had its origin in the generalization of particular factors discerned in the various natural and social sciences, in aesthetics and in religious experience. His readings in world religions had led him to conclude with Bradley that the ultimate principle of the universe must be impersonal. But his category of the ultimate, "creativity," had not proven satisfactory and the system was found to suffer from elements of incoherence. In the light of the Christian revelation of God, it becomes evident that "creativity," rather than being the ultimate principle, is but one expression of the creative process initiated and sustained in being by a Creator whose relations with the universe and man require that he be regarded as Personal.

On the other hand, Whitehead would appear to have been following a genuine insight in his rejection of extreme transcendentalism, whether of the original Semitic or the Neo-Platonic type. Through Christ there is disclosed a manifoldness within the Being of the One God, who is now declared to be Father, Son, and Holy Spirit, all equally and fully divine and each mutually operative in the work of the others, so that the work of God is one in all his manifold operations. The revelation of God incarnate in Jesus Christ is a disclosure of God as actively at work within the world, and particularly in the lives of men and women in the history of the nations; the Holy Spirit is declared to be the mode of God's operations in the world, so that every operation of God is, according to Athanasius, from the Father, through the Word, and in the Spirit. Whitehead's insight into the necessity for some differentiation in the language we employ about God as we refer to his various functions, receives confirmation and a more adequate terminology from the Christian revelation, so that it is now possible to speak about the various operations of God without falling into contradiction.

As we turn to the task of applying these Christian insights in a re-interpretation of the cosmology, our first move must be to rationalize the relationship between God and creativity. Our examination of Athanasius' *contra Gentes* disclosed that the phrase "*creatio ex nihilio*" was employed to differentiate the work of the world's creator from that of the craftsman who works with materials already to hand. We need to retain the sense of the Christian phrase while at the same time avoiding the usual philosophical counter that "out of nothing nothing comes," and I believe Whitehead has placed in our hands the tools which will enable us to do so.

[14] Ibid., pp. 154-55.

In his chapter on "Science and Philosophy" in *Adventures of Ideas*, originally delivered as a lecture in March, 1932, Whitehead speaks of "the world in its function as the theatre for the temporal realization of ideas,"[15] and calls for "a doctrine of nature which expresses the concrete relatedness of physical functionings and mental functionings," as aspects of one reality. He had come close to providing this interpretation in *Process and Reality* in which God in his primordial nature is declared to be performing mental (conceptual) functions of such magnitude as to constitute him in fact the world's creator, except for the fact that Whitehead had accepted the Platonic framework which relegated God to a subordinate position by definition. If we now bring to the re-interpretation of Whitehead's cosmology the Christian conception of God as portrayed in the New Testament and the metaphysical interpretation of the fourth-century theologians, we commence with God as a community of eternal love, with the Father eternally Father in relationship with the Son who is eternally Son or Word of God, and the Holy Spirit proceeding from the Father and the Son. The author of the Fourth Gospel informs his readers that in the beginning "The Word dwelt with God, and what God was the Word was,"[16] and then continues, "through him all things came to be; no single thing was created without him." Once the Platonic limitations are removed from God in Whitehead's cosmology, his portrayal of the primordial and the Consequent natures of God might well be his attempt to put into modern language the implications of verses 1-5 of this Prologue to the Gospel.

Bringing the Christian conception of God to the aid of the cosmology, we may now employ Whitehead's terminology and say that God's envisagement of a structured universe whose underlying principle would be that of a creative advance into novelty constitutes his initial act of creation. In this act we would include all those operations which Whitehead ascribed to God in his primordial nature, but whereas Whitehead found it necessary to say that God in his primordial nature "presupposes the general metaphysical character of creative advance,"[17] we would affirm that God in his envisagement creates this character along with all the other metaphysical principles which constitute the beginning of the world process. The creativity which Whitehead took for an ultimate is now recognized to be simply an aspect of the created universe, in fact, its most general characteristic.

The Christian revelation, moreover, provides a form of language by means of which both the transcendence and the immanence of God may be recognizsed as required for our understanding of his relation to the world and mankind. According to the Christian revelation the creative process of the universe, with its provision for the emergence and the interaction of man in society as a free and developing person in fellowship with God and other men, is the sphere in which God manifests himself and his purpose of love which embraces all mankind. The

[15] Ibid., Preface, p. viii; also p. 201.
[16] John 1:1-5 (N.E.B.).
[17] Whitehead, *PR*, p. 522 (487).

earlier insights to which Whitehead calls attention in *Religion in the Making*,[18] and to which he seeks, without much success, to give expression in the final chapter of *Process and Reality*, are now, in the light of the disclosure of the cosmic significance of Jesus Christ, seen in their full importance to an understanding of the purpose of God in the world and the relevance of Christian faith to the life of today. Jesus' proclamation of the Kingdom or reign of God as at hand constitutes an announcement of the New day of his reign and a call to all men to respond to the new situation in which they now find themselves. The Kingdom is at hand in Jesus Christ and is coming as men respond to and enter into Him, allowing Him to motivate their lives by the Holy Spirit in their life in the world.

The disclosure of God in the person of Jesus transcends the bounds of language and yet must be communicated by means of language and relationships. His disclosure of the ultimate relationship of filial love as between himself and the Father conveys a depth of significance into the terms employed which can only be understood by meditation upon his life of prayer and obedience in loving devotion to his call upon the life of the disciple. There is a depth of meaning conveyed into the relationships of man and God by Jesus' employment of the term "Abba, Father,"[19] which is later interpreted by the apostle Paul as exemplifying the relationship in which, in Christ, the individual Christian man stands before God.[20] This is a disclosure of a new depth of present personal relationship and communion between man and God, a relationship which was sustained by Jesus throughout his life and in the midst of constant activity and controversy, according to the records. He is portrayed by all the New Testament writers as abiding in the Father's love.

The notion, which stands out throughout the Johannine writings, but is the underlying motivation of all the New Testament documents, that God is love, is constituted in the Incarnation and the Cross. The Incarnation is a demonstration in a life lived out among men that "God is with us." God is a constantly abiding Presence undergirding and sustaining the life of the world and of mankind, and his nature is Eternal Love. This is the theme of the Ministry of Jesus in his teaching and his works of mercy and healing. God's loving concern and constant care for all is being expressed in and through the life of this one man in all his comings and goings among men in all the relationships of their lives. The depth of the reality and the costliness of the love that God is here and everywhere bestowing upon man is seen in stark realism in the suffering form upon the Cross. God in Christ has given himself into the hands of men and they are here doing with him as they will; in this one scene both the depth and the costliness of God's love for man and the depth of human selfishness and rebellion are portrayed.

"God is love" is at the very centre of the Christian disclosure of the nature of God, a disclosure made in and through the life of Jesus,

[18] Whitehead, *Religion in the Making* (New York: Macmillan, 1926), pp. 72-73.
[19] Mark 14:36.
[20] Rom. 8:15.

whose life was lived for others. The Epistle of John rightly interprets the situation; we know what love is only because of the love which he has poured out on our behalf, and conversely, our love, including our love for God, can only be shown, displayed, expressed, by being bestowed upon our fellow men, "for he who does not love his brother whom he has seen, cannot love God whom he has not seen."[21] It is in the love of man for man, and the concern that he shows for others that God is known by men in the world today. Here is a principle so fundamentally important as to transform all human relationships and one which is applicable in all the associations of man with man. It is the redemptive principle by the operation of which Christianity becomes an effective force of reconciliation in the world. Its application to the life of grace in the Church will correct inadequate notions about the operation of grace; in this principle and in its exemplification in the life of Jesus Christ and of his followers the insight of Plato that God is a persuasive agency is incorporated into the Christian's understanding of his relationships with God and with all men.

Whitehead's recognition of the importance of the introduction of the Logos doctrine in St. John's Gospel is now seen in its full significance. If He who lived the human life in all its limitations and under the humble surroundings of life, as the man, Jesus of Nazareth, is none other than the Creative Word, Who was with God in the beginning, and Who is God; if He who teaches and heals now in Galilee and tomorrow in Judaea is that Creative Word, through whom all things were made, in whom is life, and whose life is the light of men, then it is understandable that with his coming into the world in the person of Jesus there is inaugurated a new thing. His coming in the Incarnation constitutes the inauguration of the New Creative age in which men in all their imperfections may start afresh to live the life which God intends for all men and in him become a part of the movement for the renewal of the life of the world which he has initiated and is carrying forward among men.

This disclosure of God the Word also sheds light upon the real significance of those functions of God which Whitehead has subsumed under the "primordial nature of God" in his metaphysical system. We are now able to replace Whitehead's somewhat ambiguous term, which Archbishop Temple derogatively described as "a concatenation of vocables,"[22] with the more meaningful designation of the Word of God, but we will want to retain the insights which Whitehead's terminology does express and so avoid the pitfalls of oversimplification in our attempt to speak of the creative process of the universe. The Christian doctrine of the Creative Word who became the redeemer and who is constantly at work in the world redeeming and sanctifying life, provides further light upon much of what Whitehead was attempting to say in the final chapter of *Process and Reality*.

A fifth insight which Whitehead had earlier found in the New Testament, and which now receives illumination by the fully articulated

---

[21] 1 John 4:20.
[22] William Temple, *Nature, Man and God*, Gifford Lectures, 1932-33 (London: Macmillan, 1934), p. 258.

Christian doctrine of God, is that of the immanence of God.[23] He regarded this as an important new insight which came through Christianity, so important, in fact, that he refers to it as "a completion required by our cosmological outlook."[24] The doctrine of the Holy Spirit as the mode of God's operation in the world and as God's gift of His Presence and abiding Grace to His Church provides the language by means of which to give more adequate expression to all those aspects of experience for which Whitehead sought to account under the "consequent nature of God," who is described in *Process and Reality* as "in unison of becoming with every other creative act"[25] and as "the weaving of God's physical feelings upon his primordial concepts."[26] Christianity with the rich vocabulary received from the revelation of God in Christ, employs a number of different but related terms to account for the variety of experiences which Whitehead sought to describe by his "consequent nature of God." From the earliest days it has been a fundamental Christian conviction that the exalted Christ is nonetheless abiding with them in the world, and the gift of the Holy Spirit was promised to bring to each a realization of his presence. The Holy Spirit as the mode of God's operations in the world, provides for general immanence of God, and the Church as the Body of Christ is God's agency sent out into the world to proclaim by word and life the Kingdom of God as a present fact in process of being gathered by the joint activity of God and man—the Church into which Christ is gathering men, and through whose lives of love and sacrificial service he is seeking men and calling them into his Kingdom.

All the personalist language of the final chapter of *Process and Reality*, in which Whitehead sought to speak of the patient operation of the love of God at work in the lives of men, bringing good out of evil, and transmuting apparently hopeless situations into creative opportunities for the spiritual and moral development of character—all this language which, in terms of the definitions given to the categories of the ultimate in *Process and Reality*, was not justified—now becomes valid as an expression of the love of God at work in the world through the Spirit, bringing to men in the midst of their ordeal insights into the meaning of the Crucified and enabling them also to triumph in and through the Cross.

Some of Whitehead's terminology will be found to be unacceptable in the light of the disclosures in Christ. The idea of the "Apotheosis of the World,"[27] as it is developed in section V of the final chapter, forms a part of the Platonic framework in which the process was conceived to be ultimate, and will now be simply dropped. The universe is a created order and will not become divinized. Whitehead recognizes now, having been taught by the Alexandrian theologians, that the idea of the

[23] Whitehead, *RM*, pp. 72-73.
[24] Whitehead, *AI*, p. 206.
[25] Whitehead, *PR*, p. 523 (488).
[26] Ibid., p. 524 (488).
[27] Ibid., p. 529 (493).

World-Soul, as an emanation, "only obscures the ultimae question of the relation of reality as permanent with reality as fluent."[28] Whitehead informs the reader that he learned from the theologians "how the primordial Being, who is the sources of the inevitable recurrence of the world towards order, shares his nature with the world."[29] The Christian revelation of God discloses that he is immanent without in any sense losing his transcendence and that the laws of nature are a manifestation of his purpose and agency within the finite and contingent order of the world. Man's life is involved in this world and it is in the here and now that God would come to men, not by some impersonal process through the performance of cultic acts as in the Gentile worship, but by himself becoming man. So the crucified and risen Lord reaches out to claim our wills for his service and making us instruments of his will, incorporates us into his kingdom, by the response of faith and obedience.

Ernst Kasemann, in his essay on "the Pauline Doctrine of the Lord's Supper,"[30] draws out the contrast between the pagan and the Christian understanding of the meaning of the sacramental act. Obedience is the new dimension in which the Christian exists, an "obedience which is no *character indelibilis*, but the possibility of truly free decision and therefore also the possibility of apostasy."[31] The very freedom into which man has entered in Christ constitutes his responsibility for his own decisions. Hellenism, knowing only cosmic powers, could only describe redemption as a species of natural processes, and therein disclose the fatalistic character of this process. "But Paul knows the Lord, who does not reign as Necessity, but, according to 2 Corinthians 3:18, dispenses freedom: the freedom to decide between obedience and disobedience."[32] The sacrament mediates for the Christian "not Fate, but the possibility of obedience as *the* eschatological gift and, at the same time, as responsibility 'before the face of Jesus Christ.'"[33]

Whitehead's conception of the "consequent nature of God" has some clear affinities with the Pauline suggestion that the universe itself is waiting "with eager expectation for God's sons to be revealed"[34] and will be transfigured as man responds to the glory of God as revealed in Christ. Whitehead's language in the two closing sections of the final chapter of *Process and Reality* becomes immediately relevant as an attempt to account for that activity of God, which he had found described in the New Testament, in which he is portrayed as gathering into himself a fellowship of free and separate individuals, yet bound together into one fellowship in him and commissioned to the fulfilment of his will and purpose in the world. In and through the lives of the membership of the Church, Christ himself is assuming and exercising

[28] Whitehead, *AI*, p. 166.
[29] Ibid.
[30] Ernst Kasemann, *Essays on New Testament Themes*, trans. by W. J. Montague (London: SCM Press, 1964), p. 119.
[31] Ibid.
[32] Ibid.
[33] Ibid.
[34] Rom. 8:19.

his Lordship in and over that world for whom he became incarnate and by whom he was crucified. As Kasemann puts it, "The Body of Christ is the realm into which we are incorporated with our bodies and to which we are called to render service in the body, i.e. total service, service which embraces all our different relationships in and to the world."[35] The source of the Christian's vitality is the gift of the presence of the Risen One himself who

> continues to do what the Incarnate and Crucified One has already done. He exists for us "in the body," he gives us "bodily" participation in himself. Thus he who is now exalted can, in the Lord's Supper, continually give us that which in his death he gave us once and for all.[36]

Kasemann continues his investigation of the Pauline theology of the Church as the Body of Christ in a paper on "Ministry and Community in the New Testament." His language at many points is reminiscent of Whitehead's attempt in the final chapter of *Process and Reality*. He examines the multiplicity of charismata which Paul declares are the motivating and directing force in the lives of Christians. The key statement occurs in Romans 6:23, "The charisma of God is eternal life in Christ Jesus our Lord." This gift, Kasemann points out, "is inseparable from the gracious power which bestows it, and is indeed the manifestation and concretion of this power, so that eternal life is not one gift among many but *the* sole and unique gift of the End."[37] All the individual gifts are for service rendered by the members in their life in the world, and it is in and through this service that Christ reveals himself as the Cosmocrator, as through these he is able to penetrate ever more deeply into the secularity of the world. Once this truth has been grasped the Church can no longer be conceived as some sacred temple precinct, but must regard the world in its totality as its field of operations. Kasemann sums up the Pauline teaching in the following significant passage:

> Because and in so far as the body of Christ, the sphere of the eschatologically realized lordship of Christ on earth, is God's new world and creation: because and in so far as Christ in and with his gift calls each of his members to the *nova oboedientia*, quickens him and moves him to service and suffering, clad in the spiritual armour of Eph. 6:10 ff.; because and in so far as, in his gifts and in the ministries which they express and indeed create, he himself is present, proclaiming his title to the lordship of the world, consecrating the secular, ridding the earth of demons; therefore and to this extent can it be proclaimed in truth that he fills all things with the power of his resurrection.[38]

All this is based upon the principle, to which Kasemann had earlier called attention in his study of the Pauline doctrine of the Lord's Supper, which Paul enunciates, that "the Giver is not to be separated from his gift but is really present in it."[39]

[35] Kasemann, *Essays on New Testament Themes*, p. 130.
[36] Ibid., p. 133.
[37] Ibid., p. 65.
[38] Ibid., p. 74.
[39] Ibid.

For Paul, the man in Christ is a member of the Body of Christ and the members are severally members one of another; the passages quoted clearly have reference to the life which Christians are called to live in the world; the Church is his Body in the world today in the twentieth century, even as in the first—those early Christians scattered across the face of the earth—a mere handful as men call numbers, and yet the possibilities are incalculable if each one will but realize his true destiny in Christ and go out in faith to fulfil his spiritual worship in the world, "growing unto the increase of the body by that which every part supplies."[40] Whitehead's consequent nature of God was an attempt to describe a reality in Christian experience; the Church is an organism whose vital life is the Incarnate, Crucified and Risen Lord, present and making his impact upon the world through the members, each of whose lives thereby becomes a component in the divine-human organism, the Body of Christ, through which God's eternal purpose is being fulfilled as the life of mankind is gathered into his Kingdom.

In this section of our final chapter we have sought to draw out some of the implications of our findings by bringing together the metaphysical and theological insights provided by the Christian revelation and the final formulation of the philosophy of organism in *Process and Reality*. The results are promising, but the most we have been able to do is to suggest the framework or outline for a theology for the twentieth century which might be formulated upon this foundation. It would appear that Whitehead, in his final discovery of the disclosure of the nature of God as revealed in Christ, has at least pointed scholars in the direction of meeting Bradley's final request for a "religious belief founded otherwise than on metaphysics, and a metaphysics able in some sense to justify that creed."[41] The religion has been disclosed by revelation through Jesus Christ and has provided the metaphysical principles by means of which the process philosophy may be reformulated to conform to the larger vision of reality disclosed in Christ. This philosophy, when so re-formulated, will provide the language and the setting for an interpretation of Christian faith to mankind in the final quarter of the twentieth century.

[40] Eph. 4:16.
[41] F. H. Bradley, *Essays on Truth and Reality* (Oxford: Clarendon Press, 1914), pp. 446-47.

Bibliography

Bibliography

A bibliography of sources quoted and to which references are made in the text.

Altizer, Thomas, and Hamilton, William. *Radical Theology and the Death of God.* New York: The Bobbs-Merrill Company Inc., 1966.

Anderson, Hugh. *Jesus and Christian Origins.* New York: Oxford University Press, 1964.

Anselm, Saint. *Basic Writings: Proslogium.* Translated by S. W. Deane. LaSalle, Illinois: Open Court, 1962.

Aquinas, Thomas. *Philosophical Texts.* Selected and translated with notes by Thomas Gilby. London: Oxford University Press, 1956.

Aristotle. *The Metaphysics.* Translated by W. D. Ross. Oxford: Clarendon Press, 1958 (1924).

Athanasius. *The Letters of Saint Athanasius Concerning the Holy Spirit.* Translated with Introduction and notes by C. R. B. Shapland. London: The Epworth Press, 1951.

_____ . *Select Writings and Letters of Athanasius, Bishop of Alexandria.* Edited, with prolegomena, indices, and tables, by Archibald Robertson. *Nicene and Post-Nicene Fathers.* Second series, Volume IV. Oxford: Parker and Company, 1891.

_____ . *Selected Treatises of Athanasius in Controversy with the Arians.* Translated by a member of the English Church. Oxford: James Parker and Company, 1877.

Ayer, A. J. *The Concept of a Person and Other Essays.* London: Macmillan Company Ltd., 1963.

_____ . *Language, Truth and Logic.* New York: Dover Publications Inc., 1946. (First edition, 1935.)

Basil of Caesarea. *Nicene and Post-Nicene Fathers.* Second series, Volume VIII. Translated by Blomfield Jackson. Edited by Philip Schaff. Oxford: Parker and Company, 1886.

Bondi, H., et al. *Rival Theories of Cosmology.* London: Oxford University Press, 1960.

Bonhoeffer, Dietrich. *Act and Being.* Translated by Bernard Noble. London: Collins, 1962.

_____ . *Letters and Papers from Prison.* Edited by Eberhard Bethge. Translated by Reginald H. Fuller. London: SCM Press, 1953.

Bornkamm, Gunther. *Jesus of Nazareth.* Translated by Irene and Fraser McLuskey with James M. Robinson. London: Hodder and Stoughton, 1960.

Bradley, F. H. *Appearance and Reality.* London: George Allen and Unwin, Ltd., 1925. (First published, 1893.)

_____ . *Essays on Truth and Reality.* Oxford: Clarendon Press, 1914.

Braithwaite, R. B. *An Empiricist's View of the Nature of Religious Belief.* Cambridge: Cambridge University Press, 1955.

_____ . Review of *Science and the Modern World*. *Mind* (October, 1926).

Bright, William. *A History of the Church from A.D. 313 to A.D. 451*. Oxford and London: James Parker & Company, 1869.

Christian, William A. *An Interpretation of Whitehead's Metaphysics*. New Haven, Connecticut: Yale University Press, 1959.

Cobb, John B., Jr. *A Christian Natural Theology*. Philadelphia: The Westminster Press, 1965. See also a critical review of Cobb by Langdon Gilkey in *Theology Today*, XXII, No. 4 (January, 1966).

Cochrane, Charles Norris. *Christianity and Classical Culture*. New York: Oxford University Press, 1940; Galaxy Book, 1957.

Collingwood, R. G. *The Idea of Nature*. Oxford: Clarendon Press, 1945.

Collins, James. *God in Modern Philosophy*. London: Routledge and Kegan Paul Ltd., 1960.

Cornford, F. M. *Plato's Cosmology: The "Timaeus" of Plato translated with a running commentary*. London: Routledge and Kegan Paul Ltd., 1937. (Fourth impression, 1956.)

_____ . *Plato's Theory of Knowledge. The "Thaetetus" and the "Sophist" of Plato translated with a running commentary*. London: Routledge and Kegan Paul Ltd., 1935. (Paperback, 1960.)

Cox, Harvey. *The Secular City*. London: SCM Press, 1965.

Cross, F. L. *Athanasius' De Incarnatione*. London: S.P.C.K., 1957.

_____ . *Early Christian Fathers*. London: Duckworth, 1960.

Danielou, Jean. *Origen*. Translated by Walter Mitchell. London: Sheed and Ward, 1955.

Descartes, Rene. *Philosophical Writings: A Selection*. Translated and edited by Elizabeth Anscombe and Peter Thomas Geach. London: Nelson, 1963 (1954).

Dodd, C. H. *The Apostolic Preaching and its Developments*. London: Hodder and Stoughton, 1936.

_____ . *Historical Tradition in the Fourth Gospel*. Cambridge: Cambridge University Press, 1963.

_____ . *History and the Gospel*. London: Hodder and Stoughton, 1938.

_____ . *Interpretation of the Fourth Gospel*. Cambridge: Cambridge University Press, 1953.

_____ . *The Parables of the Kingdom*. London: James Nisbet, 1935.

Emmet, Dorothy. "The Ground of Being." *The Journal of Theological Studies*, XV, Part 2 (October, 1964), 280.

_____ . *Whitehead's Philosophy of Organism*. London: The Macmillan Company, 1932. Republished with a new Introduction, 1966.

Eusebius of Caesarea. *The Proof of the Gospel*. Translated by W. J. Ferrar. London: S.P.C.K., 1920.

Farrer, Austin. *Finite and Infinite*. 2nd ed. Westminster: Dacre Press, 1959.

Feuerbach, Ludwig. *The Essence of Christianity*. Translated by George Eliot, 1850. New York: Harper Torchbooks, 1957.

Florovsky, George. "The Concept of Creation in Saint Athanasius." In *Studia Patristica*, Vol. VI, pp. 36-57.

Foster, Michael. "Christian Theology and the Modern Science of Nature." *Mind* (New Series), XLIV, No. 176 (October, 1935).

_____ . "The Difference between Modern and Ancient Rationalism." *Mind* (New Series), XLV, Nos. 177, 178 (January, 1936), 1-27.

_____ . *Mystery and Philosophy*. London: SCM Press, 1957.

Franks, Robert S. *The Doctrine of the Trinity*. London: Gerald Duckworth and Company Ltd., 1953.

Fuller, R. H. *The New Testament in Current Study*. New York: Charles Scribner's Sons, 1962. Revised British edition, London: SCM Press, 1963.

Grant, Robert M. *Gnosticism and Early Christianity*. New York: Columbia University Press, 1959.

Gregory of Nazianzus. *Nicene and Post-Nicene Fathers*. Vol. VII. Translated by Edward Hamilton Gifford, 1893.

Gregory of Nyssa. *Nicene and Post-Nicene Fathers*. Vol. V. Translated by William Moore and Henry Austin Wilson, 1892.

Grillmeier, Aloys, S.J. *Christ in Christian Tradition*. London: A. R. Mowbray and Company Ltd., 1965.

Grube, G. M. A. *Plato's Thought*. New York: Methuen and Company Ltd., 1935. Boston: The Beacon Press, 1958.

Gwatkin, H. M. *Studies of Arianism*. Cambridge: Cambridge University Press, 1900.

_____ , ed. *Selections from Early Writers Illustrative of Church History to the Time of Constantine*. London: Macmillan and Co., Ltd., 1911. (First edition, 1893.)

Habgood, John. *Religion and Science*. London: Mills and Boon, 1964.

Hamilton, William. *The New Essence of Christianity*. London: Darton, Longman and Todd, 1961.

Hardy, Edward Rochie, ed. *Christology of the Later Fathers*. Written in collaboration with Cyril C. Richardson. In *The Library of Christian Classics*. Vol. III. London: SCM Press, 1954.

Harre, R. *An Introduction to the Logic of the Sciences*. London: Macmillan and Company Ltd., 1960.

_____ . "Philosophical Aspects of Cosmology." *The British Journal for the Philosophy of Science*, XIII, No. 50 (August, 1962).

Harris, Errol E. *The Foundations of Metaphysics in Science*. London: George Allen and Unwin Ltd., 1965. See also the favourable review by W. H. Thorpe in *The British Journal for the Philosophy of Science* (November, 1966).

Hartshorne, Charles. *The Logic of Perfection and Other Essays in Neo-classical Metaphysics*. LaSalle, Illinois: Open Court Publishing Company, 1962.

_____ . *Man's Vision of God*. Hamden, Connecticut: Harper and Row, Inc., 1941. (Reprint ed., 1964.)

_____ , and Reese, William L. *Philosophers Speak of God*. Chicago: University of Chicago Press, 1953.

Heisenberg, Werner. *The Physicist's Conception of Nature*. Translated by Arnold J. Pomerans. London: Hutchinson and Company, Ltd., 1958.

_____ . *Physics and Philosophy*. New York: Harper, 1958.

Hodgson, Leonard. *The Doctrine of the Trinity*. London: James Nisbet and Company, 1943.

Hook, Sidney, ed. *Religious Experience and Truth: A Symposium*. New York: University of New York, 1961. London: Oliver & Boyd Ltd., 1962.

Hume, David. *Dialogues Concerning Natural Religion, 1779*. Hafner Library of Classics No. 5. Edited with an Introduction by Henry D. Aiken. New York: Hafner Publishing Company, 1948.

Jaeger, Werner. *The Theology of the Early Greek Philosophers*. Gifford Lectures, 1936. Oxford: Clarendon Press, 1947.

Kasemann, Ernst. *Essays on New Testament Themes*. Translated by W. J. Montague. London: SCM Press, 1964.

Kelly, J. N. D. *Early Christian Creeds*. London: Longman's, 1950.

_____ . *Early Christian Doctrines*. London: Adam & Charles Black, 1958.

Kline, George L. ed. *Alfred North Whitehead, Essays on His Philosophy*. Englewood Cliffs, New Jersey: Prentice-Hall, Inc., 1963.

Lawrence, Nathaniel. *Whitehead's Philosophical Development.* Berkeley, California: University of California Press, 1956.

Leclerc, Ivor. *Whitehead's Metaphysics: An Introductory Exposition.* London: George Allen and Unwin Ltd., 1958.

———, ed. *The Relevance of Whitehead.* London: Allen and Unwin Limited, 1961.

Leitzmann, Hans. *A History of the Early Church.* Translated by Bertran Lee Woolf. London: The Lutterworth Press, 1961.

Levi, Albert William. *Philosophy and the Modern World.* Bloomington: Indiana University Press, 1959.

Lewis, H. D. "The Idea of Creation and Conceptions of Salvation." Chapter VII of *The Saviour God.* Edited by S. G. F. Brandon. Manchester: Manchester University Press, 1963.

Lightfoot, R. H. *The Gospel Message of Saint Mark.* Oxford: Oxford University Press, 1949. (Oxford Paperback edition, 1962.)

Mascall, E. L. *Christian Theology and Natural Science.* London: Longmans, Green and Company, 1956.

———. *He Who Is: A Study in Traditional Theism.* London: Longmans, Green and Company, 1943.

Mays, W. *The Philosophy of Whitehead.* London: George Allen and Unwin Ltd. New York: The Macmillan Company, 1959.

Momigliano, Arnoldo, ed. *The Conflict between Paganism and Christianity in the Fourth Century.* Oxford: Clarendon Press, 1963.

Moule, C. F. D. *The Epistles to the Colossians and to Philemon.* Cambridge: Cambridge University Press, 1957.

The New English Bible: The New Testament. Oxford: Oxford University Press, 1961.

Newton, Sir Isaac. *Theological Manuscripts.* Selected and edited by H. MacLachlan. Liverpool: Liverpool University Press, 1950.

Norris, R. A. *Manhood and Christ.* Oxford: Clarendon Press, 1963.

Origen. *contra Celsum.* Translated by Henry Chadwick. Cambridge: Cambridge University Press, 1953.

———. *The First Principles.* Translated by G. W. Butterworth. London: S.P.C.K., 1936.

Photius. *The Epitome of the Ecclesiastical History of Philostorgius.* Translated by Edward Walford. London: Henry Bohn, 1855.

Pittenger, W. Norman. *The Christian Understanding of Human Nature.* Digswell Place, London: James Nisbet and Company Ltd., 1964.

———. *The Word Incarnate.* New York: Harper Brothers, 1959.

Plato. *The Dialogues of Plato.* Translated by B. Jowett. Oxford: Clarendon Press, 1892.

Plotinus. *The Enneads.* Translated by Stephen MacKenna. 3rd edition, revised by B. S. Page and with an Introduction by Professor Paul Henry, S.J. London: Faber and Faber Ltd., 1956.

Polanyi, Michael. *Personal Knowledge.* London: Routledge & Kegan Paul, 1958.

Popper, Karl. *Conjectures and Refutations.* London: Routledge & Kegan Paul, 1962.

Poteat, William H. "Birth, Suicide and the Doctrine of Creation." *Mind,* LXVIII (July, 1959), 309ff.

Prestige, G. L. *God in Patristic Thought.* London: William Beinmann, Ltd., 1936.

Price, Lucien. *Dialogues of Alfred North Whitehead.* London: Max Reinhardt, 1954.

Ramsey, I. T., ed. *Biology and Personality.* Oxford: Basil Blackwell, 1965.

Reese, William L., and Freeman, Eugene, eds. *Process and Divinity.* LaSalle, Illinois: Open Court Publishing Company, 1964.

Robinson, J. A. T. *Honest to God.* London: SCM Press, 1963.

————. *The New Reformation.* London: SCM Press, 1965.

Russell, Bertrand. *A History of Western Philosophy.* New York: Simon and Schuster, 1945.

————. *Mysticism and Logic.* Middlesex: Penguin Books, 1918.

————. *Our Knowledge of the External World.* London: Unwin Brothers Ltd., 1914.

————. *My Philosophical Development.* London: George Allen and Unwin Ltd., 1959.

Schilpp, Paul Arthur, ed. *The Philosophy of Alfred North Whitehead.* New York: Tudor Publishing Company, 1941. (2nd ed., 1951.)

Sherburne, Donald W. *A Whiteheadian Aesthetic.* New Haven: Yale University Press, 1961.

Sozomen. *Ecclesiastical History.* Translated by Edward Walford. London: Henry G. Bohn, 1855.

Stead, S. C. "*HOMOOUSION.*" In *Studia Patristica,* III. In *Texte Untersuchinge,* Vol. 78, p. 397.

Stebbing, L. S. "Critical Review of Process and Reality." *Mind* (October, 1930), p. 475.

Stevenson, J. A. *A New Eusebius. Early Christian Writings in Translation.* London: S.P.C.K., 1960.

Stockwood, Mervin, ed. *Religion and the Scientists.* London: SCM Press, 1959.

Taylor, A. E. *Commentary on the "Timaeus."* Oxford: Clarendon Press, 1928.

————. *Plato, the Man and His Work.* London: Methuen, 1925.

Temple, William. *Nature, Man and God.* Gifford Lectures, 1932-33. London: Macmillan and Company, 1934.

Thomas, George F. *Religious Philosophies of the West.* New York: Charles Scribners & Sons, 1965.

Thornton, Lionel Spencer. *The Incarnate Lord: An Essay Concerning the Doctrine of the Incarnation in its Relation to Organic Conceptions.* London: Longmans, Green and Company Ltd., 1928.

Tollinton, R. B. *Selections from the Commentaries and Homilies of Origen.* London: S.P.C.K., 1929.

Toulmin, Stephen. *The Philosophy of Science.* London: Hutchinson's University Library, 1953.

Urmson, J. O. *Philosophical Analysis: Its Development between the Two World Wars.* Oxford: Clarendon Press, 1956.

van Buren, Paul. *The Secular Meaning of the Gospel.* London: SCM Press, 1953.

Webb, C. C. J. *God and Personality.* London: George Allen and Unwin, Ltd., 1919.

Welch, Claude. *The Trinity in Contemporary Theology.* London: SCM Press, 1953.

White, Victor, O.P. *God and the Unconscious.* London: Harvil Press, 1952. (Collins Fontana Book, 1960.)

Whitehead, A. N. *Adventures of Ideas.* New York: The Macmillan Company, 1932. Cambridge: Cambridge University Press, 1933.

————. *The Aims of Education and Other Essays.* New York: The Macmillan Company, 1929. (A Mentor Book, 1956.)

————. *The Concept of Nature.* Cambridge: Cambridge University Press, 1920.

————. *An Enquiry Concerning the Principles of Natural Knowledge.* Cambridge: Cambridge University Press, 1919. (Reprint ed., 1955.)

————. *Essays in Science and Philosophy.* New York: Philosophical Library, 1947.

————. *The Function of Reason*. Princeton: Princeton University Press, 1929. (Beacon Paperback ed., 1958.)

————. *Modes of Thought*. New York: Cambridge University Press, 1938.

————. *Process and Reality: An Essay in Cosmology*. New York: The Macmillan Company, 1929. (Harper Torchbook ed., 1960.)

————. *Religion in the Making*. New York: The Macmillan Company, 1926. (Reprint ed., 1933.)

————. *Science and the Modern World*. Cambridge: Cambridge University Press, 1926. (Reprint ed., 1933.)

————. *Symbolism: Its Meaning and Effect*. Virginia: Virginia University Press, 1927. Cambridge: Cambridge University Press, 1928.

Wisdom, John. *Philosophy and Psycho-Analysis*. Oxford: Basil Blackwell, 1957.

Witt, R. E. *Albinus and Middle Platonism*. Cambridge: Cambridge University Press, 1937.

Wittgenstein, Ludwig. *Philosophical Investigations*. Translated by G. E. M. Anscombe. Oxford: Basil Blackwell, 1963.

————. *Tractatus Logico-Philosophicus*. Translated by D. F. Pears and B. F. McGuinness. London: Routledge and Kegan Paul, 1961.

Wolfson, Harry Austryn. *The Philosophy of the Church Fathers*. Cambridge, Massachusetts: Harvard University Press, 1956.

Journals

Proceedings of the American Catholic Philosophical Association, for the year 1970.
The Southern Journal of Philosophy, Winter, 1969.
Theology Today, XXII, No. 4 (January 1966).

Index

Index

Absolute, 4, 35-39, 45, 100, 126
Abraham, 107, 118, 119
Actual entity, entities, vi, 26, 35, 42-4, 48-9, 50-1, 53, 59, 60, 67, 77, 81, 100, 101, 102, 132
Actual occasions, actualities, vi, 26, 31, 50-1, 74, 76, 77-8, 82, 131, 134
Aeschylus, 105-6
Albinus, 123
Alexander, Bp. of Alexandria, 128, 129, 147, 159
Alone, The, 127, 130, 135
Altizer, Thomas, 3-4
Alexandria, 99, 123, 126, 127, 128-9, 134, 138, 139, 140
Alexandrians, 103, 137, 140, 147, 150, 180
Anselm, 22
Anthropology, -ical, 3, 106
Antioch, 99, 140; Antiochenes, 103, 162-3
Apochalyptic, 110
Apotheosis of the World, 134, 180
Appetition, 31, 88
Aquinas, 25, 73
Arian, 97, 102, 122, 126-7, 128, 130, 132, 134, 141, 142, 146, 147, 155, 156, 157
Arianism, v, viii, 102, 138
Aristotle, Aristotelian, 16-7, 32, 34, 42, 45-6, 59, 60, 70, 99, 122-3, 125, 135
Arius, viii, 99, 126-7, 128-30, 155, 165, 166; *Thalia, The,* 129-30, 158
Asiatic, 21, 89
Athanasius, viii, 126, 127, 128, 138, 139, 142-70, 174
  contra Gentes, ix, 144-9, 168, 176
  De Synodis, 142, 158
  Discourses Against the Arians (contra Arianos), ix, 129, 142, 155-60, 165-6

Epistle Concerning the Council at Ariminum, etc., 130
Letters on the Holy Spirit, ix, 160-3, 167, 168
On the Incarnation, ix, 149-55, 168
Tome to the Antiochenes, 162, 163
Athanasius' contribution to theology, 163-5
Athena, 105-6
Atticus, 123
Augustine, 22, 73, 97, 105
Ayer, A. J., 2, 3, 5-7

Basil of Caesarea, 142
"Being," 124, 130, 134, 157, 176
Bergson, Emile, 30
Bonhoeffer, Dietrich, 10-11, 141
Bradley, F. H., vi, 18, 30, 35-40, 70, 100, 183
Buddhist, 23
Butterworth, G. W., 128

Caesarea Philippi, 111
Cambridge, 13, 137
Cappadocian Fathers, 142
Categories, 6, 41; categoreal, 8, 79, 82
Catholic Church, 162
Causa, sui, vii, 56-7, 81
Chalcedon, Council of, 97, 103, 165
Chance, 19, 76, 149
Change, 36, 43, and the changeless, 36
Chaos, chaotic, 9, 102, 105
Christ (see Jesus Christ)
Christian, 73, 78, 80, 92, 97, 138, 140, 142; doctrine, 93, 96, 99, 102, 144, 152, 164, 165, 168; doctrine of creation, 96, 144-49; revelation of God, 108, 145
Christian Church, 10, 101, 112, 114-5, 121, 122, 130, 182, 183
Christianity, 21, 76, 97, 98-9, 102, 103, 126, 129, 132, 143, 148